Home Away from Home

SAWA KUROTANI *Home*

DUKE
UNIVERSITY
PRESS

DURHAM
AND LONDON
2005

JAPANESE CORPORATE WIVES

IN THE UNITED STATES

Away from Home

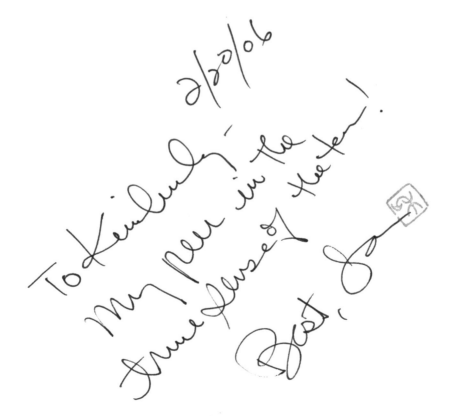

© 2005 DUKE UNIVERSITY PRESS

ALL RIGHTS RESERVED

PRINTED IN THE UNITED STATES OF AMERICA ON ACID-FREE PAPER

DESIGNED BY REBECCA GIMENEZ

TYPESET IN GARAMOND 3 BY KEYSTONE TYPESETTING, INC.

LIBRARY OF CONGRESS CATALOGING-IN-PUBLICATION DATA APPEAR ON

THE LAST PRINTED PAGE OF THIS BOOK

TO MY PARENTS,

Hideo and Tsuyoko Kurotani

Contents

Acknowledgments

WHEN I FIRST left my family in Japan and came to the United States as an undergraduate exchange student, it was not even in my wildest dreams that I would someday write and publish a book. Many years have passed and many things have happened since, and here I am, cobbling together a few words to acknowledge and thank those who have helped make this book possible. It seems, truly, uncanny.

When you move away from home, you become nobody, a person with no name, a person without history. When you begin to build a life in a strange place, you have no place to start from, and this complete freedom, this arbitrariness, is far more frightening than liberating. But from my early years in the United States all the way to the present, I have been extremely fortunate, as I always had people around me who were willing to help, to go a little further than what their duty called for, to offer unconditional support, to anchor me in this new place. To recollect their names and the time, care, and resources that they invested in me is to recollect the process of my self-making as a transnational migrant, an anthropologist, and a person with history. I name here only those whose help directly contributed to the making of this book, though I acknowledge that there were many others without whom I would not exist as the person I am now.

I would like to acknowledge two organizations for providing me resources that made this project possible. My dissertation fieldwork was funded by the National Science Foundtion Dissertation Improvement Grant. The postdoctoral phase of my field research was made possible by a Rockefeller postdoctoral fellowship at the University Center for International Studies, the University of North Carolina, Chapel Hill, during the academic year 1999–2000. Multisited fieldwork such as mine is costly and practically impossible without substantial funding. I appreciate the generous support of these organizations. I would also like to state that the views and findings presented in this book are solely mine and do not necessarily reflect those of the funding organizations.

Among those whose presence in my life contributed directly to this book project, I would like to thank, first and foremost, Anne Allison. From the first moment I met her to this day, she has been a constant source of inspiration, both as an anthropologist and as a person. She has seen me through those years when I was unsure of my academic future, through the challenging transition from graduate school to the "real" world of academia, through times of rejection and disappointment, and through moments of elation and joy. Just as she acknowledged her indebtedness to her own mentor in her first book, I acknowledge my debt, which can never be repaid in full, to her. I only hope that I can return her kindness, as I try to be as good a teacher to my students as she has been to me.

I would also like to thank Charles Piot, who taught me many, many things, most important among them, how to *really* read and write critically. He did this not by telling me how, but by example. I will never forget that summer when he read draft after draft of my grant proposal and sat down with me weekly with detailed comments. At the end of each meeting, I remember his saying, "It's getting close." I also remember that he never said, "It's there." The way I work on my writing today is very much a reflection of that experience: to take the reader's comments seriously, to scrutinize every aspect of my writing, to keep working on it until I can't stand it any longer.

At the University of Colorado at Boulder, I was also very fortunate to find a supportive dissertation advisor, Dennis McGilvray, who adopted me after Anne Allison departed for Duke University and who was always generous with his time whenever I needed his attention. He gave me much needed stability through my graduate work and allowed me the space to pursue my ethnographic passion.

My year at the University of North Carolina, Chapel Hill, was an exciting and productive time, when I expanded my dissertation project and began to formulate the shape that this book was going to take. James Peacock, then director of the UCIS, made possible the intellectually stimulating environment in which we thrived. I am particularly indebted to Donald Nonini, who generously spent many afternoon hours talking with me and gave me invaluable feedback on my work. He also understood, from his own experience, the complications that one encounters in transnational ethnography. I greatly appreciate his supportiveness in this regard as well.

There are many others who helped me think through my ethnographic project over the years. Teresa Wilkins, my dearest friend and colleague, has been a source of support and encouragement as we went through the thick and thin of graduate school and the transition into tenure-track jobs. She has also been an important intellectual peer to me, and our bouncing back and forth over the years helped me tremendously to clarify, sharpen, and flesh out my ideas, many of which are included in this book. Here at the University of Redlands, I have met many students who took an interest and became involved in my research. They have been my sounding board over the past four years, against which I was able to bounce my manuscript ideas and to do some reality checks. My first thanks go to three students who read an earlier draft of this book in spring 2004: Jeanette Meliska, Amanda Porter, and Summer Glenney. I would also like to thank M. G. Maloney, who cotaught with me the spring 2003 Johnston Seminar, "Writing across Gender Lines," as well as other participants of the seminar who also read portions from an earlier version of this manuscript. Their responses, both positive and challenging, helped me make this an accessible yet substantial reading for a broader audience. I would also like to thank Lino Alexander Barraza for his feedback and support at the final stages of manuscript preparation.

Last, my sincere thanks go out to those women who generously shared their time with me during my fieldwork and beyond. Although I will not mention their real names in this book for the sake of confidentiality, I will never forget their insights and humor.

CHAPTER ONE

Domesticating the Global

ON A CLOUDY AFTERNOON in early August 2001, Kawagoe-san and I sat in the living room of her home in a suburban town thirty miles south of Tokyo, drinking a glass of cold barley tea after the delicious noodles she served for lunch. Gloominess outside reminded us of the Midwestern city where we used to live, Kawagoe-san as the wife of a Japanese businessman who was stationed there by his Japanese employer, I as an anthropology graduate student on my first fieldwork project. We began thinking about how we met for the first time. I told her that it was one of those famous *yam cha* days.

"That was an overly daring move, I must say," said Kawagoe-san. "For the first-timer, *yam cha* ought to be a bit too much."

I nodded in agreement. "It sure was. I was completely overwhelmed."

The thought of *yam cha* brought a smile to our faces. I asked her, "Have you done it recently, since you got back to Japan?"

"Not since we left Centerville—it's already been four years! How about you, Sawa-san?"

"Oh, I've been to several," I said grinning. "New York, Chicago, San Francisco, and most recently, Los Angeles. I have to say that New York is the best, closely followed by L.A."

On hearing this, Kawagoe-san folded herself in half and pretended to be in pain. "Aaaah, yam cha shitai [I want to do *yam cha*]!"

THIS CONVERSATION WAS one of the postfieldwork episodes in our relationship that began in September 1996. I visited her for the first time in her home in a town that I call Centerville in the American Midwest, when she was hosting a big lunch of take-out *yam cha* (dim-sum, an assortment of Chinese dumplings and other small dishes). It was just several weeks into my first ethnographic fieldwork, and I was anxious, to say the least, to make the first contact with this woman who, I was told, regularly organized social gatherings with other expatriate Japanese wives. Unfortunately, Kawagoe-san was too busy getting the lunch going and was unable to talk to me (or anyone else, for that matter). Takeda-san, who brought me in as her guest, quickly deserted me to help Kawagoe-san. Everyone else seemed to know each other well and was talking loudly and fast all at once. Even though Japanese is my first language, I quickly found the noise of twelve incessantly talking women and their fourteen screeching children entirely exhausting.

We could hear Kawagoe-san's three children, Michi, Mika, and Tadashi, right outside in the tiny front yard, arguing excitedly. The excitement was apparently about some bugs they had just caught. Michi, the older girl, appeared to be trying to convince her unsure younger sister and baby brother that it really would be all right to take the bugs into the house. Kawagoe-san, without missing a beat, yelled out, "Michi, sonnamon uchini motte hairunjanaiyo [Michi, you will not bring such things inside the house]!" Her voice was loud and her tone stern, and as usual, she spoke in an extremely casual and almost masculine language.

There was a brief moment of silence outside, then three cheery voices replied in unison, "Haai [yes]."

"Mattaku mo," Kawagoe-san turned to me with exaggerated exasperation. (*Mattaku mo* roughly means "Entirely so," a phrase often used to indicate desperation or exasperation.) "Listen to my kids, they are so bratty sometimes! They are always pushing the envelope. Just wait and see. In no time, they will bring those bugs inside."

I knew that, behind this roughness, Kawagoe-san loved her kids to pieces. I had known her and her children a long time, since before Tadashi was born, before Mika could pronounce her own name correctly, before Michi went through her toilet training. Five years later, back in Japan, where we both came from but had never met before, Kawagoe-san did not remember how, when, and where we met for the first time in Centerville. When I reminded her about the yam cha lunch, she recalled it as a particularly large and chaotic event among many similar gatherings that she hosted while she lived in Centerville.

An awful lot of shuffling sounds came from the foyer, and Kawagoe-san yelled out once again. "I hope you aren't bringing in those bugs, or else!" There was no response, but a hushed chuckle.

Kawagoe-san and I looked at each other and burst into laughter. "Mattaku mo," Kawagoe-san said again under her breath.

"Your children are growing up so fast, Kawagoe-san. No wonder we are getting old!"

THE PASSAGE OF TIME and change of location are integral parts of my relationship with Kawagoe-san and other women with whom I became close friends during their temporary residence in the United States. Many of them stay in regular contact, even after their husbands have been reassigned back to Japan or to another location in the United States, with the phone and the fax and now, increasingly, through the Internet. They also try to get together whenever they are back in Japan. In that sense, my meeting with Kawagoe-san was nothing extraordinary, just part of life for many middle-class Japanese women like her. These translocal friendships are one of the most concrete manifestations of *gurobaruka*, or globalization, that is otherwise abstract and distant for most of these women but that suddenly, and often unexpectedly, becomes real when they are sent abroad, along with their husband, on a *kaigai chuuzai*, a corporate job assignment in a foreign country far away from home. Most of the Japanese corporate employees who are chosen for foreign assignments are men—not surprising, because the core corporate workforce in Japan, despite some recent changes, remains predominantly male. Therefore, when Japanese women speak of going abroad "on a job assignment," they usually are referring to their husband's (or their future husband's) assignment rather than their own. At the same time, they also know that they have an important role to play during their corporate-driven temporary migration: to create a Japanese home away from home and make a foreign place livable for their family members. These Japanese corporate wives and their homemaking in the context of corporate-driven transnational migration are the focus of this book.

With this ethnographic study, I wish not only to analyze the specific form of globalization that middle-class Japanese wives experience as spouses of "corporate warriors," but more important, to shed light on some key aspects of globalization that have not received adequate anthropological attention. First, we need to consider more carefully how class affects the experience of globalization. Highly mobile transnational professionals and their family members experience globalization in their middle-class positions and from the vantage point constructed through their professions (Hannerz 1998; Ribeiro 1994; Wulff 1998).[1] Previous studies of transnational migration tended to center on underprivileged groups, including labor migrants and refugees whose undesirable political-economic positionings in the home country motivate their movement. The mobility practices of those who are relatively affluent and privileged are expected to differ significantly from those who are not. The fact that they have the means to (and often do) return to their home country, either permanently or on a temporary visit, also changes the significance of transnational mobility. Transnational professionals—who reside abroad for an extended period on a corporate job assignment, government service, or for other professional purposes—often behave more like sojourners than migrants, because they almost invariably expect to return to their home country after a period of residence overseas. The economic and social privileges that these expatriates carry from their home country also allow them to keep a distance from the host society and form their own exclusive community. Thus, we may expect that the Japanese corporate families in posh New York suburbs share some class-specific experiences with South Asian professionals in Silicon Valley and entrepreneurial Cuban émigrés in Little Havana that they do not share with other migrants of Japanese ancestry, including the Japanese Americans who arrived in the Americas in the early twentieth century as labor migrants and Japanese women who married American GIs during the occupation period and came to the United States in the 1950s as so-called war brides.

The domestic space and homemaking practices are another area in the study of globalization that has not received the close analytical attention they deserve. The critical importance of the domestic—an insight explicated by feminist anthropologists and in theories on modern power—has not been fully explored in relation to the process of globalization, as existing studies have tended to focus on the public domain, such as paid labor, consumption, and popular culture (e.g., Appadurai and Breckenridge 1988; Constable 1997; Ong 1987; Pinches 1999; Wilson and Dissanayake 1996; but see Rapport and Dawson 1998). By contrast, the interconnection between the domestic arena and the public interest of transnational capitalism is at the heart of my study. As I argue in the following chapters, the transnational migration and homemaking of expatriate Japanese wives are driven by the specific and often contradictory demands of Japanese capitalism, which makes the homes of Japanese transnational migrants a novel ethnographic site in which to examine the connection between the domestic space and larger social and economic systems.

I also examine the ambivalent outcomes that the global-local articulation generates and consider how the results of my ethnographic study speak to recent theoretical developments regarding modern power and resistance. Despite the conservative cultural roles and social positioning of middle-class Japanese women, the experience of transnational homemaking often has unexpected effects on these women's relationships to their family members, their conception of home, and their own gender and cultural identity. The range of responses that middle-class Japanese housewives have toward corporate-driven transnational migration indicates that intersecting identities of gender, class, and national culture complicate the individual subject's experience of global processes and that the consciousness of transnational subjects always remains split and ambivalent.

Finally, the complexity and hybridity of mobility practices in today's globalizing world urge us to reexamine our conception of mobility itself. Many studies indicate that it is quite common among today's transnational migrants to go back and forth between their home country and host country, or to hop from one host country to another, all the while maintaining close economic, cultural, and personal ties with their origins. Many others have scrutinized the arbitrary distinction between "traveling" and "dwelling" (Clifford 1997; also see Bammer 1994; Gupta and Ferguson 1997; Hannerz 1996) and analyzed the construction of local identity in which transnationality is an integral part (e.g., Levitt 2001; Piot 1999; Tsing 1993). These realizations influence my approach to the study of transnationally mobile Japanese corporate families. Rather than fixing them in an existing category, I analyze how intersecting economic interests, ideologies of nation, class, and gender, and daily practices of homemaking produce a very particular experience of the global for middle-class Japanese women who are charged to manage the impact of transnational mobility on the core corporate workforce, and how that experience may affect the ways those women think of their relation to the global.

In the next several sections, I outline the set of theoretical questions that drive this ethnography. It is a way of placing my ethnography in the context of existing studies and key theoretical thoughts and of suggesting how the study of this particular group of transnational migrants connects with the broader anthropological concerns regarding two intricately related spheres of our experience in the late capitalist world that may seem distant at first: globalization and domesticity.

GLOBALIZATION AND CULTURE

Economic, social, and cultural changes that characterize the late twentieth and early twenty-first centuries are often glossed as *globalization*, in which the increased geographic mobility and the global flows of information and commodities appear to disintegrate national and cultural boundaries, produce a new global culture that is at once hybrid and homogeneous, and make identity formation more fluid with fewer necessary links to a geographic location (Appadurai 1991; Hannerz 1996; Jameson and Miyoshi 1998). Cultural aspects of globalization, such as the development of homogenized global cultural trends and hybrid identities, are considered simultaneously the product of and the impetus for flexible accumulation—or the newly deterritorialized strategies of capitalism—and thus the unique historical phenomenon of late capitalism (Harvey 1989). This materialist-historical explanation of cultural change associated with globalization carries an unmistakable sense of evolution or linear progression, however (Kearney 1995, 550). Such an implication is particularly troublesome for anthropologists, whose disciplinary legacy includes the physical and intellectual distance between the educated cosmopolitan anthropologist and their "natives" who live quaint lives, untouched by the trappings of modernism. To say that formerly discrete cultures have just recently *become* deterritorialized is to accept the static and geographically bound notion of culture that needs to change only now, in response to the "changing" realities in which we conduct our anthropological research. By contrast, many anthropologists resist the essentializing notion as they focus on hybridity and mobility as always important aspects of cultural development (Hannerz 1996, 4–5). In fact, the notion of a pristine culture itself is questioned through the analysis of historical contacts that various cultural groups have had with others and constant renegotiation of cultural identities through such encounters (e.g., Comaroff and Comaroff 1991; Fox 1985; Mintz 1985, 1996; Wolf 1982).

To say that transcultural relationships are an old norm rather than a recent exception fundamentally changes the nature of our inquiries and raises profound questions about the ways we investigate local knowledge and identity (Clifford 1997; Marcus 1998). Whereas earlier thinkers, for example, tended to assume the stability and self-containment of cultures and identities and to assign flexibility exclusively to non-Western selves in contrast to bounded Western "individuals" (Carrithers et al. 1985; Shweder and LeVine 1984; but see Mead 1934; Strathern 1988), current works on alterity and transnationalism challenge us to see all identities, non-Western and Western, as the outcome of negotiation and contestation between self and other, shifting, multiple, and even paradoxical by nature (Battaglia 1995; Bhabha 1994; Rosaldo 1989; Tsing 1993). To extend this insight, we also need to reconsider the category of the local itself that is often positioned against the global (Gupta and Ferguson 1992). If identities are always the outcome of negotiation, then there is no a priori identity of the local to stand in opposition against the global. The local never exists without the global, as it is always already shaped within the world system, and the forces of global capitalism appropriate the uniqueness of places around the world (Dirlik 1999; also see Mintz 1985; Ong 1987). In turn, the global must also become localized, grounding itself in a specific place and taking advantage of its local resources, labor, and social organization, to operate effectively. Furthermore, social actors have to conceptualize and come to terms with globalization in their given cultural and social milieus. Thus, the study of globalization necessarily becomes the study of the local construction of the global, and the study of local knowledge also has to take into account its connection to the global (Marcus 1995).

This complex global-local articulation results in two seemingly contradictory outcomes. On the one hand, the increased global flow of people, ideas, and material objects in the late capitalist world appears to homogenize and generate the possibilities for creative mixture and cultural hybridity in every corner of the world at an unprecedented rate in world history (e.g., Featherstone 1996). On the other hand, as the rise of (neo)nationalism and religious fundamentalism indicates, the attachment to the local—symbolized in real or imagined places of origin, age-old cultural practices, or archaic social relations—continues to be an important constituent of collective identity, despite, or perhaps precisely because of, the deterritorialized conditions of the late capitalist world (see, e.g., Appadurai 1990; Ong 1998; Ong and Nonini 1997). Place-based identity in the globalizing world can become a naturalized and predominant ideology, which in turn gains the power to construct the subjective experience, determines the choices of social actors involved, and affects the ways they view and interact with global forces. The need for careful analysis exists in the production of the local as an ideological construct grounded in a historical and political-economic context, its process of depoliticization, and the function for which it serves. Even in the constantly changing, unsettling conditions of post-modernity, people construct—or attempt to construct—their sense of who they are based on shared beliefs and practices of identity making. They also tend to act according to the collective norms as they perceive them. This is not to say that the boundary around a cultural group is solid and stable, or that no one would challenge the values and defy the norms. Yet, at certain moments and places in history, people tend to uphold particular constructs of identity that are hegemonic, that which is covertly inserted into our understanding of the world as natural and "official," something to be taken for granted and beyond reproach, and thus to be acted on without question. Globalization has not fundamentally changed that. Instead, it has encouraged the development of novel forms and flexible strategies of identity making that often transcend the geopolitical boundaries.

In his consideration of the ethnography of the world system George Marcus (1995, 112) writes, "Sorting out the relationships of the local to the global is a salient and pervasive form of local knowledge that remains to be recognized and discovered in the embedded idioms and discourses of any contemporary site that can be defined by its relationship to the world system." No globalization takes place in a cultural or ideological vacuum, and no one faces globalization as a cultural and historical blank slate. Instead, people appropriate, stretch, and renegotiate the linguistic and conceptual repertoire available to them in order to construct their own sense of what globalization is. Through this process, the existing idioms and discourses are also transformed and the meaning of the local itself continues to shift. A good anthropological study of globalization, then, must ask, and attempt to answer, two complementary questions: How is the local constructed vis-à-vis the global, and, in turn, how do locally constructed cultural ideas and practices influence social actors in their engagement with global processes?

When we think of the "Japaneseness" of the Japanese experience of transnational mobility in this way, instead of in the essentialist sense, the question of cultural specificity also takes on a different—and more intriguing, I argue—meaning. Certain idioms have been very important conceptual tools for Japanese subjects in a transnational situation, and Japanese cultural nationalism, a form of nationalism justified by the perceived cultural singularity of the Japanese, also plays a prominent part in the Japanese discourse of globalization. As I examine in more detail below, this sense of cultural uniqueness that the majority of today's Japanese seem to accept and share is a product of local-global articulation through Japan's modern history. At the same time, middle-classness and gender seem to be equally, if not more, powerful forces in shaping the experience of Japanese migrants/sojourners/travelers.

Japaneseness is, then, just one of the many pieces that make up this particular picture of globalization. Both my academic peers and lay audience have asked me on a number of occasions whether expatriate Japanese families become "American," "Western," or "cosmopolitan" because of their experience of living in the United States and other places outside Japan. Some inquisitors are more direct and declare my ethnographic project fatally flawed, because those sheltered housewives, they assert, remain "Japanese" throughout their time abroad and thus never truly experience the global. These comments and questions implicitly assume that local identities are stable and discreet and that being "Japanese" and being "American" are mutually exclusive. Equally problematic is that they also seem to suggest that the mobility experience of "sheltered" Japanese housewives is less authentic, and therefore not worthy of anthropological attention, than that of, say, hardscrabble Mexican immigrants.

I can only respond to these assertions with more questions: Whose idea of Americanness are we talking about here? Yes, I have seen many subtle and not so subtle changes in the lives of expatriate Japanese wives, but they are not necessarily American in the way Americans think of themselves. Then are their changes to be considered Americanization, or the localization of *Amerika* (see Tobin 1992a; Watson 1997)? "Japan," bracketed to emphasize its always already constructed nature, makes an intriguing case of the local as an ideological construct that shapes the worldviews and actions of its citizen-subjects in today's globalizing world. What sojourning Japanese may see outside their national and cultural home is in itself the product of local-global interaction, that is, the knowledge of the "other" generated through their perceived Japaneseness. Here we come full circle: the local is global and the global is local.

CORPORATE, MIDDLE-CLASS, AND MOBILE

The daily life of middle-class Japanese overseas became popular reading throughout the 1980s and into the early 1990s, when the Japanese economy experienced a long period of global expansion and when those Japanese corporations that were traditionally reluctant to go outside Japan began to transnationalize (see below for a more detailed discussion). Many kaigai chuuzai returnees and others with the experience of living in the United States and elsewhere around the world published memoirs detailing their encounters with the foreign, chronicling the trials and triumphs of transnational mobility. Many of those memoirs were written by former expatriate workers (e.g., Kawai 1992; Yamazaki 1984) and wives who accompanied their husband to his foreign assignment in the 1970s (e.g., Fukunaga 1990; Taniguchi 1985) and were read widely by the wives of prospective foreign assignees. By the early 1990s, kaigai chuuzai, or at least the possibility of it, became a common feature in middle-class Japanese life; at the same time, the typical age at which Japanese corporate workers and their families experience their first foreign assignment also began to drop. These changes are reflected in popular readings in the kaigai chuuzai genre in the 1990s that are targeted toward younger readers, using *manga* or cartoons as the medium and taking a more light-hearted, even mocking approach to kaigai chuuzai. For example, the popular cartoon series *Amerika Chuuzai Monogatari* (American Job Assignment Story) features a young Japanese couple and their son who have just been stationed in New York. In each installment, they make a funny mistake due to a lack of language skills or cultural knowledge, and through their errors, the reader is introduced to useful English idioms or unique American customs (Okada and Shimamoto 1993). Another example, *Chuuzaiin Fujin no Deepu na Sekai* (The Deep World of Expatriate Wives), is split between the written text and manga (Mori and Saike 1997). The book is both a memoir of a former expatriate wife and a "manual" for young corporate wives who are about to embark on their first foreign assignment. One of the authors (Mori), who spent five years in Los Angeles with her husband, imparts her clever strategies as a young expatriate wife to maneuver smoothly around what she calls ironically the "deep world" of expatriate Japanese wives; all the while, she is poking fun at the "peculiar ways" in which expatriate Japanese, particularly those who are older and in higher corporate ranks than she and her husband, behave in their tightknit and gossip-laden community.

The increasing familiarity of kaigai chuuzai in middle-class Japan, however, has not necessarily resulted in a better understanding of its impact on corporate families, particularly the experience of those house-wives who are expected to take care of their family members through the period of transition and uncertainty before, during, and after kaigai chuuzai. These topics have largely escaped anthropological scrutiny, too, perhaps because of the assumption that their corporate affiliation and the nimble-footedness of their mobility practices shielded them from any experience of profound consequences. Just about everyone to whom I asked the question about the everyday life of expatriate Japanese wives—including middle-class Japanese women in Japan, male corpo-rate managers, and, most of all, expatriate Japanese wives themselves—were generally dismissive of the significance of what middle-class Japa-nese housewives did during the kaigai chuuzai. Many did admit that those women who went to underdeveloped countries experienced many challenges, as their homemaking was made difficult by lack of access to Japanese goods, climate change, the threat of unfamiliar illness, and safety concerns. However, regarding those in the United States and other industrialized countries, the predominant perception has been that their daily lives changed very little during their temporary resi-dence abroad, and in some cases, they were thought to enjoy a life of luxury and leisure.

Such perceptions of the lives of middle-class corporate Japanese fam-ilies in the United States are only a partial truth, and a quickly fading truth at that. There was a time when "five years in the United States would build a house," meaning that the U.S. assignment was so well compensated that a transferred family could save enough money in five years to build a house on their return to Japan. This was partly due to the strong U.S. dollar against the Japanese yen, and partly because of the elite status of many expatriate corporate workers who received generous *chuuzai teate*, or foreign assignment benefits and subsidies. These financial advantages quickly disappeared through the 1980s, however, when kaigai chuuzai became a much more common occurrence and the number of kaigai chuuzaiin dramatically increased; the tendency was further exacerbated during the economic downturn in the 1990s. Today, it is a common understanding among expatriate Japanese families that they are lucky if they financially break even during the foreign assignment.

Throughout these changes, the wives of expatriate corporate workers have been asked to extend their role as a domestic manager to ensure the productivity of their husband in a foreign location. This sometimes means that the wives have to remain in Japan and take care of the children and elderly family members so that the husband can concentrate on his job far from home. In other situations, wives are encouraged, expected, and even required to accompany their husband to the foreign assignments to help him, as well as their accompanying children, manage the impact of geographic mobility and ease the difficulty of living in a foreign social and cultural environment. The latter has been the choice of the overwhelming majority of Japanese corporations that send their male workers to the United States, where, particularly in and around larger cities, the living conditions are considered equal to or better than those in Japan and where amenities necessary for expatriate Japanese families, including Japanese schools and Japanese-speaking local businesses, are available, if only to varying degrees. As a result, an increasing number of Japanese corporate families has been sent to the United States over the past three decades, not only to major coastal cities such as New York and Los Angeles that have long been important hubs for Japanese businesses in the United States, but also to less cosmopolitan cities in the Midwest, the Southeast, and the Southwest.

The job that middle-class Japanese wives perform in the United States and other places outside Japan is to create a bubble of Japaneseness in the middle of foreignness. The women, like worms in cocoons, are to stay in the domestic space that they create with their daily labor. Such drawing and reinforcing of cultural boundaries is, perhaps, a universal phenomenon at the site of cross-cultural contact and a common experience among all types of transnational migrants and sojourners—military personnel, missionaries, colonial officers, governmental and NGO staff, migrant workers—from all places in all different circumstances. Expatriate Americans, for example, are known to live clustered in particular neighborhoods of Tokyo and develop their own social circles of other Americans, expatriate Europeans, and perhaps a few cosmopolitan Japanese. The ethnic enclaves around larger cities in the United States—Chinatown, Little Italy, Little Saigon—also remind us of the immigrants and migrants who came and went since the turn of the last century and reshaped the urban space in their adopted home in the image of their place of origin. They also seem to employ similar strategies of identity making and marking, including spatial clustering, the emphasis on national/ethnic cuisine, display of cultural artifacts in domestic spaces, and the importation of popular culture from their place of origin.

Therefore, my claim is not that the creation of the cultural bubble is a unique invention by the transnationally mobile Japanese corporate families. Rather, my interest lies in *how* this bubble is established and maintained according to what this particular group of transnational migrants believes to be necessary to protect the cultural boundaries around them, and more important, how it is challenged and renegotiated, if inadvertently, through their experience of transnationality. For instance, the closedness of the home and women's innate domesticity are largely assumed by the male corporate managers, the husbands of these women, outside observers, and sometimes even by the women themselves; thus, it is a largely shared conception that transnational migration does not affect these housewives much, if at all, as they perform the same mundane household tasks day in and day out. Japanese women themselves regard these responsibilities as their duty as women, and they appear to define their feminine selves through the fulfillment of their domestic roles, at least in part. Every act of homemaking produces "ideal" femininity in these women that not only conforms to the normative concepts of gender and Japaneseness, but also propagates them by providing a space of cultural reproduction in a foreign environment.

Expatriate Japanese wives are, by and large, a conservative bunch, who have chosen to live by this ideal of female domesticity. However, a closer look at their daily lives reveals that these women often have complicated feelings about their domestic labor, and they may find ways to contest this otherwise all-consuming requirement of femininity. Their relationship to ideal femininity is always already ambivalent, and even contradictory: while taking their roles as wives and mothers seriously, middle-class Japanese women question the imposition of the ideal of feminine domesticity during their temporary migration to the United States, both in their words and in their actions. This gray area between the hegemony of feminine domesticity (or the connection between women and domesticity that is presented as beyond reproach) and the reality of women's everyday life and consciousness is what I highlight throughout this book.

It is important to acknowledge that this gray area, as well as all the negotiations that may take place in it, is not solely the product of transnational migration. But it is the function of the built-in ambiguities, contradictions, and flexibility in the construction of femaleness. The self exists only in and as a process of negotiation, and, in the case of middle-class Japanese housewives, this negotiation takes place mainly in the home, through homemaking activities of the everyday that they perform as wives and mothers. Thus, the question that we ought to be asking is not how a previously stable identity of middle-class Japanese women is suddenly disrupted in a foreign country, but how transnational homemaking affects the ongoing process of self-making for these women. Transnational mobility has a certain jarring effect of exaggerating contentious aspects of self-making and bringing to the surface what is unspoken and unquestioned in ordinary circumstances. Does the transnational mobility create an opening in which these women can begin to reconsider, challenge, and rework what they have taken for granted as a natural part of their feminine selves? And how do they, or do they not, take advantage of such openings? Why, or why not?

THE DOMESTIC AS THE POLITICAL

The realm of the domestic seems oddly absent in transnational studies, and the critical importance of the domestic—an insight explicated by feminist anthropologists and in theories on modern power—in the context of globalization has not been fully explored. Perhaps this tendency is hardly surprising, given the highly visible material practices of translocality and hybridity. I propose, however, to turn to the domestic as the critical juncture between the global and the local, where the multitude of global and local forces intersect, collide, and negotiate with one another.

The materialist-feminist theory situates the privatization and feminization of reproductive labor at the root of female subordination in societies, most prominently in advanced capitalist societies, with a strict division of labor in the public and domestic spheres. Although this has been a pervasive practice through time and space, in which culturally classified males and females are assigned different productive and reproductive tasks, women in many non-Western and premodern societies reportedly have enjoyed high status and power based on their critical roles in food production, economic management, and ritual activities (Brown 1975; Draper 1975; Strathern 1981). By contrast, in modern capitalist societies, particularly among the middle and upper classes, the division of labor between women and men tends to be synonymous with the separation of paid versus unpaid labor, or the private sphere as the locus of reproduction versus the public sphere as the locus of production. Male labor is exploited outside the household for the production of exchange values, and women are confined at home as specialists in the production of use value and reproduction of labor (Rapp 1978; Sacks 1975). As capitalist interests center on the increase of exchange value, the labor of men is compensated in the form of wages, whereas women's domestic and reproductive labor is unpaid and unrecognized (Miller 1995).[2]

The devaluation of women's labor has a dire consequence in women's access to social power in highly stratified and/or capitalist societies. Sacks (1975) argues that social power and status do not originate from the ownership of private property, but from the participation in social labor; thus, women's work at home cannot translate into social or political power in the public sphere. This is in stark contrast to societies with less social and economic stratification, according to feminist researchers, where women's labor in the domestic sphere not only gives them authority within the household, but also gives them a certain amount of power and unique influence in the public arena (Friedl 1967; Sanday 1981). The strict physical and social divisions between the domestic and public domains in modern capitalist societies exacerbate this differ-ence. Women's indirect participation, by coercion or manipulation of the male members of the household, might prove effective in less strat-ified societies where the boundaries between the public and the private spheres seem more flexible (Strathern 1981). However, the effectiveness of this "female" strategy is curtailed in contemporary society, where work and home are carefully separated, and the formal versus informal or social versus domestic powers are clearly distinguished and rigidly ranked (Kanter 1977; Nippert-Eng 1996; Rapp 1978).

This gendered assignment of domestic labor is also historically con-nected with the emergence of the middle class (Davidoff and Hall 1987; also see my discussion below). The domestic space and the domesticity of women who create it continue to be "crucial sites for producing middle class-ness" in today's globalizing world (Sen and Stivens 1998, 4). Even as women's unpaid reproductive labor marginalizes them, well-managed homes become the source of class identity. Women-as-housewives become the conservative agents of state and global power not only for the reproduction of labor, but also for the construction of cultural and national identities, and their middle-class femininity is produced and reinforced by their reproductive labor (see Chodorow 1989; Sacks 1975; Sanday 1990).

Domesticity continues to be the hallmark of middle-class femininity in Japan, despite some recent signs of change.[3] In recent labor statistics, Japanese women's labor participation continues to take the traditional "M" shape, as they withdraw from the labor market during their re-productive years (Bowman and Osawa 1986; Inoue and Ebara 1995). The nature of their participation in extradomestic work is also prob-lematic: women's employment during and after the reproductive period is in largely part-time, unskilled jobs with nearly no job security or nonwage benefits (Inoue and Ebara 1995). Many analysts have pointed out that the notion of feminine domesticity, which is still prevalent in Japanese society today, is the ideological constraint behind these phe-nomena (Inoue and Ebara 1995; Ueda 1992). With the prospect of a serious labor shortage in the near future, Japanese public opinion ap-pears to sway between the increased emphasis on women's reproductive roles and the impetus for furthering women's participation in social labor (Ohinata 1992; Ueda 1992; Yoshitake 1994). Marriage avoidance is a widespread phenomenon among contemporary Japanese women in their twenties (White 2002), but by their late twenties or early thirties the majority ultimately choose the life of a full-time housewife over a stressful juggling act between domestic duties and professional jobs (Ogura 1998). Even when they remain in the workforce beyond their twenties, many are on the clerical track and are not likely to be sent on a kaigai chuuzai. Therefore, for many middle-class Japanese women, participation in transnationalism typically happens *to* them, not as a consequence of their paid labor outside the home, but as an extension of their domestic roles as wife and mother, to make a Japanese home and take care of their husband and children in a foreign country to which corporate employers decide to send the husbands.[4]

As feminist scholars have pointed out, women's reproductive labor has long been appropriated in the capitalist system, of which modern Japan is a stark example. Throughout Japan's modernization process, productive and reproductive labor was increasingly gendered and segregated (see further discussion in chapter 2). In the period during which modern industrial labor practices called "Fordism" developed, corporations provided generous benefits and took an active part in the workers' private lives to ensure an effective reproduction of labor (Martin 1997). In other words, the corporations benefited from the shifting of the costs of labor reproduction from the realm of corporate responsibility to that of individual workers and their households, by using the unpaid labor of the housewives and mothers to take care of corporate workers and raise future corporate workers at home. The reproductive strategy in the post-Fordist era pushes this privatization even further and requires the homes of their workers to reproduce workers who can adapt to ever changing conditions of work and to absorb all the impact of a flexible labor regimen. For instance, the impact of long-distance travel and increased mobility—ranging from the health risks of frequent flyers to the financial loss incurred by frequent moving and the complex psychological effects of dislocation—are less a concern of corporations and governments, but are shifted to the domestic space as private matters for individual workers and their families to deal with (Martin 1997). At this stage, the incorporation of the domestic space into capitalist machinery is complete. It is no longer spoken of, and what comes without saying goes without saying. The domestic space, from this perspective, is simply the location in which capitalism cultivates and harvests the docile and productive bodies that populate its factories and offices and submit to strict work routines.

This view of the domestic space also reflects the decentered nature of modern power itself that permeates every aspect of our lives and consciousness (Foucault 1978). Some theorists resist this implication by emphasizing the autonomy of the domestic space from the larger society. Michel de Certeau, for instance, considers the everyday life an opportunity for "microresistances" and "minitransgressions" (de Certeau et al. 1998, xxi). To him, the taken-for-granted activities, or ways of "doing" and "using" things in everyday life, constitute a vehicle of resistance rather than oppression, no matter how small its effects may be (de Certeau 1984). De Certeau sees these "minor" practices as the source of plurality beneath the monopoly of power, escaping totalization precisely because of this seeming lack of importance. His theorization stems from his skepticism toward the antihumanist implication of the conception of power as all-pervasive, which minimizes the role of individual agency in social processes (Althusser 1971; Foucault 1978). Similar to Pierre Bourdieu (1977; Bourdieu and Waquant 1992), who conceives of social actors as resourceful individuals who maneuver around the structural constraints and negotiate their way through the existing system to their own ends, de Certeau's idea of microresistance projects the image of active, clever, and self-aware human beings who, despite the appearance of obedience, act on their own will and do not hesitate to subvert the dominant power in their minor practices of the everyday. At the same time, his conception of the domestic space as a sanctuary contradicts my earlier observation of how the domestic space and reproductive labor have been incorporated into the capitalist system. The making of productive bodies under Fordist and post-Fordist labor regimes has been so successful precisely because it operates at this very level of the mundane and minute. De Certeau's conception of the domestic as a private sanctuary cannot account for this and therefore ultimately is dissatisfying as a theoretical model.

We can instead conceive of the domestic as a space in which social actors can more successfully exercise their agency and negotiate with structural power than in any other institutional location. Daniel Miller (1995, 1998), for example, locates the possibility of individual agency within the diffuse power itself. On the one hand, power in modern society is literally everywhere; on the other hand, the nature of this power is inherently ambivalent: liberating and oppressive, enabling and repressive all at once. Furthermore, every "little decision-making" act of the everyday can eclipse the "big political decision-making" (Miller 1995, 10) mechanism in consumption-oriented late modern society, as the power in this social context becomes so diffuse that every one of us comes to have a share in it, relative to our social and economic positions. It seems that, as our subjectivities become infused with power, the question is not so much the resistance of the powerless against the powerful, but the internal negotiation between the repressive and the enabling aspects of power within ourselves. The everyday practice, and the identity that is performatively constituted through the everyday practice, thus take on the same ambivalent character as power itself and become the point of contestation between the structural forces and individual agency.

This is a particularly important insight in our attempt to understand the transnational experience of middle-class Japanese housewives, whose oppression may not be so immediate or brutal but nonetheless limits their choices in expressing their dissent. Their acts of resistance or subversion require the façade of compliance while effectively undermining the structure of power from below. If power is "subtly, pervasively diffused throughout habitual daily practices" (Eagleton 1991, 114) then the opportunity to subvert is also found in that same location (Foucault 1978; Gramsci 1971; Jameson 1984). In modern societies, Homi Bhabha (1994, 11) points out, the domestic space is incorporated into the world, and it becomes "the space of the normalizing, pastoralizing, and individuating techniques of modern power and police: the personal-*is*-the political; the world-*in*-the-home." However, there is an irony in this doubling of the home: by meddling with the boundary between the world and the home, modern power opens itself for resistance from within, as domestic spaces become *unheimlich*, or "unhomely," the place where the hidden becomes revealed and where the unfamiliar is made familiar and the familiar strangely distant. This hybridity of home, in turn, embodies "the disjunctive, displaced everyday life" of an interstitial subject (13). The split or doubling of domestic space that is simultaneously the public and the private, the world and the home, the self and the other makes it a place of political struggle, where the dirty laundry (i.e., what our world and ourselves are made of) is in everyone's plain view in the intimate space of a home. Thus, as soon as Japanese corporations explicitly urged their employees' wives to mind homely responsibilities, they unintentionally started the process of transformation that makes the location of Japanese self-making such an unhomely place. In this moment, everyday life and the homemaking labor that is intended to protect its mundaneness come to bear the possibility of generating alternative historical voices, as Harry Harootunian (2001) asserts, that contradict official narratives.

A question remains, however: How does transnational mobility affect the domestic, as unhomely as it already is? If the domestic is quietly (and sometimes not so quietly) incorporated into the machinery of global capitalism for the reproduction of labor, will the everyday practices of homemaking also provide opportunities for the negotiation between ideal and alternative subjectivities? Are middle-class Japanese housewives, despite their conservative positioning, seduced by these opportunities as they go abroad with their "corporate warrior" husband? To put it another way, is the assumed everydayness of homemaking disrupted through the process of transnational mobility, creating an opening in which to question, challenge, and modify their taken-for-granted assumptions about gender difference and national identity?

TO TRAVEL, OR TO LIVE

Somewhere between my first two field projects in Centerville and New York, I opened James Clifford's *Routes: Travel and Translation in the Late Twentieth Century* (1997). In his thought-provoking introduction, Clifford examines "traveling" and "dwelling" as implicit yet critical conceptual oppositions in the development of anthropological epistemology and implores, "Why not focus on any culture's farthest range of travel while *also* looking at its centers, its villages, its intensive field-sites?" (25). I realized that my ethnographic work in expatriate Japanese homes was necessarily dually focused and that the duality of my vision was further complicated by the fact I, too, was an expatriate Japanese woman, although my transnational migration was motivated by my own professional aspirations. At that moment, an obscure ethnographic observation of mine suddenly clicked with the theoretical concerns that were reshaping the anthropological conception of mobility and motivated me to situate the rhetorics of "home" and "travel" at the center of my ethnography (also see Gupta and Ferguson 1997).

The notion of home is complicated and loaded, with double and triple entendres. On the one hand, it is the place of domicile, the place where one lives, the house that one goes back to at the end of the day. On the other hand, it is the place of origin and identification, a community, a city, or a country to which one "belongs," the place in which one may or may not live at the moment but to which one always looks back as the location of one's cultural and personal roots. In today's globalizing world, the split between these two "homes" has become a familiar experience not only to people in diaspora, but to all types of permanent and temporary migrants, refugees, extended and perpetual travelers, and transnational workers. Among some cultural groups, mobility has long been part of their collective identity: Jews and diaspora Chinese, for example. Among others, a strong physical attachment to a geographic location has been at the core of their identity, and mobility poses a problem, or at least a complication, in that self-construct.

For contemporary middle-class Japanese, two homes have become increasingly separated and distant, as movement within Japan for educational and economic reasons has become more and more common. Many urban families have *inaka* (country home) or *furusato* (an old home place), where they trace their family origins, where Grandpa and Grandma live on the farm, where they spend every summer vacation and go to visit ancestral graveyards. To many corporate workers and their families, *tenkin*, or relocation to take a new job assignment, is a way of life (Okifuji 1986). In a way, kaigai chuuzai is an extension of this mobility experience in the sense that people in both situations encounter the effect of uprooting and labor to create a home of their own in a new and unfamiliar place away from their place of origin. In many other ways, it is a radically different experience from mobility within the national and cultural borders of Japan. After all, one can count on certain things no matter where one goes in Japan: communicating in Japanese, having the same administrative procedures at government offices, finding familiar brands of toothpaste, and buying staple food items, like rice and soy sauce, at a nearby grocery store. In urban areas, where newcomers are numerous and family ties are no longer the primary factor in social networks, there are public resources that one can use to make friends, entertain oneself, and receive information, even if for a fee. Above all, the people are all Japanese and thus never have to think twice about shared language, cultural identity, and citizenship.

When a job assignment takes one outside Japan, none of these assumptions stand true, as one finds oneself living among foreigners. Even more shocking is the fact that one becomes a foreigner and feels that one is treated differently because of that. Suddenly, it becomes meaningful that one is Japanese and, with other Japanese, distinct from the Americans, French, Chinese, and so forth. When the two homes are split across national borders because of kaigai chuuzai, the domestic space in a foreign country also becomes a little bubble of Japaneseness that floats in the sea of foreignness. I have already discussed how women are expected to maintain this bubble as an extension of their roles as wife and mother. This job is often perceived by corporate employers and male workers (i.e., the husbands) as not significantly different from homemaking in Japan. Yet, homemaking in a foreign place brings many constraints and also opportunities to the daily life of middle-class Japanese housewives, as they go back and forth between the *uchi* (the inside, a home) and *soto* (the outside, a strange place) to construct their Japanese home in a foreign place.

As the globalization of Japanese capitalism makes foreign job assignments more frequent and prolonged, more and more expatriate Japanese families begin to develop an attachment to their home away from home. Particularly for the corporate wives, whose womanly job centers on turning a foreign place into a familiar place in which to live, the contradiction of living and traveling at once dominates their transnational experience. At the same time, they wonder whether they can ever go home to Japan, or whether they will become a modern version of Urashima Taro, a tragic hero in a Japanese folk tale who, after a prolonged visit to the kingdom under the sea, found himself a stranger in his own village. At the same time, admitting that one is living (as opposed to staying or traveling) in the United States is a frightening prospect that shakes the Japan-centered worldview of most Japanese who reside outside their national and cultural home (Rapport and Dawson 1998). If they live in the United States, does that mean that this foreign place has become their home? And, if so, what is Japan to them? Can they possibly call both places home? This ambivalence at the core of transnational mobility is what I explore in my ethnography of middle-class Japanese housewives' everyday life in the United States.

SOON AFTER I BEGAN fieldwork in Centerville, I noticed that many of my informants considered their temporary residence in the United States a sort of prolonged travel or a "long vacation" (see Flory 1989). In the accounts of my informants, kaigai chuuzai is often described as a form of travel and kaigai chuuzai families as travelers. Many women called themselves a *ryokosha* (literally, "traveler"). Others refer to their *Amerika chuuzai* as a *ryoko* (travel), *bakeeshon* (vacation), or *kyuuka* (vacation or holiday), in spite of their acknowledgment that it is of an "extended" (*choki* or *nagai*) nature. Other phrases capture kaigai chuuzai as the opposite of the home and permanent dwelling. They include, for example, *ichiji taizai* (temporary stay), *choki taizai* (extended stay), *kari no sumai* (temporary domicile), *ichiji taizaisha* (a temporary visitor), and *yosomono* (a stranger to the area).

The language of temporariness, particularly of "vacation," seemed disjoined from what these women did every day in the United States: making a home and turning a foreign country into a livable place. Why do they speak of traveling when they actually try to live in the United States, though temporarily? Why do they call their life in the United States a vacation when they work so hard at homemaking every day? What does the metaphor of travel convey about the meanings of transnational homemaking as Japanese corporate wives perceive them? And what effects does it have on the experience of transnationality to perceive it as traveling as opposed to dwelling?

The vacation motif also raised questions in my mind about the work-driven nature of Japanese wives' and mothers' daily routine. A vacation has a connotation of escapist pleasure, relaxation, excitement, and perhaps luxury. The temporary transnational migration of Japanese corporate families is obviously not a vacation in the literal sense of the word. It comes with many responsibilities, and both the corporate worker and his wife dutifully perform their tasks every day. The women can hardly escape from the mundaneness of homemaking or the obligation-driven social life as they continue to be part of the expatriate Japanese community and are bound by social constraints similar to those in Japan. Transnational migration also lasts much, much longer—an average of three to five years—than a vacation, and return home involves careful preparation and at times painful adjustment.

Making a home, even a temporary one away from their true home, is a practice in dwelling in both meanings of the word: living in a place and contemplating something at length. Yet, expatriate Japanese wives always seem conscious of the transient nature of their lives during kaigai chuuzai. Just about everyone wonders when and where their husband's next job assignment might be. Some dread the day when they will have to return to the social obligations and responsibilities that await them in Japan. Many wonder how they might turn their temporary residence in the United States into cultural capital that they can take back with them to Japan. With all these ambiguities, why do Japanese corporate wives choose to use a word with the connotation of escape and leisure?

FIELDWORK IN THREE U.S. CITIES

Like homemaking, ethnographic fieldwork is an act of constructing places and spaces in which to work. My fieldwork in three expatriate Japanese communities in the United States is no exception. Each of my three "anthropological locations" (Gupta and Ferguson 1997), in fact, consists of a unique combination of multiple social and cultural locations that middle-class Japanese families occupy and share with others. These locations are at once conceptual and concrete. Here, my intention is to provide a succinct yet substantive account of these sites on which I can develop a more complicated narrative in the following chapters.

My ethnographic fieldwork in three U.S. cities—a Midwestern city that I call Centerville, the Greater New York area, and North Carolina's Research Triangle—took place in part by design and in part by chance. My field projects took place between 1996 and 2000. First, I spent ten months in Centerville, then six months in New York, and an equivalent of four full-time months in North Carolina. At each site, I had my own place to live, and my fieldwork activities included semistructured interviews, group interviews, and informal conversations, as well as participant observation of my female informants' daily activities. These activities included attending Japanese community events, being a member of interest groups that included expatriate Japanese wives, teaching at a Japanese-language school, and, on a few occasions, staying over at my key informants' homes.

My primary informants in all these sites were married Japanese women who accompanied their husband on a corporate job assignment in these cities. I sought out women from different age groups, family compositions, educational levels, and occupational histories in all three sites. I interviewed and interacted with more than 120 women and worked closely with several key informants and their circles of friends in the three sites. I also interviewed and interacted with the husbands of some of my female informants. In addition, I interviewed Japanese and American professionals who provided needed services in and around expatriate Japanese communities, including teachers at both local U.S. and Japanese-language schools, psychological counselors, local government employees, translators, and corporate representatives. Through a mail-in survey, I gathered information from approximately 150 additional informants (a small number of informants responded to both the survey and interview, but the exact number is unclear due to the anonymity of the survey). Serendipity often played a role in my ability to meet, interact with, and get to know many of the informants, who in turn introduced me to their friends if they so wished. Self-selection by informants was a major factor, particularly in the process of forming a closer and longer-term relationship. Some women actively sought me out or made a concerted effort to work with me (Kawagoe-san and Takeda-san being prime examples); many allowed a limited engagement in a controlled situation (e.g., group interaction away from their home, or a strictly confidential, private conversation over the phone); and others tactfully avoided any interaction with me beyond polite greetings. There were moments of an unexpected shift from one mode of communication to another, such as a previously distant person warming up to me after we discovered a common interest, and a woman who limited her interaction with me to a public setting suddenly calling me at home to confide in me about a very sensitive situation that she was dealing with.

These field projects form a string of strategically situated single-site ethnographies (Marcus 1995, 110–113). Although the three sites were discrete and independent in many ways, they all fit together in a broader scheme of the transnationalization of Japanese capitalism, as I elaborate in chapter 2. Here, I describe the key features of each location.

As a rule, an expatriate Japanese community in the United States is structured around a corporation or a network of corporations in the area, and the geographic location of the community is also determined by the specific needs of transnational capitalist operations, both indicative of the corporate-driven nature of transnational movement and community formation. Although each expatriate Japanese community has its own history and well-defined boundary around it, corporate presence is a common structural force everywhere. All the Japan-based companies usually form an association that is at once a cooperative business organization, social structure, and information exchange network for expatriate Japanese families, and also serves as a conduit of information between the expatriate corporate community and Japanese government agencies (e.g., Japanese consulate's office and Japan External Trade Organization). It also requires some key Japanese resources: a Japanese-language school within driving distance, a comfortable living environment, and at least one source of Japanese food items. Some of the key differences include the size of and the diversity within the expatriate community, the existence of a predominant corporation, and the relationship with the local American community, which are also influenced greatly by the corporate interests and preselection of the type of expatriate workers to be sent to these locations.

I suspected that there were several different types of expatriate Japanese communities around the United States and wanted to sample at least a couple of different types. I chose Centerville and New York as manufacturing-centered and trade- and finance-driven examples and anticipated that these two communities consisted of different types of expatriate workers. I took local history and ethnic diversity in these two areas into consideration as well. After I completed these two field projects, an opportunity presented itself for me to continue my fieldwork in yet another expatriate community, this time in the technology-driven Research Triangle area of North Carolina. Although this was not a comparative study in a strict sense, I gained important insights about the breadth of transnational experience among corporate Japanese families through this multisited research.

To protect the confidentiality of my informants, I use pseudonyms for all personal names, and also for my first field site, which is closely associated with a well-known Japanese company (I may otherwise give away too many clues about my informants' identities). By contrast, the size and diversity of the Greater New York area eliminate such possibilities, and the expatriate Japanese community in North Carolina's Research Triangle lacked the kind of corporate center that characterized Centerville, making the identification of individual subjects by abbreviated description impossible.

Centerville (1996–1997). Centerville is one of the older locations in the United States to which subsidiaries of Japanese manufacturing industry ventured about twenty years ago. It was then an overgrown college town with little prior experience with manufacturing sectors. The areas surrounding Centerville had been productive agricultural areas, and even today, one may see corn fields at the edge of the city, although they are quickly being replaced with housing developments. The long-term residents in this state are predominantly whites of British, German, and other Northern European origins. For a long time, ethnic diversity here meant Jews and Southern and Eastern Europeans, with some African Americans and, more recently, Spanish-speaking groups in Centerville and other metropolitan areas.

In the early 1970s, Centerville's Midwestern state began an aggressive campaign to recruit direct foreign investment, the most important being from Japan, to boost its sagging economy. In the mid-1970s, Maveric Automotive decided to build its first manufacturing plant overseas just outside Centerville. Initially, there were next to no critical Japanese resources in the area, such as Japanese grocery stores and Japanese-language schools. There were a small number of Japanese permanent residents, many of whom acted as intermediaries between the expatriate workers and local Americans. ESL classes in local schools were small and qualified teachers few, reflecting a relatively small number of students whose first language was not English. With the increase of the expatriate Japanese population, more and more Japanese resources, ranging from educational institutions to stores that carry Japanese goods and personal services in Japanese, became available in the Centerville area. The first Japanese grocery store opened in the early 1980s, and the second one, combined with a Japanese bookstore and video store, followed shortly after. The Japanese Saturday School of Centerville started teaching a Japanese school curriculum to expatriate Japanese children in the early 1980s and soon became an approved *hoshuukou* (the supplemental overseas Japanese school), loosely supervised by the Japanese Ministry of Education. In the meantime, local public schools, most notably those in the town of Dunville, a wealthy

Centerville suburb with a heavy concentration of Japanese corporate families, began to expand their ESL programs to accommodate the ever increasing number of Japanese students whose English-language skills ranged from low to nil.

Maveric Automotive of Centerville (MAC) has become a powerful center of the Centerville expatriate community, with its financial resources and its well-established presence in the state and more generally in the United States. It seemed that most of the Japanese who lived in and near Centerville depended on MAC in one way or another. In fact, every Japanese corporate wife I met there had a husband who either worked for MAC proper, a Maveric-affiliated company, or a company that did business with MAC. Centerville, at least in its expatriate Japanese segment, has become a virtual "corporate castle town," where one powerful corporation dominates the economy of an entire community and its influence permeates every aspect of the life of its citizens (Kinoshita 1983). The hierarchical relationships between MAC and others were felt among the expatriate wives on an everyday basis; one of the most visible differences was the access to the MAC Family Center, where MAC's Japanese employees and their families can get an interpreter to go with them to their doctor's appointments, take English classes, join a variety of hobby groups, get referrals for children's tutors, and ask questions about living in Centerville. Many Maveric wives were quite dependent on the Family Center's services; Japanese families without access to the expatriate services of the Center were at times resentful of the poor family support that they received from their own employers.

Greater New York (1997–1998). The second research location, in the Greater New York or Tri-State area, where the corners of New York, New Jersey, and Connecticut meet, has the largest expatriate Japanese population in the United States, and perhaps in the world (Ministry of Foreign Affairs of Japan 1997). The cosmopolitan ambience and ethnic diversity of this area contrasts sharply with Centerville and its surroundings. In the first part of the twentieth century, the Japanese presence in the Tri-State area was relatively small in scale, as the mass immigration from Japan around the turn of the century came through the West Coast. The Japanese immigrants who settled in New York before World War II tended to be intellectuals and professionals. During and right after the war, *Nisei*, or second-generation Japanese Americans, began to form a sizable community in New York and established social and political organizations, such as Nikkeijin Kai (Japanese-American Association). A small number of Japanese expatriates began to arrive in New York several years after the end of World War II. Reflecting the nature of this city as the center of trade and finance, many of those expatriates represented the Japanese government's international trade interests, private financial institutions, and trading companies. The expansion of Japanese exports to the United States through the 1950s and 1960s supported the increasing number of corporate expatriates in the New York area. Simultaneously, Japanese industries represented in the area diversified into a wide range of manufacturing industries.

A major change occurred in the demographics of the New York Japanese-speaking community in the 1980s. Nisei citizens were aging and their community presence was diminishing. Many of their children became assimilated into mainstream middle-class America and no longer had a strong connection to the ethnic community; many others left the New York area for better quality of life and job opportunities in other parts of the country (cf. Newman 1993). At the same time, the expatriate corporate Japanese population was growing dramatically in size and strength. The number of corporate Japanese in New York, New Jersey, and Connecticut more than doubled during the 1980s, from approximately 17,000 in 1982 to more than 35,000 in 1988 (Ministry of Foreign Affairs of Japan 1997; Consulate General of Japan in New York 1997). With the strong and continuous economic growth through the mid-1980s to 1990, Japanese corporations' activities were visibly expanded and upgraded, as symbolized by their offices opening up one after another in Manhattan's expensive business districts.

The trend of expanding Japanese corporate activities and expatriate population was reversed at the end of Japan's "bubble" economic boom in the early 1990s, when many Japanese corporations were forced into eliminating or downsizing their operations in the United States. In 1992, the number of expatriate Japanese in the Tri-State area decreased for the first time since 1981, and this downward trend continued for the first half of the 1990s. By 1996, however, the trend shifted again, and the number of long-term Japanese residents showed a slight increase. The most current figures indicate that there are approximately 56,000 Japanese residents in the Tri-State area (Ministry of Foreign Affairs of Japan 1997).

Today, there are a number of Japanese corporations and their local subsidiaries in the New York area, whose names are readily recognized in this country: Sony, Toshiba, and Panasonic, from the electronics industry; Marubeni, Mitsui, Sumitomo, and Mitsubishi, in the trading and contracting business. These corporations not only have large revenues from the U.S. market, but also stake their corporate future on their long-term success in the United States. Thus, many of them are intent on creating and maintaining a positive corporate image in American society at large. They unfailingly appear in the list of corporate donors to such New York institutions as Lincoln Center for the Performing Arts, Carnegie Hall, the Metropolitan Museum, and the Museum of Modern Art. They also support community events, give endowments to major universities, and sponsor Japanese cultural programs. For example, one of the most talked-about events in New York in 1997 was Fuji Photofilm's attempt to sponsor a public *Seinfeld* farewell party in Bryant Park, which the Mayor's Office quashed for fear of a mob situation in the heart of Manhattan.

Unlike in my first field location in Centerville, no single company formed the center of the expatriate community in the Tri-State area. The early arrivals from Japan are acknowledged, by others and by themselves, as elites who were selected to carry on the international agenda of their corporations and the nation. As privileged as they may have been, these elites in finances and trading were small in number, and lacked the overwhelming presence of Maveric in Centerville. They also tended to form their own cliques within the expatriate community, excluding more recent arrivals, a tendency that continues even today. Since the late 1980s, however, the rapid expansion of the manufacturing industries in the Tri-State area resulted in another power shift in the expatriate Japanese community. Giant corporations, including Sony and Panasonic, are taking over some of the high-profile positions in the New York Japanese community and replacing bankers and traders as the central force that leads the expatriate community and represents it to the outside world. Yet, there are literally hundreds of Japanese corporate subsidiaries and branch offices that operate in the Tri-State area, aside from these high-profile corporations. This expatriate community is simply too big, too diverse, and too complex for one company to preside over.

The preferred residential areas for expatriate Japanese have shifted around the Tri-State area over the past few decades. Largely of middle-class, white-collar background with little experience of ethnic diversity, expatriate Japanese almost always prefer to live among middle-class white Americans. Their strong commitment to their children's education also drives them to communities with good public schools. Manhattan has a limited number of corporate Japanese residents; they are *tanshin funin*, or "single transfer" employees: those who left their family in Japan, young couples without children, and middle-aged corporate executives and their wives whose grown-up children remained in Japan. In the 1960s, suburban communities in Queens (e.g., Flushing) were the most popular areas for expatriate Japanese families. As these neighborhoods became more ethnic and less middle class, Westchester County, New York, began to attract more and more Japanese throughout the 1970s and 1980s. For instance, Riverdale, at the southern end of Westchester County, was called "JJ town" in the 1970s, as it became the home of many Jewish and Japanese families. After Riverdale, Scarsdale and Hartsdale further north became the favorites of Japanese expatriates. In the 1990s, the expatriate Japanese population was moving even further north, to the northeastern corner of Westchester County and toward Fairfield County, Connecticut. This movement is often attributed to the presence of a full-time Japanese school in Greenwich, Connecticut, that opened in 1992. On the New Jersey side, Bergen County has been a very popular area among expatriate Japanese since the 1970s, but the overall number of Japanese residents has been slightly decreasing in recent years. The center of the population is also moving northward, from the Fort Lee area toward smaller communities, such as Englewood, Tenafly, and Teaneck. Many of my New Jersey informants attributed these movement patterns to the Japanese preference to live away from the large and expanding Korean population in the southern part of Bergen County. The relationship between Korean and Japanese groups tended to be distant and even confrontational at times.

The development of businesses and services that cater to the expatriate Japanese community closely follows this population growth and movement. Twenty years ago, there was only one Japanese grocery store in Westchester, where every Japanese wife in Westchester County shopped. There were a few Japanese restaurants in Manhattan, but none in the suburbs. Today, there are multiple Japanese grocery stores in Westchester, Manhattan, and Bergen County. There are Japanese department stores, bookstores, video rental shops, clothing stores, shoe stores, traditional confectioners, kitchen stores, souvenir shops, golf shops, and just about any kind of store you can imagine, scattered throughout the Tri-State area. A good example is Yaohan Plaza, which opened up in Bergen County several years before my fieldwork. It is a Japanese shopping mall that includes a supermarket, bakeries, confectioners, video store, bookstores, stationer, souvenir shop, drug store, language school, cosmetics counter, beauty salon, dentist, coffee shop, take-out food stalls, a food court, and a full-service restaurant catering to customers who speak Japanese and/or have a taste for Japanese things. Yaohan also hosts various social events: a prefectural product show and sale, the end-of-the-year rice cake pounding, and a children's calligraphy competition, all resembling the popular events at shopping malls and department stores in Japan and targeted at, albeit not exclusively for, expatriate Japanese patrons. A whole range of services is available in Japanese as well. Doctors, dentists, beauticians, masseurs, either Japanese or Japanese-speaking Americans, offer all needed services to live a healthy and comfortable life. There are hobby groups that teach various handicrafts that are popular among Japanese wives, English conversation classes, computer classes, tennis and golf lessons—all taught in Japanese.

Educational resources for children are very important features of expatriate Japanese community life. Twenty years ago, the only Japanese educational institutions were supplemental Japanese schools in Long Island and Bergen County. Every Japanese child in the Tri-State area went to local schools during the week and to the Japanese schools on Saturdays. Today, a wide variety of Japanese educational institutions and services are available to expatriate children in this area. There are three Japanese-language schools in Long Island, Westchester County, and Bergen County. There are also two full-time Japanese schools, partially funded and supervised by the Japanese Ministry of Education, a handful of private full-time/boarding schools, and a number of *juku* or cram schools. These institutions and services can provide all the instruction and guidance needed to succeed in the Japanese educational system, even better than in Japan, in some cases. For example, the New York Japanese School in Greenwich is known as one of the top *shingakuko* (prep schools geared toward rigorous entrance examination) in or outside Japan (Okada 1993). Local school districts also have extensive ESL programs, and in some schools, there are bilingual teachers who teach certain subjects in Japanese. Because of this wide selection of Japanese services and resources, it is quite possible in the Tri-State area to live as Japanese as in Japan itself, a seductive possibility for many corporate wives who are ill-prepared for a life in an English-speaking country. The urban environment also offers many exciting opportunities that are much publicized and admired in Japanese media: an evening at a Broadway musical, a visit to "Museum Row," window-shopping on Fifth Avenue, gallery hopping in SoHo, none of which requires much contact with local Americans.

North Carolina's Research Triangle (1999–2000). The Research Triangle area of North Carolina—between Raleigh, Durham, and Chapel Hill—is one of those "second-tier cities" (Markusen et al. 1999) that grew rapidly over the past three decades as the epicenter of technology-intensive industrial development. As a state-sponsored initiative to increase foreign direct investment, the Research Triangle is extremely important. The opening statement of the Japanese executive summary prepared by the Business/Industry Development Division of the North Carolina Department of Commerce pitches North Carolina to potential Japanese investors as an internationalized, business-friendly state: "Imagine a state where one can have a comfortable and fulfilling life. In that state, workers are productive and they would not start a strike. From the president to the new employee, everyone is enjoying the mild climate and rich living environment" (translation by author).

Research Triangle Park, or RTP, and its adjoining areas are a successful case of planned economic development that has attracted industrial ventures in microelectronics and biotechnology. Unlike the traditional manufacturing sector, these post-Fordist manufacturing industries are environmentally clean and are able to create well-paying jobs for highly trained and educated workers. Although the conceptualization and building of RTP began much earlier, 1980 was a benchmark year in its global aspirations, when the State of North Carolina, in cooperation with the Research Triangle Foundation and local chambers of commerce, began an aggressive campaign to invite foreign investment to the Triangle. Japan was one of the target countries whose previous direct investment in North Carolina was virtually nonexistent. The state tried to make North Carolina attractive to potential Japanese investors by introducing tangible economic benefits as well as cultural programs and symbolic gestures, including the establishment of the state development office in Tokyo, the founding of Japan centers throughout the state, active participation in the Japan-U.S. Southeast Economic Consortium, and deferential treatment of Japanese corporate representatives from initial contact to well after actual relocation.

These statewide efforts resulted in increased Japanese direct investment in the State of North Carolina throughout the 1980s, to $353 million in 1990 (Kuroda n.d.). Major investors included Mitsubishi Semiconductor (1983), Sumitomo Electric Lightwave (1983), Konica Manufacturing (1986), and Matsushita Compressor (1989); in particular, Mitsubishi and Sumitomo Electric chose the Research Triangle as the location of major manufacturing facilities. North Carolina's Research Triangle became one of the popular destinations for Japanese corporations that aimed to take full advantage of innovative technologies and proximity to a large consumer market. This trend was greatly facilitated by the rising value of the yen against the U.S. dollar, the availability of superfluous capital, and the optimistic mood in the late 1980s, which loosened the purse strings of otherwise fiscally conservative Japanese corporations.

During the time of my fieldwork, the majority of expatriate corporate Japanese families lived in the fast-growing suburban city of Cary, located conveniently between Raleigh and RTP, and a smaller number of corporate families lived in middle-class neighborhoods around Raleigh. There were also small pockets of expatriate Japanese in Chapel Hill and Durham who were visiting researchers or students at local universities. Many of the expatriate Japanese in the area were affiliated with Japanese corporations in communications, microelectronics, and the pharmaceutical industry, involved in research and development and/or the management of highly specialized small-scale production sites. Some of them were not on the work assignment per se, but were sent by their corporate employers to study at one of the universities in the area as research fellows, visiting scholars, or graduate students. They presented themselves in our conversations as always already globalized. Even before they arrived at their foreign posts, their work activities (in Japan or elsewhere) routinely crossed geographic and national boundaries. I also detected a much less paternalistic corporation-employee relationship in high-tech companies; as a result, workers had a greater sense of control over their professional development in general and their foreign assignment in particular.

The expatriate Japanese community there was also much more diverse than the Centerville community, despite its relatively small size and short history. It was a mixture of expatriate Japanese workers and their families who were affiliated with Japan-based corporations as well as U.S.-based multinationals, scholars and research fellows affiliated with universities in the region, and permanent residents. The Japanese Firms Association, the organization of Japan-based businesses in the Research Triangle and eastern North Carolina, listed approximately thirty companies on its membership roster. Included was Japan Tobacco, the oldest Japanese business concern in North Carolina, founded in the mid-1960s, which has maintained very close ties with North Carolina's tobacco industry, as well as high-tech ventures of several internationally known corporations and many small to midsize companies. In addition, there were the Japanese employees of IBM, one of the largest employers in the region, who were transferred from its subsidiary in Japan. Area universities regularly hosted visiting scholars and researchers from Japanese universities and corporations, who also belonged to many Japanese organizations and networks in the area. It appeared that there was no single corporation to form the solid core of the community or to exercise enough control over the Japanese-speaking community to be a dominant figure. Yet, the relatively small size of the community (the expatriate community leaders estimated in 1999 that approximately five hundred Japanese families lived in the Research Triangle area, given the number of chuuzaiin reported by Japan-based corporations in the area and the enrollment in the Japanese Language School of Raleigh) made it possible for the expatriate Japanese families to know and exchange information with one another.

With historically very little connection to Japan and Asia generally, North Carolina's Research Triangle area had practically no Japanese resources that are critical to expatriate Japanese families prior to the state initiative in the 1980s. The Japanese Language School of Raleigh was the only comprehensive educational facility for expatriate Japanese children in the eastern half of the state throughout the 1980s and 1990s. There were no Japanese-speaking doctors and dentists, as far as my informants in Raleigh, Durham, and Chapel Hill could tell, and a Japanese grocery store in Raleigh was the only specialty store where

Japanese housewives could count on purchasing all of the necessary food items. Some of the local churches provided language instruction and cultural programs for foreign women and actively recruited expatriate Japanese housewives to participate. Although these free programs were very popular among Japanese women of all ages, they did not often serve as an entree to the local community or religious faith. Unlike Centerville, where cultural activities were primarily the women's responsibility, many male Japanese in the Research Triangle actively participated in local community events side by side with their wives and children, including the International Festival, held each fall in Raleigh, with representatives from ethnic communities from the region putting up food booths and cultural performances.

THE WORK OF ETHNOGRAPHY

It is a deliberate choice that this book is *not* a sweeping overview of Japanese corporate wives in the United States, although I introduce certain generalizations as a backdrop to my stories that center on several Japanese women, all of whom I met in Centerville. At the end of my fieldwork, I was confronted by the enormity of my writing task. How could I best represent the complexity of transnational lives that I came to know in three U.S. cities, and in some cases followed back to Japan? How could I situate the subjective experience of Japanese corporate wives within the larger framework of globalization and transnationalism without losing the individual voices of those women to whom I became close? And what role should these three sites play in my book? Also, I wanted my ethnography to be beautiful and interesting to read. I didn't want to prove Mary Louise Pratt (1986) correct one more time by taking interesting experiences and rich stories and turning them into an incredibly dull book.

In Centerville, I became a regular face in the gathering of Japanese wives of my own age group who spent much of their free time together at the home of Mitsuru Kawagoe, a woman in her midthirties who played a leadership role in the group. I spent many afternoons with Kawagoe-san and the key members of this clique, and I got to learn the intimate details of their lives in the United States, and then in Japan. Other informants from Centerville and the two later research sites also appear throughout the book whenever their similarities and differences can help contextualize the experience of my key informants and shed a different light on their narratives. I made this decision not only because it is too complicated to talk about the three separate populations with whom I worked, but also in favor of the thickness of description that I can provide when I focus on this particular group of women whom I know best.

The organization of the book also reflects my interest in providing an intimate view of globalization from the vantage point of those women. Strung together along the theme of home and journey, many of my chapters evolve around one conversation, one statement, or even one phrase, exchanged casually among the women in my presence. It was with these conversations, statements, and phrases that I came to formulate my otherwise incoherent and inarticulate thoughts; in them, all of the pieces of the puzzle in my head suddenly fell into place. I hope that the experience of reading this book also tells the reader something about the process of discovery and comprehension that I experienced during my fieldwork, and later, throughout the process of analysis and interpretation. This strategy also gives me the flexibility to go back and forth between theoretical framework and ethnographic description, to juxtapose, and I hope connect meaningfully, the abstract and the concrete.

The book consists of six chapters, including this introductory chapter. In chapter 2, I place transnational mobility and homemaking in the context of transnational capitalism through examination of the connection between the needs of transnationalizing Japanese corporations and the Japanese home away from home, in which particular everyday practices are legitimized and the boundaries around middle-class femaleness delineated. The relationship between domestic labor and women's subjectivity is the main focus of chapters 3 and 4. Domestic management and family caretaking are two important jobs for married Japanese women, and women themselves often speak of the fulfillment of these responsibilities as their own priority and source of satisfaction. However, a close examination of their narratives of domesticity reveals that there is an inherent ambivalence in this role-oriented construction of self-identity and that, in the context of transnational migration, this ambivalence is amplified by a sense of transiency. In chapter 3, I specifically focus on the domestic space and the work that goes into creating and maintaining this space. The women's work routine is filled with mundane, repetitive, and tedious details that dissect and fragment their day into the succession of tasks necessary to fulfill the needs of their family members. In the foreign cities where they do not speak the local language well and lack certain local knowledge to get around smoothly, their work of domestic management and child care can become quite burdensome. As these women labor to maintain the domestic space for the comfort of their husband and children, they themselves become the boundaries between the self/inside/home and the other/outside/ strange place.

I continue my analysis of women's reproductive labor in chapter 4, particularly in terms of the concept of the "relational self." Expatriate Japanese wives also belong to a larger community outside the home, which I discuss in chapter 4. Living in a foreign country where their neighbors are all strangers, the network of relationships among expatriate Japanese women often becomes the only source of extradomestic social ties through which women seek friendship, advice, and support that make their lives in the United States possible and even enjoyable. Only in the homosocial space in which no woman is expected to be the provider of comfort for others can they let go of their caretaking responsibilities and "play." However, belonging to a tightknit community of women comes with a price. The requirement of reciprocity and competitiveness often complicates the relationships among expatriate wives, and their husband's corporate connections and pressing needs for extradomestic support often make these relationships obligatory and quickly turn the women's friendships into an extension of their domestic work.

In the final two chapters, I shift my focus to traveling and mobility. In chapter 5, I turn to the phrase "a long vacation" that plays a key role in my exploration into the "traveling" side of the stories and the many layers of meaning that Japanese women find in their transnational mobility and homemaking. During the "vacation" abroad, many unexpected—and largely inadvertent—changes take place in and around the homes of expatriate Japanese families, from changes in the conjugal relationship to new personal interests and a redefined sense of Japaneseness. Many of these changes register in the minds of middle-class Japanese housewives as positive and enjoyable, although they are unsure about what these changes may mean to them in the long run. Like all vacations, kaigai chuuzai assignments do come to an end for most expatriate Japanese families, and I discuss divergent endings to the story of kaigai chuuzai in chapter 6. By looking at different groups of women who ended their "long vacation" with different choices, I seek to address the questions of agency, contradictory consciousness, and resistance. In the end, what does corporate-driven transnational migration mean to middle-class Japanese wives, and how does it affect the sense of who they are as a person, as a woman, and as a Japanese? The outcomes of my research indicate the multiplicity of choices these women may make and the ambiguity of implications that transnational experience may have in their lives after kaigai chuuzai.

THE CLOUDS SEEMED to grow thicker and lower, the air heavier with humidity—a warning that heavy summer rain was on its way. Looking out the window toward the small patch of brown grass encased in the cinder block walls, Kawagoe-san and I recalled those lazy afternoons that we spent sitting and talking in her sunny living room in Centerville, with an expanse of green grass in front.

"Centerville seems like a long time ago," Kawagoe-san mused. "It almost seems like a dream, if you know what I mean."

"No," I replied, "yes, in a way, but not exactly."

Kawagoe-san paused for a moment to put her thoughts into words. "I'm back here now, talking to you, Sawa-san, in my new home. My house in Centerville is where we met, but, I mean, the house is still there, I'm sure, but we aren't anymore. It feels really strange to think about it."

I knew what she was getting at. In Centerville, Kawagoe-san started her family; there, I started doing anthropology. She organized yam cha, and I went to pick up the dumplings for her. She invited me into her home, and we became friends. People dispersed, the scene evaporated, and Centerville wasn't her home any longer. Yet, the children who were born there were growing up fast, and the ties that began there remained.

When it was time for me to go, she offered to walk me to the bus stop. She yelled upstairs to her children. "You behave yourselves and watch over the house!" she demanded.

As we walked out the front door, three heads came out the second-floor window. "Good bye, Sawa-san. Please come and play with us again!" They waved, and I waved back.

On the crowded bus, my thoughts lingered on what Kawagoe-san had said about the strangeness of being in Japan and thinking back on life in the United States. Watching raindrops beat on the steamed window, I was back in that place that Kawagoe-san and her friends once called home.

CHAPTER TWO

Managing Transnational Work

KAIGAI CHUUZAI, OR THE practice of sending employees on a job assignment abroad, has played a critical role in the recent transnationalization of the Japanese economy (Hamada 1992). The core word in this phrase is *chuuzai*, which means a station or assignment, or the state of being stationed or assigned, at a remote post. The word appeared during the Meiji era, particularly in reference to government officials who were stationed in foreign locations (Nihon Kokugo Daijiten, s.v. "chuuzai"). The person who is being stationed, on the other hand, is a *chuuzaiin* (*in* means a staff member). The direction of movement implied here is clearly from the center to the periphery: a person is sent out and away from his or her home office in the center to a post in the periphery. The adjective *kaigai* literally means "overseas." So together, *kaigai chuuzai* becomes "a station at a remote post overseas" and *kaigai chuuzaiin* "a staff person stationed at a remote post overseas."

My aim in this chapter is to decipher Japanese corporate visions of ideal labor and to examine the economic and ideological factors that compel Japanese corporations to send their skilled workers and experienced managers to their subsidiaries around the world. Despite its critical importance to globalizing Japanese corporations, however, a close look at corporate discourses and practices reveals that, from the point of view of corporations and individual workers alike, kaigai chuuzai is fraught with uncertainty and anxiety. This ambivalence is the very reason Japanese corporations appropriate the domestic space to become a Japanese bubble in which to ensure the reproduction of efficient and loyal labor in the unfamiliar environment outside Japan.

TRANSNATIONAL MOBILITY OF JAPANESE CORPORATE WORKERS

The postwar history of kaigai chuuzai in the United States is directly connected with Japan's economic reconstruction and its positioning in the global economy as a supplier of consumer goods for the affluent consumer market. Only a few years after the end of World War II, Japan was already threatening the U.S. garment industry with inexpensive products. Throughout the 1950s and 1960s, Japan became one of the major suppliers of consumer electronic appliances for the United States, such as transistor radios and TV sets (Johnson 1988). In other words, Japan's economic recovery was made possible by consumer demands in the affluent U.S. market and by Japan's ability to quickly produce coveted consumer goods at a lower price than the U.S. manufacturers'. Many world-class corporations based in Japan came out of the chaotic economic booms of postwar Japan. Prominent examples include Matsushita (better known in the U.S. as Panasonic), Sony, and Toshiba in consumer electronics, as well as Honda's motorcycles and Nissan's Datsun brand pickup trucks in the automotive industry.

The patterns of kaigai chuuzai are closely tied to these national economic interests of postwar Japan and Japanese corporations' continuing dependency on revenues from U.S. markets and their more recent move toward direct investment overseas. Several years after World War II, a small number of corporate Japanese began to arrive, mostly in Los Angeles and New York, to rebuild their businesses with the United States and to find a way to better meet the U.S. consumer needs and expand their market share in the United States. As challenging as it might have been, *Amerika chuuzai* (a job assignment in the United States) in the early postwar era had its rewards. It was a rare opportunity that signaled a prestigious business career and promised a higher standard of living both during and after the assignment. At this stage, the major tasks for chuuzaiin in the United States were the marketing and distribution of Japan-made products; thus, the majority of chuuzaiin were white-collar sales specialists operating out of small offices in large urban centers. These pioneering chuuzaiin often likened themselves to *tokkotai*, the World War II suicide bombers. Their projects were risky and their responsibilities were enormous, yet, there was a distinct sense that they were part of Japan's postwar economic recovery. Their wild success stories made these early kaigai chuuzaiin the stuff of corporate legend.

The changes in the relative strength of the U.S. and Japanese economies through the 1970s and 1980s resulted in a major shift in Japanese corporate interests and strategies abroad. While Japanese manufacturing industries enjoyed a dramatic increase in consumer demand for the made-in-Japan automobiles and consumer electronics, they also began to face complex and highly politicized trade issues and the threat of tightened trade sanctions against the import of Japanese products through the 1970s. In response to increasing pressure from the U.S. government to reduce the widening trade imbalance between the two nations, Japanese manufacturing industries began to "localize" their production, that is, to assemble or manufacture their products for the U.S. market within the United States, instead of bringing in finished products from Japan. The most notable example was the automobile industry, in which the U.S. domestic industry aggressively rallied for political intervention against their "unfair" Japanese competitors. Japanese automobile manufacturers attempted to dodge the threat of strict import quotas by the U.S. government by first bringing assembly processes to the United States, thus producing "American-made" cars mostly from Japanese parts. When "domestic content" issues surfaced in the early 1980s, they moved to procure locally produced parts and components for their cars either from American vendors or from the U.S. subsidiaries of their regular Japanese vendors. The strong yen and rising labor costs in Japan also reduced the advantage of production in Japan. By the early 1990s, the domestic content rates of automobiles manufactured by Japanese corporations in the United States were typically 70 percent to 80 percent.

The expansion of the Japanese manufacturing industry in the United States had direct consequences for the kaigai chuuzai practice at large. First, it dramatically increased the number of expatriate Japanese corporate workers in the United States. Unlike the sales- and marketing-driven subsidiaries, which required only a handful of chuuzaiin to run their business at a foreign location, the operation of large manufacturing plants—Maveric's Centerville plant, which I examine below, is a good example—required a much larger number of expatriate workers, at least in its initial phases. The number of expatriate Japanese, according to estimates by the Japanese Ministry of International Trade and Industry (MITI), more than doubled during the 1980s, which coincided with the period of increased localization in the automobile and other manufacturing industries. The Japanese manufacturing sector overseas continued to grow even in the early 1990s, when the overall number of expatriate Japanese companies in the United States temporarily declined due to a severe economic recession in Japan (MITI 1996).

Transnational production strategies, which initially affected only major manufacturers of consumer end products, eventually filtered down to the second-tier subcontractors. Until about 1980, the second-tier companies provided high-quality parts and components to their first-tier corporate clients from their usually small, less automated production facilities located in Japan. However, as the U.S. government kept on pressuring Japanese manufacturers to localize their production, major manufacturers urged, coerced, and enticed their smaller affiliates and suppliers to build their own production facilities in the United States to locally provide the needed supplies to their parent/customer company. Thus, the small to midsize companies with little overseas ambition or experience were dragged out by their parent/customer companies who were already located in the United States. By 1993, the majority of newly established Japanese-owned businesses abroad were small to medium size (MITI 1996).

The increased presence of Japanese manufacturers in the United States, particularly that of second-tier corporations, forever changed the type of kaigai chuuzaiin who were sent to the United States. Setting up a manufacturing plant requires that the home-grown efficiency of Japanese manufacturers be transplanted quickly and faithfully to new, foreign soil. This necessity facilitated the mass transfer of experienced Japanese engineers and semi-blue-collar technicians to their overseas plants, instead of the white-collar managers and sales representatives of previous decades. These production-oriented chuuzaiin generally had an educational background in engineering and hard science, with very little emphasis on language and international training. They were also less interested in international business than their sales and managerial counterparts.

The locations of kaigai chuuzai have also been diversifying. Thirty years ago, Amerika chuuzai meant only a handful of metropolitan locations, including New York, Los Angeles, and San Francisco, with the urban amenities and cultural diversity of world-class cities. These cities also had established Japanese American and/or Japanese permanent resident populations, and the resources in these Japanese-speaking communities helped in the initial transition of corporate newcomers. Until the late 1970s, Chicago was considered a hinterland, and few Japanese knew of Columbus, Ohio, Houston, Texas, and Atlanta, Georgia, all of which today have sizable expatriate Japanese populations (Ministry of Foreign Affairs of Japan 1997). Japanese corporations looked for suitable sites for manufacturing facilities with different criteria than in earlier decades, focusing on locations with abundant land, lower energy costs, nonunionized labor, tax incentives, and so on, where they could keep the production costs low. Through the 1980s and 1990s, with the establishment of Japanese-owned manufacturing businesses, the expatriate Japanese population moved inland to the Midwest, then Southeast and Southwest, to smaller cities and rural towns where chuuzaiin and their families often found themselves amid local residents who had never seen any "Orientals" before, let alone experienced living and working side by side with them (Hettinger and Tooley 1994; Kim 1995).

My three field sites represent these patterns of diversification over the past three decades. New York, which has the largest and most diverse expatriate Japanese population among the three (and one of the largest in the world), is a center of international commerce. A large portion of New York expatriates are white-collar workers and managers in trading, marketing, finance, and administration. Centerville is a manufacturing mecca that developed around a major auto manufacturer in the late 1970s, and the great majority of expatriate Japanese workers there are engineers and other technically trained workers. North Carolina's Research Triangle has the newest expatriate Japanese community among the three, where many Japanese companies relocated their research and development and highly specialized small-scale manufacturing facilities in the late 1980s to early 1990s. I found expatriate Japanese workers there to be a mixture of engineers in the traditional manufacturing sector and knowledge workers and researchers in microelectronics and biotechnology.

These recent changes in the condition of kaigai chuuzai have, in turn, resulted in the transformation of its significance in the lives of Japanese corporate workers. It is no longer a privileged career step of white-collar elites in major corporations, but a familiar experience for many corporate employees, regardless of the type of industry, the size of their corporation, or their job category; in short, kaigai chuuzai is becoming increasingly commonplace in Japanese corporate life today. The types of corporate workers who would not have expected only fifteen or twenty years ago to ever have a job assignment abroad—plant technicians from a small parts company in a rural town, for instance— now experience a foreign assignment or two just about anywhere in the world throughout their careers. Foreign residence is becoming part of the mainstream middle-class experience rather than a sign of elite status. As kaigai chuuzai becomes less elitist and an increasing number of expatriate Japanese with next to no international training move into rural locations in the United States, the management of cross-cultural problems that arise between internationally inexperienced expatriate Japanese managers and their equally provincial local workforce has become a larger concern for Japanese corporations (Kim 1995). At the same time, increased global competition has motivated many Japanese corporations to manage their expatriate workforce "on the cheap."[1] This tendency was exacerbated in the mid- to late 1990s with increasing global competition and the economic recession that hit Japan in 1991. One of the strategies for cost reduction is to "normalize" kaigai chuuzai as a routine in the corporate world of work and to gradually reduce, or even entirely discontinue, the special stipends, subsidies, and other forms of support that used to be the norm for an overseas assignment. For example, the company may reduce the monthly allowance for the housing expense, thus increasing the burden on the employee; change the criteria for the English-instruction subsidy so that some of the family members no longer qualify for it; or simply cease to provide cars for the expatriate employees, who then must purchase a car on their own while in the United States with no corporate support. If these examples do not seem convincing, consider the fact that these expatriate workers and their families are bearing the double burden of living in Japan and the United States. Many own homes in Japan, whose mortgage they continue to pay during their foreign assignment; the same can be said about those who own a car in Japan. English-language instruction and tutoring is a necessity for those who come from a country where English is not used in daily life and is an added expense to the usual school tuition. There are many other added costs for expatriate families that are not covered by the corporate subsidy, such as additional international travel, overseas phone bills, and purchasing additional items of clothing and home furnishing. As a result, many expatriate families have come to call themselves *chuuzai binbo*, or "foreign-assignment poor."

In the past, there was also a general assumption that successful kaigai chuuzai returnees ought to be rewarded with promotions on their return to headquarters; this no longer holds true in most Japanese companies. As transnational mobility affects an ever larger portion of their workforce, companies are subtly redefining foreign assignments, from "prestige" to "routine," thus justifying the reduction of special benefits and opportunities for promotion. While Japanese corporations with transnational ambitions view this routinization of transnational labor as the key to surviving global competition, the families of these expatriate workers have to manage the impact of prolonged transiency with ever diminishing corporate support.

Another common corporate strategy to cut the cost of kaigai chuuzai is to recycle their expatriate workers, identifying a specific group of workers as generic overseas specialists who are given longer and/or repeated foreign assignments and spend ten or more years of their corporate career overseas. The emergence of Japanese corporate workers who specialize in foreign assignments adds complexity to the changing patterns of kaigai chuuzai. The standard length of foreign assignments has always differed by industry, typically from one to two years in trading, banking, and finance to five to six years in manufacturing. More recently, there is a polarizing trend among kaigai chuuzaiin even within an industry, between those who come to the United States on a short-term assignment (under two years) for well-defined projects or for training purposes, and those who stay over ten years and become, more or less, "foreign experts" within their corporations. It also seems a common corporate practice to keep the terms of kaigai chuuzai quite vague for their workers and their families. Most of my informants expected to stay in the United States between two and five years on their current assignment, but none of them knew exactly when it would end. It could be extended indefinitely, or be abruptly cut short. Nor were my informants sure whether they would be sent back to Japan or to another foreign location after the current assignment. The higher degree of deterritorialization in production and marketing in the late twentieth century has made multiple and extended chuuzai assignments quite common in many corporate workers' careers. Some of these perpetual kaigai chuuzaiin spend twenty or more years of their professional careers abroad and even reach their retirement on their foreign assignments.

MAVERIC AUTOMOTIVE OF CENTERVILLE

Maveric Automotive has always been "not quite Japanese" in their own views and in the public image that it has cultivated. Reflecting the ways of its iconoclastic founder, its corporate culture is widely known as relatively egalitarian, individualistic, and innovative. Maveric management and employees alike take pride in individual initiative and entrepreneurship, and have looked outward, particularly to Europe and the United States, for inspiration and opportunities. When its Centerville plant began operating in the late 1970s, Maveric management promised that, in fifteen years, Maveric Automotive of Centerville would be completely "American" in its corporate structure and achieve 99 percent localization of its personnel, leaving a few Japanese liaisons as a communications conduit with Tokyo. MAC's vision, then, was to become one of the autonomous affiliates of the global Maveric family, which would design, manufacture, and market its own products tailored to the consumer demands and tastes of the local market.

Nearly two decades later, in 1996, MAC had no prospect of achieving its localization goals. They had more than three hundred expatriate workers and managers on site, most important technological innovation flowed unidirectionally, from Tokyo to Centerville, and the most critical management decisions were still made in Tokyo. Two of my informants, who worked for MAC at the time, told me that MAC tried in vain to reduce the number of expatriate managers and engineers in the mid-1980s, but they had to discontinue this effort as the productivity dropped to a level that threatened MAC's viability. This convinced the MAC management that the expertise of expatriate engineers and managers was necessary, if problematic, to maintain its productivity.

As Maveric managers sought to balance two contradictory needs to make MAC profitable—the local demand to hand over management to the Americans and Maveric's own desire to maintain Japanese control—their explanation for the necessity of expatriate engineers and managers, ironically, pointed to the same corporate climate that made Maveric one of the pioneers in localized production to begin with. First, Maveric manufactured a wider range of products in the United States than their Japanese competitors did; thus, they needed more Japanese-trained specialists to run their manufacturing facilities with an efficiency equal to those in Japan. Second, Maveric's corporate culture defied standardization. Some of my MAC informants explained that at other Japanese auto manufacturers, production was 100 percent "manualized," so that "anyone who can read and understand the production manual can replicate the same result." By contrast, they contended, Maveric production sites were run by people, with their own expertise and idiosyncracy. Thus, Maveric had to continue sending their Japanese engineers and managers in order to transfer its production knowledge and maintain its efficiency abroad.

MAC's expatriate policies are also fraught with contradiction, reflecting the conflicting requirements of its localization effort. Maveric management saw complete localization of their U.S. operation as the ultimate goal, but they seemed to lack careful planning in their international human resources strategies. Nor did they make a concerted effort to establish a comprehensive internationalization training program or to identify suitable candidates for foreign job assignments ahead of time. In fact, the determination of kaigai chuuzai assignments is closely tied to the changing market conditions and production goals of MAC, and the pressing need for technical expertise drives the typically haphazard process in which Maveric employees are assigned to Centerville as chuuzaiin. For example, say that marketing research identifies that the SUV is going to be the hottest product line in the U.S. market in the next five years. MAC then sets out to plan a new production line, determines specific technical needs for the new operation, and asks Tokyo to send a specialist on an as-needed basis. The assigned (and often reluctant) specialist takes regular trips (e.g., once every three months) to Centerville as a troubleshooter. Eventually, the need for this specialist increases, and his trips become more frequent, until he is spending half of the year in Centerville. If the project is a success and the demand for his service continues at the same level or increases further, the company officially sends him as a full-time chuuzaiin and relocates his family to the United States as well.

As unpredictable market trends, rapid technological advancement, and ever-changing production procedures make it difficult to forecast future personnel needs, it appeared to me that there was little attempt on the part of corporate management to prepare their employees for foreign assignments in advance. This unpredictability of kaigai chuuzai in Maveric's corporate organization makes it necessary for the corporation to find an alternative solution to the possible maladjustment of their kaigai chuuzaiin and their families in the form of corporate-supported comprehensive family services. A MAC human resources manager in charge of expatriate family programs estimated that, if the company did not intervene, approximately half of an expatriate employee's time abroad would be "wasted" taking care of the family's everyday needs, and "there is no way MAC can do its business [*shigoto ni naranai*]" while losing so much of the expatriate employee's productivity. In other words, MAC is trying to ensure the productivity of its expatriate employees—and by extension, the productivity of its U.S. operation—by helping the expatriate families live as trouble-free as possible. For this reason, the company allocates a substantial budget to the Expatriate Family Program each year that supports the space for the program, several interpreters, English-language classes, hobby groups, a Japanese library, and newcomers' orientation.

All the support and attention that the Expatriate Family Program receives from corporate management is no surprise when we consider the importance of the U.S. operation to Maveric Automotive at large. Maveric's market share in Japan is respectable but not enough to sustain the corporation in this highly competitive industry. Its cash cow has been the United States, and, considering the way Maveric is situated in today's globalizing economy, it will continue to be in the future as well. Ensuring MAC's productivity thus has a direct effect on the future of Maveric at the corporate level. If the Family Center can efficiently and single-handedly fill the expatriate family needs and prevent the absenteeism of their male employees, every bit of money the company spends there is more than worth it. Maveric's needs for the extensive family assistance program also relate back to its human resources management, which is necessarily market-driven. When Maveric selects employees to send to the Centerville plant, the first and foremost criterion is technical expertise in certain areas of production. These plant technicians, with highly specialized educational background and little international training, often have trouble communicating in English at work and, more generally, adjusting to life in a foreign country, requiring constant attention from their corporate employer.

In the first fifteen years of localized production, the corporate logic of cost-effectiveness has validated the existence of the family program as an integral part of Maveric's transnationalization strategy. It was a far less costly alternative to *tanshin funin*, or "single transfer," in which the employee would leave his family in Japan and go to the new job location by himself. The Maveric compensation system dictates that, if a chuuzaiin's family remains in Japan, they will receive a very generous "chuuzaiin family support," commensurate with the chuuzaiin's salary. This family support is paid in addition to the regular salary to the chuuzaiin himself. Let's say that one kaigai chuuzaiin cost Maveric about $100,000 a year in wages and other compensation; the additional support to his family in Japan, at the rate of 80 percent, will be $80,000. If there are three hundred expatriate employees at MAC, and every one of them left their family in Japan, then the family support alone will cost the company $24 million annually. By contrast, if the chuuzaiin's family accompanies him to the United States, Maveric provides a much smaller amount of special bonuses and subsidies to cover housing and other expenses, as well as family support services at the Family Center. Corporate management calculates that, even after spending "quite a bit of money" on the expatriate family program and paying some extra chuuzai bonus, it is still a lot cheaper to have the families accompany their chuuzaiin to the United States.

How the need for expatriate workers is construed and how kaigai chuuzai is practiced at Maveric Automotive highlight several important aspects in the globalization process of Japanese capitalism and the possible responses of an individual corporate entity to manage related difficulties. The first and most important point is the persistence of the Japan-centered worldview, even in a company that boasts its "not-so-Japanese" corporate identity and dreams of a global corporate family. Centerville, despite its strategic importance to Maveric's transnationalization, remains on the periphery. The most advanced technology and production techniques, the heart and soul of a manufacturing company and of technically oriented workers, always flow unidirectionally, from

Japan to Centerville. Even though Maveric has been expanding a research facility in its Centerville plant and sending more and more corporate researchers from Japan each year, the outcomes of research activity there are sent back to Japan and reexported to Centerville. This is not to say that no local innovation takes place; in recent years, the designs and products that were developed in Centerville and other overseas subsidiaries were "reverse-exported" to Japan's affluent consumer market in the 1980s and 1990s. Yet, the center-periphery mentality persists in the corporate worldview, particularly among those expatriate workers in technical fields. Kaigai chuuzai often meant being away from the center of technological innovation and required an extraordinary effort just to keep up with the rapid advance in production know-how.

The second important feature in the Maveric case is closely connected to the fact that manufacturing is the center of its U.S. operation. Although Maveric steadily expanded its market share in the United States since the 1950s, all of their products were made in Japan and exported to the United States and elsewhere until the early 1980s. Although they were among the first group of Japanese auto manufacturers that made the historic switch from export to localized production, they did so without fundamentally changing their Japan-centered worldview and organizational structure. This was, as we have seen, initially conceived of as a transitional state to last only until the corporate ideology is thoroughly globalized and their structure almost completely localized. Although Maveric management appears to have made a serious attempt to actualize these visions, it was also quick to determine that they would not work. In a sense, then, Maveric never stopped exporting, but simply switched what it exported: from products to workers who produce. Maveric achieved the current state of its U.S. production through a series of reterritorializing moves. The first switch was from the finished products to Japan-made components, which were assembled in the United States. Only when the domestic content became the center of the issue did Maveric move to the next stage, making cars mostly from the components acquired within North America. Even then, the entire production process is ultimately under the supervision of highly trained Japanese managers and engineers at all levels, from the manufacturing of the smallest parts to the finished products.

As is the custom in most Japanese corporations, Maveric invests much in the training of their core workers, and highly skilled and well-socialized workers are extremely valuable yet perishable assets of the company. Thus, the transnational export of workers requires careful management decisions, particularly in an industry driven by unpredictable shifts in the consumer market, to balance the conflicting needs of nurturing and maintaining productive workers and meeting the immediate market demands. This balance, however, often eludes Maveric's corporate management, which often leans toward sacrificing individual workers for the sake of corporate survival in the global market.

THERE IS A GREAT DEAL of variation in the human resources strategy of Japanese companies with extensive transnational business interests and overseas investments. Among white-collar corporate workers in the fields of international trading, banking, and management, for example, a kaigai chuuzai assignment or two are a planned—and expected—part of corporate life and a necessity for career advancement. Even within the manufacturing industry, I have seen examples that significantly diverge from the Maveric case. One such example is Green Mountain Photographics (GMP), the manufacturer of photographic material and equipment with a large stake in the U.S. market. Having maintained and expanded a manufacturing and distribution facility in the New York area and in several other cities around the United States for three decades, GMP has invested heavily in internationalized management workers by hand-picking executive candidates and sending them to business schools around the United States and/or giving them shorter foreign assignments early in their career, when they are in their late twenties or early thirties, in preparation for later, longer foreign assignments with heavy management responsibilities. In these corporations, transnational work is readily recognized as important to the future of the company itself as well as the specific worker's career path, and becomes incorporated into the taken-for-granted reality of corporate work life in general.

These tendencies were even more exaggerated among the knowledge workers in microelectronics, many of whom I encountered in the Research Triangle in North Carolina. After several interviews with male Japanese workers in this technologically driven corporate environment, I was struck by a matter-of-fact, almost nonchalant attitude common among them toward their U.S. assignment. When asked how they reacted to the news of a foreign transfer (one of my stock interview questions), many of my male informants responded that it was not a surprise at all; some even said that they were getting impatient waiting for it, and thought that it was "about time" that they were finally assigned to the United States. Some of them had had other assignments in the United States or other foreign countries; many others had extensively traveled abroad on business. Also common were the ability to communicate well in English and the ease with which they adjusted to their bicultural work environment and living situation in the United States. These globalized knowledge workers in the Research Triangle downplayed the significance of their North Carolina assignment in their narratives of transnational work experience and appeared to regard these assignments as a truly commonplace occurrence in their deterritorialized occupational niche. They presented themselves in our conversations as always already "globalized": even before they arrived at their foreign post, their work activities (in Japan or elsewhere) routinely crossed geographic and national boundaries, made possible by the extensive use of advanced technology and English as the lingua franca of technical communication.

THE AMBIGUITY OF FLEXIBLE LABOR

I was sitting in a crowded upscale restaurant in Yokohama, Japan, having a late lunch with Bessho-san, a long-time friend of my father and an upper-level manager in a large Japanese corporation with extensive business interests in the United States. When the first course of our *kaiseki* (traditional Japanese cuisine of small, intricately prepared dishes) lunch arrived, he was explaining to me how difficult it was to fill the personnel needs of their New York subsidiary and, at the same time, look after the well-being of the individual workers and managers whose careers were affected significantly by a prolonged assignment away from Tokyo. If an expatriate worker stayed away from Japan too long, he risked losing his touch and becoming marginalized in the intricate network of human relations that governs many aspects of corporate work life in Japan.

"As a rule," he said, "if the kaigai chuuzai assignment is five years or less, the worker can usually manage to reintegrate into the Japanese workplace with some effort. If it extends much over five years, there is an increasing risk that the damage to the expatriate worker's career becomes irreversible, and he becomes obsolete [*tsukaimono ni naranai*] in the corporate organization."

It normally takes an expatriate worker two to three years to become truly productive in a foreign environment; thus, companies operate at a narrow margin of error between benefiting from a seasoned kaigai chuuzaiin and condemning him to a career dead end.

AT DIFFERENT STAGES of its development, capitalism requires a particular kind of body that serves its changing needs. In the era of Fordist mass production, corporations actively produced, through coercive and covert means, efficient and docile bodies "geared to producing large quantities of standardized products put together from standardized components" (Martin 1997, 544). By contrast, flexible late capitalism requires its productive bodies to be flexible as well. In more concrete terms, capitalist practices today include constant technological innovation, small-batch and just-in-time production, niche marketing, and reterritorialization in all aspects of production and distribution processes. These practices require workers who can readily adapt to the specific and fast-evolving demands of late capitalist operation and can absorb the impact of periodic under- and unemployment, continuous retraining and reassignment, deskilling, and geographic mobility (545–548). Recent studies also suggest that a new form of stratification among the workers is emerging: while the majority struggle to keep up with rapid changes in their work environment, a small segment succeeds in actively capitalizing on their ability to manage the flexibility of their work (Harvey 1989). "Transnational professionals" are among that new elite class who specialize in the organization and management of transnational capitalist operations (Hannerz 1996). Perhaps the most crucial aspect of this new privileged identity formation is, as Jonathan Friedman (1999, 197–200) argues, the hybridity of a generalized "top-down" variety in which "the particularity of mixture is never at issue," in which the identity of this global elite class is defined by the ability to harness, consume, and incorporate differences and the highly abstracted sense of globality that frees emerging elites from the specificity of places and place-based identities.

Today's Japanese corporate workers are also expected to be more flexible than ever before and to keep up with changing requirements in the Japanese corporate world, where the foreign tour of duty is now considered a normal and routine aspect of a corporate career in all types of business and industry. However, transnational Japanese workers are also expected to remain Japanese, even as their work becomes increasingly global: they are required to function well in their respective foreign business environments and bring positive results within a few years, but they must also stay in close touch with their colleagues and superiors in Japan, keep up with technological advancements, and, more generally, remain Japanese in their demeanor, worldview, and behavior.

Central to the understanding of this Japanese globalization dilemma is the belief in the unique Japanese national-cultural character, widely shared among contemporary Japanese (Yoshino 1992). Japanese self-analysis of their national-cultural character is known as *nihonjinron* (literally, the discussion or theory of the Japanese), which centers on the ahistoricized, self-essentializing notion of cultural uniqueness—and often superiority—of the Japanese people (Minami 1994). This notion of cultural singularity is a double-edged sword as the Japanese economy continues to globalize. It serves as the basis for the nationalistic sentiment that flourished at various moments in Japan's modernization process (Morita and Ishihara 1989). The explanation for Japan's postwar economic achievement, put forth by both Japanese and foreign observers, is a prime example in which essentialized Japaneseness explains Japan's capitalist success, and that success in turn validates the unique character of the people (Harootunian 1993). Whether objectively accurate or not, both outside researchers and Japanese corporate insiders have often cited in their Weberian analysis the presumably uniquely Japanese combination of attributes, such as strong work ethic, group solidarity, loyalty, modesty, and self-sacrifice, as a major factor that made "Japan, Inc." uniquely competitive in the world (Kumon and Rosovsky 1992; Vogel 1979; Yoshino 1992, 188–191). If being Japanese, that is, being unique and different, is the key to beating the dominant West in its own game of capitalism, then the loss, or the blurring, of the self-other difference is a threat to Japan's success. Increasing globalization of the Japanese corporate world of work has created the condition in which an unprecedented number of core Japanese workers have kaigai chuuzai experience. Whether their direct encounters with the foreign affect their Japaneseness in some fundamental, and thus debilitating, fashion continues to haunt Japanese corporate management and workers alike.

At the same time, Japanese have been keenly aware throughout their modern history that they must maintain relationships with the outside world for their own survival. Particularly after World War II, the Japanese economy depended heavily on the export of industrial products to the United States and other foreign markets; it also appears to be the recent consensus among Japanese industrial leaders and academic observers that Japan must globalize even further, learning to actively participate and seize new opportunities in the global economy, if it is to overcome recent economic difficulties and continue on its path to affluence and power (Nakasone and Ishihara 2001; Takeuchi 1998; Tsurumi 1994). Thus, increasing globalization in the late twentieth century and into the twenty-first century requires that Japanese corporations have to be both Japanese and global, or to manage a balance between the preservation of Japaneseness and the adaptation to global economic conditions in terms of both organizational structure and the individual worker's psyche. Some "transplant" factories (particularly those jointly owned by Japanese and U.S. companies) appear hybridized in their corporate organization and workplace culture (see Milkman 1991); many others are structured on the assumption that the Japanese style of management is critical in maintaining productivity, and for this reason, they need expatriate Japanese managers and engineers who are fully trained and socialized in the Japanese corporate world of work. In addition to technical expertise, these kaigai chuuzaiin are believed to bring and maintain Japanese workplace culture and corporate loyalty and are expected to nurture the Tokyo-centered worldview in their foreign subsidiaries.

As a result of this ambivalence between Japaneseness and globality, some social scientists observe, transnational business experience has had only a marginal effect on the Japanese corporate structure and worldviews, and Japanese management style and corporate organization have thus far inhibited fundamental changes in corporate structure and worldview. They have also noted that the traditional Japanese corporate practices of consensus building, relational decision making, and complex networking will ultimately be harmful to the globalization of Japan-based corporations as a whole (Hamada 1992; Lifson 1992; Mannari and Befu 1983). Thus, in the context of a globalizing economy, the retention of Japaneseness does not always guarantee high performance, but potentially threatens the long-term survival of Japanese corporations. If "traditional" cultural traits have aided Japanese corporations to succeed thus far in the capitalist world, the same sets of traits appear to prohibit them from going truly global. In turn, the dual concern of globality and Japaneseness filters down from the corporate organization to the individual identities of their expatriate workers, who have to function well in a foreign environment but must not become so cosmopolitan that they lose their steadfast loyalty to their company and their country of origin. This fundamental requirement of transnational labor in Japan-based corporations becomes vividly—and cruelly—apparent in the cases of those who are seen to have crossed the boundary and whose innate Japanese character is thought to be irreversibly damaged.

In the official corporate discourse, corporation-worker identification is presented as mutual, and mutually beneficial, to both parties: while male workers cultivate the sense of belonging and gain an avenue of self-realization through corporate work, the corporation, acting as a benevolent parent, can count on a degree of loyalty and productivity from its employees that cannot be achieved otherwise. The utilitarian calculation that goes into the cost accounting of transnational labor, however, betrays the duality in the corporate conception of male work, in which the objectification of male work/ers is a prominent theme. As Bessho-san called the expatriate worker who stayed overseas "too long" *tsukaimono ni naranai*, labor (and, by extension, the laborer himself) is conceived as *mono*, literally, a thing or an object. Furthermore, the value of this object is measured in terms of its usefulness in the corporate organization, as indicated in the word component, *tsukai-*, which is a derivative of the verb *tsukau*, "to use." In the scheme of capitalism, the productive labor of a male worker is a commodity that is bought and sold for money; the sense of belonging, so essentialized in Japanese corporations, also makes the worker a member of a close-knit social group within which his contribution is used for the benefit of the group. Thus, the predominantly male core workers in the Japanese corporate world of work must be useful both in the production of exchange value and for the maintenance of the collectivity. There is also a certain sense of responsibility and care in Bessho-san's comment, even as he objectifies expatriate workers. The loss of productivity in an expatriate worker is perceived here as a loss for the corporate collective as well as for the individual worker himself.

Yet, "the thing for use" that is no longer useful is to be discarded, and the paternalistic relationship between the corporation and the individual worker does not extend beyond a certain breaking point.

THE CHOSEN, THE EXILED, AND THE SENILE

Kawagoe Takeshi (the husband of one of my key informants), worked for a midsize trading company that specialized in mechanical tools. Because he had always had a strong interest in a foreign assignment, he volunteered to be sent to the United States when his company was planning to open its first branch office on the East Coast. Five years later, after the first branch office was established, Takeshi moved to Centerville to develop more business with expanding Japanese automobile manufacturers in the Midwest. He began to think about returning to Japan in his eighth year, and asked his superiors to transfer him back to Tokyo. Takeshi's supervisors in Tokyo were reluctant to transfer him back to Japan for two reasons: first, Takeshi knew their U.S. operations so well that having to replace him could be a costly and time-consuming endeavor; second, the company did not seem to know what to do with him in Japan. In his late thirties, Takeshi had worked independently as a manager (though in a very small branch office) and handled much heavier responsibilities and a larger latitude of freedom than his cohorts back in Japan; thus, he presented a bit of a conundrum in a Japanese corporate organization, where seniority is often an important criterion for promotion. After nearly ten years of managing two successful offices in the United States, they feared Takeshi may have become too independent to fit back into the tightknit corporate community in Japan.

Yet, Takeshi's company could not simply reject him, even if it was perturbed by his repeated transfer requests and was skeptical of his usefulness back in Japan. While the corporation, as a "parent," exercises control over its employees' work, and even their private lives, it also bears the moral obligation to take good care of its employees/children (Cole 1977; Kondo 1990; Rohlen 1974). As the corporations place their employees in exceptionally stressful, demanding positions overseas, kaigai chuuzai should compel the moral sensibility of their corporate parents to grant special consideration and treatment to their employees/children in return.[2]

After nearly two years of negotiation, Takeshi's superiors agreed to bring him back to Tokyo. At the same time, they punished Takeshi's transgression in covert ways. They waited until the last minute to make his transfer back to Tokyo official, which meant that he and his family had to make the transition back to Japan very quickly. They also appointed as Takeshi's successor a former colleague of his with whom he had had an awkward relationship for years. The successor arrived only three months before Takeshi's departure, and he had to be trained quickly and while Takeshi was busy dealing with his departure. Moreover, Takeshi was sent back to Centerville a month after his return to Japan to supervise one of his projects to its completion. It was three more months before he was allowed to take his new position in Tokyo.

I ARRIVED AT THE OFFICE of Metal Technologies, Inc., in Research Triangle Park a few minutes earlier than the time of my appointment with Saito-san, the president of this U.S. subsidiary of a large Japanese manufacturer. There was no one around the entrance area, but through the partitions I could hear the voices of a few men speaking in English, and I was struck by the familiar and informal tone of their exchange. Then an Asian man in his forties emerged from behind the partition; he saw me standing at the reception desk and quickly bowed. That was Saito-san.

Saito-san is a very serious-minded and intelligent man who speaks English quite well and is an effective manager of both American and Japanese workers. His background and work history confirm this impression: he originally came from the northeastern region of Japan (which is known for its hard-working, single-minded ethos), studied science at a highly regarded university there, and, upon his graduation in the mid-1970s, entered a large company with strong ties to the steel industry. In his late thirties, he was sent to the company's New York branch as a midlevel manager; five years later, in 1995, the company opened up a new venture in North Carolina, and he was reassigned there as president.

In response to my question regarding the nature and scope of his subsidiary's operation, Saito-san stated that it was a "very important project" for his company despite its relatively small scale. The Japanese as well as the U.S. steel industry had been in decline for some time, and his company, which manufactures materials for steel production, had been looking to diversify. This North Carolina venture represented his company's serious attempt at diversification, and thus was key to its future in the global economy. Saito-san felt both a heavy responsibility and a sense of excitement to be put in charge of such a critical operation, and he found the opportunity to manage a U.S. subsidiary an invaluable management experience that he never would have been granted had he stayed in Japan.

Metal Technologies, however, had difficulty becoming profitable, and Saito-san, at the helm of this struggling venture, seemed to be deeply concerned. Japanese corporate management was not prepared for the degree of customization required by high-tech industry clients, and recouping its rather sizable initial investment would take many years. Moreover, Saito-san himself had to face a major adjustment due to the shift from one industrial culture to another. Steel was considered the critical basis of Japan's postwar industrial development, and government-protected giant corporations operated less like profit-motivated capitalist organizations and more like government agencies. When Saito-san dealt with clients in the Japanese steel industry, relationship building was of the utmost importance, and price negotiation, product specification, and other relevant issues were handled in the context of a stable, long-term association in which everyone was "in on it together." Coming into the world of high-tech industry with this work history, Saito-san was astonished by the lack of client-vendor loyalty and the utter competitiveness that places tremendous pressure on vendors to continuously improve their products, to meet a tight delivery schedule, and to be light-footed enough to keep up with the ever changing climate of a consumer-driven industry.

Several weeks after our first meeting, I ran into Saito-san again at a local business conference. During lunch, I joined him and another Japanese businessman, Tanaka-san, who was visiting from New York in preparation for the opening of the North Carolina office of his company, a well-known general contractor. On hearing about Tanaka-san's situation, Saito-san offered that he, too, had been stationed in New York and was transferred to North Carolina several years ago. This was an interesting revelation, as Saito-san never mentioned his previous assignment during our interview. After reminiscing about his days at the busy subsidiary in the bustling city, Saito-san said, in an ironic tone, "Yah, miyako-ochi desuyo [Oh, it was the removal from the capital]." In Japan's early history, one of the most feared consequences for a nobleman who fell from grace was *miyako-ochi*, banishment from Kyoto on an indefinite appointment to a remote location far away from the political and cultural center. In today's corporate world of work, too, the transfer from the center to the periphery implies a downward mobility in professional and social terms. Tanaka-san chuckled nervously and explained for my behalf that many Japanese companies were moving their U.S. subsidiaries away from costly metropolitan cities, and that his company also found it more advantageous to move its U.S. base to the South, where their (Japanese corporate) clients were building more and more manufacturing plants.

Throughout the 1980s and early 1990s, Japanese direct investment in the United States shifted away from large-scale manufacturing toward technology-intensive post-Fordist ventures, particularly in microelectronics and biotechnology. Even those corporations in conventional manufacturing sectors began to move their research and development functions to the United States and/or start exploratory enterprises in these fast-growing industries. The increased Japanese direct investment in North Carolina's Research Triangle was part of this larger trend. There were miscalculations and unforseen changes, however. For one thing, Japan's economic "bubble" collapsed in 1991, instantly drying up investment money from Japan, and Japanese direct investment in North Carolina quickly dropped after it peaked in 1989. Some of the established Japanese subsidiaries also divested from North Carolina in the mid-1990s. The close correlation between the patterns of Japanese direct investment in the United States and that in North Carolina suggests that the state of Japan's national economy and the foreign investment trend among Japanese corporations are the primary determinants of Japanese direct investment in North Carolina, and that other, more regionally specific incentives and advantages are after all insufficient to overcome macroeconomics.

Also, some of the Japanese-owned subsidiaries were ill conceived from the beginning. By the mid-1980s, the Research Triangle was recognized among Japanese corporate planners as the new Mecca of high-tech industry and a prime site for relocation. This knowledge resulted in two types of Japanese direct investment. The first type is made by those Japanese corporations with a long-standing and substantial history in microelectronics who sought to establish manufacturing sites in the United States. The other type is made by those who saw a new business opportunity in supplying materials and components for major microelectronic manufacturers in the area, of which Metal Technologies is one. It appears that the latter type of Japanese-owned ventures in and around RTP experienced difficulty for two main reasons. First, neither the managers in charge of these subsidiaries nor the corporate management in Tokyo were prepared for the competitiveness, the high degree of customization, and the short product cycle that characterize the high-tech industry. Particularly those corporations that previously operated in the economy of scale, the steel industry being a prominent example among them, experienced much difficulty as they struggled to shift to highly customized, small-batch production in this competitive environment. Second, many Japanese managers began to realize that the production cost around RTP was too high to remain competitive against products made in off-shore locations, while physical proximity to microelectronics giants, including IBM, did not give them much advantage.

THESE TWO STORIES are telling examples of where the breaking point of corporate paternalism may be. Kaigai chuuzaiin may see their corporate career take a sudden and dramatic turn, from the chosen to the exiled, and then to the senile. Takeshi, like many other male corporate workers whom I have encountered, set out on his foreign assignment not only with his own career ambitions, but also with a sense of mission. Kaigai chuuzaiin often feel that they are the "chosen," charged to lead their company's transnational ambitions to success. It is important to remember that personal ambition and dedication to the corporate collective are not mutually exclusive for these men; in fact, they are experienced as one and the same by many, as their masculine selves are so tangled up with their corporate work (see Allison 1994). One of the New York informants expressed this sentiment succinctly: "Otokoto umaretakaraniha, ichidoha New York de shigoto wo shitemitakatta [Because I was born male, I always wanted to work in New York]." In this brief statement, he made three important connections. First, being male comes with certain expectations and assumptions, as the expectant ending, -karaniha, indicates. Second, the expectations of maleness are, in this instance, related to his work or career (*shigoto*). And the prestige of a New York assignment makes it a definite and concrete goal to aspire to: it is not just any kind of work assignment, but an important job at the center of international business. His comment was made as a recollection of his hope in the past (*shitemitakatta*), but it also implies his pride in the achievement of a masculine and professional ideal or, perhaps, his excitement over working at such an achievement. Third, his statement suggests a certain sense of control over his own career: it was his own will and effort that brought him to New York.

In contrast to the way expatriate male workers spoke of New York, no one said that they "always wanted to work" in Centerville. After all, Centerville is not one of those prestigious chuuzai destinations, and it appeared that the expatriates with technical specializations—with a few exceptions—generally lacked the kind of interest in international business that I found among largely white-collar New York expatriates. Even then, many Centerville chuuzaiin took pride in their work and made explicit connections between their kaigai chuuzai, their own identities as workers, and their corporation's future. By contrast, always already globalized knowledge workers in the Research Triangle tended to downplay this sense of chosenness, which in turn suggested their elite consciousness in the deterritorialized world of global capitalism and high-tech industry vis-à-vis others in the Japanese corporate world whose careers remained largely geographically bound.

Despite such a sense of mission, kaigai chuuzaiin often find out that they have a short shelf life—five years, maybe seven at the outside—before they become so out of touch with their corporate home in Japan that their return is neither desired nor welcomed. *Kaigai boke*, literally, "overseas senility," is the phrase that summarily and cruelly describes the out-of-touch expatriate workers and returnees; it connotes the condition of long-term chuuzaiin who have spent too much time away from Japan on the foreign assignment and have lost their usefulness in the Japanese world of work. Many of my male Centerville informants referred to the fear of "falling behind" for more technology-oriented reasons. In the minds of Japanese automobile technicians and engineers, Japan was the center of technological innovation. During five or so years of kaigai chuuzai, they did their best to keep up with their colleagues in Japan, who had access to the most current technical information. But they also knew that there was much work to do when they returned to

Japan to fill the five-year gap and catch up with their cohorts as soon as possible. A similar sentiment preoccupied some of my nonengineer informants, but for a slightly different reason. They were not concerned about falling behind technically; they were worried that they would be "out of the loop" and "off the fast track" since they were sent away from the center of decision making.

More than any other tangible reasons, however, a kaigai chuuzaiin is afraid of losing his spot because of his distance from the relational network, the bread and butter of Japanese work life. In the formal language of Japanese corporate management, his status in a foreign subsidiary is that of a *shukko shain*, a corporate employee who still belongs to the home company but has been "sent away" to a subsidiary or an affiliate. The ambiguity of his position comes from the fact of not sharing the same daily scene (*ba*) required for membership in a close-knit Japanese social group (Nakane 1967). Even in large Japanese corporations, human resources policies can be quite unsystematic and murky, and how well one is connected in a corporate organization may have a significant impact on one's career advancement. Being abroad for an extended period of time, many kaigai chuuzaiin feared that they would lose their spot in the network of *ningen kankei* (human relationships) and might be passed over for the promotion that should have been theirs.

Radical structural shifts in the corporate, industrial, and economic environment in Japan can take place while a corporate worker is on a foreign assignment, and he may miss the subtle cues of change and/or lack the resources to reposition himself in the corporate organization accordingly. In some cases that I documented, formerly elite employees in major Japanese manufacturers were sent on multiple long-term assignments in foreign locations as the priorities of their corporations shifted from heavy industry to post-Fordist ventures and consumer products. Each time, they were further removed from the strategic positions in their respective corporate organizations and, therefore, from opportunities for advancement. Exiled in remote places with little hope of returning to the position of future promise, these expatriate workers are often transferred from one foreign location to another, performing duties at the margin of corporate organization, their rank potentially rising with their experience and years of service to the company, but who are painfully aware that they can never "go home."

Finally, expatriate workers may become accustomed to the increased autonomy in work life that frequently exists in foreign subsidiaries of Japanese corporations, and thus become difficult to reintegrate into a more tightly controlled work organization in Japan. The great majority of U.S. subsidiaries and branch offices of Japanese corporations are managed on the bottom line of "not losing money." In the first three to five years, particularly, the concern is to get the business going with minimum investment, which usually means as small an office and staff as possible. Many subsidiaries, even of major corporations, start humbly with just a few expatriate managers and a dozen or so locally hired workers; I have also run into branch offices that consisted of an expatriate worker, a fax machine, and his wife as a volunteer answering service. In these small offices, the usual decorum of corporate hierarchy is less rigidly observed and human relations tend to be informal and uncomplicated. Kawagoe Takeshi's work environment was a good example of this. For the first few years in the United States, Takeshi worked alone, but even in his tenth year, his office had only one other expatriate Japanese worker and a couple of locally hired staff members. In many cases, the presence of locally hired American workers further encourages the informality of the work environment, as Japanese managers try to adapt to the expectations of American employees by calling one another by their first name, making casual small talk, exchanging stories about family life, allowing food and drink in the work area, and sometimes even inviting them home for dinner. Even at a sizable concern such as MAC (with more than three hundred expatriate workers and literally thousands of local workers), where Japanese expatriates occupy most of the upper management positions and all the workers on the floor are locally hired Americans, the hierarchy is underplayed, as every "associate" is asked to wear the same uniform on the factory grounds and no one, not even the president, has the privilege of a reserved parking spot. Minami-san, a former MAC executive and one of my key informants in Centerville, once told me jokingly that, in fact, the higher one's rank, the farther away one's parking spot: by the time the managers show up at the office at 8 A.M., assembly line workers and engineers have already taken all of the nearby spots.

Ultimately, the motives for these organizational modifications are quite self-serving on the part of Japanese corporations that would like to run their foreign subsidiaries effectively with less expense and minimize any possibility of a cross-cultural conflict (see Kim 1995). Yet, because of these necessary alterations in the work environment, expatriate corporate workers enjoy more autonomy during their foreign assignments that often require them to be assertive, innovative, and adventurous. Furthermore, when sent away to the periphery of the Japanese corporate world of work, a definite sense of frontier defines the experience of kaigai chuuzai. These changes in the corporate work environment affect many expatriate workers and their views toward work. Many workers, in fact, grow to like the simpler ningen kankei and informal working environment in the United States, and, though they look forward to going back to Tokyo and resuming their career at headquarters, they dread the thought of having to go back to the "same old stuffiness" of a Japanese corporate office.

From the perspective of the corporation that is bent on going global while remaining Japanese, the changes that its foreign subsidiaries and expatriate employees may exhibit are inevitable yet alarming results of transnationalization. On the one hand, the company depends on the flexibility and adaptability of the organization and workers in a foreign environment, without which transnational business ambitions would be severely limited. On the other hand, the same flexibility may inadvertently threaten the integrity of the worker's personal and collective self. As the ongoing transnationalization of Japanese capitalism increases the need for more and more transnational workers, the gap between two contradictory implications of flexible labor also grows. Creating a core of exilic workers—those employees who have outlasted their usefulness to the corporation, who have criticized their superiors once too often, or whose kaigai boke is deemed beyond repair—can help contain the effects of kaigai chuuzai. They become the transnational *madogiwa-zoku* (the "by-the-window tribe"), whose physical positioning at the periphery of the workplace signifies their symbolic marginalization in the corporate organization. These effects of kaigai chuuzai are undesirable, if inevitable, to Japanese corporations that have invested in their core male workers, trained them on the job, and socialized them into their particular brand of corporate masculinity in the hope of cultivating their career-long dedication and productivity to support the future of the company at large. So it is a keenly felt necessity, from the point of view of Japanese corporate employers, to devise a way of prolonging the shelf life of their workers abroad and to delay (if not so much to avoid) the inevitable as much as they can.

DOMESTIC BLISS AS CORPORATE NECESSITY

The pressing question for transnationalizing Japanese companies is, ultimately, how to keep their overseas workers "productively Japanese" and bring them back into the fold of the Japan-based corporate network before they are damaged beyond repair by extended kaigai chuuzai assignments. As transnationalization progresses and foreign assignments are redefined as a normal course of a corporate worker's career, this also has to be done cost-effectively. This is where the reproductive labor of women becomes key to the management of transnational male work. The unsettling changes in the work routine and dislocation are offset by the familiarity of the domestic space, of the "Japanese" homes in a foreign place, in which the basic needs of male workers outside of their cultural space are fulfilled in a familiar and specific fashion, and in which the dislocated workers are assured of fundamental stability in their lives, if only in the limited time-space of their home away from home.

This perceived necessity for labor reproduction drives the corporate vision of a Japanese home and the appropriate behavior of employees' wives in a foreign environment. When Maveric and other Japanese corporations began directly investing in the United States, their overriding concern was for their male expatriate workers "in trouble." Reportedly, Japanese men left alone in a foreign country without a caretaker would soon fall ill, become homesick, and/or engage in extramarital affairs. These diversions would reduce their productivity, tarnish the corporate image, and make these employees useless. To avoid such disastrous outcomes, the employee's wife has to be there with him, managing the home, taking care of the children, and making sure that her husband gets up every morning to a hearty breakfast and encouraging smile. In Maveric's visions and policies, the reproductive role of women is articulated along this line, vaguely defined as providing the material and mental needs of the male workers (*seikatsu-men* and *seishin-men*). It all goes without saying: everyone should know what it means and whose responsibility it is to "take care" of a man. However, in the context of transnational migration, some things have to be mentioned, and mentioned emphatically at times, to drive the message, to ensure that the job is done properly.

In my conversations with male Japanese managers and executives, they stated that women's domestic work is very important and highly appreciated by the company. There are rules and policies for expatriate wives, and even though grossly inadequate, many corporations provide cross-cultural training to wives of their kaigai chuuzaiin and conduct orientations in which a representative from the human resources department gives a pep talk, praising the sacrifice of expatriate families and hailing the devotion of dutiful wives. However, companies pay practically no attention to the wives' interests or ability to live in a foreign country and provide minimum international training for them. Asked whether these two positions were contradictory, male informants often dismissed the concern by saying that women, after all, "just stayed home" and did not need specific training because they "did pretty much the same thing whether in Japan or America."

The expectation for the wives' reproductive contribution abroad is not only greater among those highly transnationalized corporations, but also more implicit. For example, the wife of a GMP manager stated that no one ever mentioned before or during her kaigai chuuzai the importance of women's caretaking work at home; yet, she *knew* that she was expected to manage a perfect home wherever her husband was assigned, and that her failure to do so diminished not only her value as a wife but also her husband's value as a worker. The qualifications of a transnational elite in a Japanese corporation, then, include a wife who willingly follows him to foreign assignments and single-handedly manages the domestic space and raises the children in an unfamiliar environment, freeing the male worker of all domestic concerns (Taniguchi 1985).

While many Japanese corporate employers find women's reproductive work critical to their foreign operations, the wives of their workers are, after all, not their paid employees, and therefore, their domestic work must be disciplined indirectly through appeal to the norm of feminine domesticity and its significance to their husband's career ambitions. For the most part, Japanese companies seem to encourage the wives of their expatriate workers to accompany their husband to their foreign station through verbal praises and minor financial incentives (such as free or subsidized English instruction) and justify their imposition of domestic work by way of these nonsalary compensations. Some corporations offer a short international training program and language instruction to the wives of outgoing kaigai chuuzaiin (which lasts between two days and a week); many others include the wives in their overseas orientation (usually one to two days). Although these programs come across to many outgoing chuuzaiin wives as grossly inadequate and even as a "useless waste of time" (Mori and Saike 1997, 18–23), they are for many corporate wives the first "official" inclusion in any corporate-sponsored events. In earlier decades, when only select groups of Japanese corporate workers were stationed abroad, it was not unusual for accompanying wives to receive kudos from their husband's employer for being the "model of feminine virtue" (Taniguchi 1985). Both in official corporate rhetoric and in informal exchanges among the members of a corporate community, it is asserted that good wives and mothers happily accompany their husband to their foreign assignment and fulfill their "duty" of homemaking. If a woman should show any reluctance, she is labeled a bad wife, whose selfish act will reduce her husband's chance of professional success because, in the ideology of corporate masculinity, "a man who can't even control his own wife" cannot be a good corporate worker (see Mori and Saike 1997; Okifuji 1986). Many of my female informants, particularly those whose husband considered kaigai chuuzai a critical career step, felt that they simply could not fail these expectations because their ability to manage a perfect home in a foreign country was assumed by everyone in the corporate community.

CHAPTER THREE

Homemaking Away from Home

TO UNDERSTAND THE SIGNIFICANCE of domestic space in the Japanese cultural universe, we need to take into account the cultural idiom of *uchi* (inside) and *soto* (outside). *Uchi* is a polysemic word that encompasses people, space, and emotions associated with one's in-group. Japanese stereotypes of uchi evoke comfort, warmth, safety, and familiarity: the cluttered coziness of a small living room, the smell of miso soup, mother's dishpan hands, and carefree interactions among family members (Hara 1989; Kondo 1990). *Soto*, by contrast, connotes dirtiness, strangeness, isolation, and danger. The boundary between uchi and soto is observed quite literally on one level, and physical discipline is an integral part of early childhood training to instill this distinction (e.g., Tobin 1992b). On another level, it is metaphorical and affective, albeit connected to a physical space or a social relationship. Uchi is a private space where people can relax and be themselves in the company of others who share a sense of belonging. The same image of a relational person nurtured in the uchi/in-group often informs anthropological understandings of Japanese selfhood as well (Bachnik and Quinn 1994; Doi 1973; Lebra 1976; Nakane 1967; Smith 1983). A mother, at the center of uchi/home, often becomes the embodiment of uchi-ness, and the mother-child relationship the prototype of the affective relationship throughout a Japanese person's adult life (Allison 2000).

Idyllic as it may sound, however, the vision of uchi as an innocent in-group smoothes over its disciplinarian aspects and pastoralizes its normalizing function in the construction of subjectivity. The opposing domain of soto (an outside, a strange place, or "the other") indicates that uchi is defined in contrast to marginalized "others," for example, Korean residents versus the mainstream population (Yoneyama 1995), or the "newcomers" versus the "natives" (Robertson 1991). Deemed dangerous and undesirable, these others mark the boundaries around their ideal selves and caution against the risk of divergence from the norms of uchi. Moreover, when a certain social relationship is metaphorically declared an uchi, it gains a similar emotive influence as an in-group and obliges its subjects to act accordingly. For instance, Japanese employers often attempt to cultivate the sense of uchi-ness among their employees to promote loyalty in the workplace and to assert patriarchal hierarchy (Kondo 1990; Yoshino 1992). Moreover, the uchi-soto binary is a highly gendered concept. Uchi, as the space of comfort, relaxation, and reproduction, is a female domain, and creating uchi-ness is distinctively female labor, whereas maleness is more readily identified with the productive labor in the soto/outside (Allison 1994). The central role in the uchi makes women as domestic managers an influential presence at home. However, the domestic-female connection has had two negative effects on women. First, they are marginalized in the public domain because of their ascribed role of reproduction, and second, the home becomes a place of work for them, robbing them of a place of relaxation and comfort.

Karen Kelsky (2001, 29) argues that the uchi-soto binary has been overused in anthropological studies to explain everything and anything Japanese. This is an important critique because, when we take for granted idioms and categories in cultural analysis, we always risk the possibility of becoming complacent and neglecting to examine them as the cultural constructs that they are. At the same time, binaries such as inside-outside, self-other, and domestic-public are the components of the ideological framework with which Japanese recognize, understand, and talk about the world around them. Uchi is a frequently used word in daily conversation, particularly among middle-class Japanese women who are responsible for reproductive labor in the domestic space in Japan and during kaigai chuuzai. Instead of thinking of uchi and soto as prearranged domains, I propose to look at these categories as arbitrary and shifting constructs, which people, whether consciously or not, manipulate and maneuver around in their daily life. To look at uchi and soto this way is to pay attention to the process of defining, negotiating, and reworking them and to make explicit how the boundaries around uchi are endowed with particular meanings and how that signification affects people, particularly those who are charged with its production and maintenance.

The ideology of uchi affects Japanese corporate wives overseas in two specific and important ways. First, the labor of creating and maintaining uchi is closely connected with their femaleness, as I explore in detail below. Second, uchi-ness becomes synonymous with Japaneseness in the foreign environment. While "others" in Japanese society are assigned positions at the margins of uchi/inside/self, foreign others constitute a more problematic and dangerous category of soto, as they often represent powerful forces beyond such cultural categories (Yoshino 1992). Japan has had ambivalent relations with foreign others since its early historic times (Hall 1988; Hane 1972). The United States over the past hundred years has represented to many Japanese all that is Western—dazzlingly superior, yet bewilderingly alien. *Amerika*, as it is customarily referred to by Japanese people, has been a parent figure against which Japan has measured its own development, particularly since the end of World War II. Even through the decades of a rapidly changing economic relationship between the two nations, America's cultural influence has remained powerful in Japan (Miyoshi and Harootunian 1990). At the same time, the United States is a potentially dangerous foreign other, and contact with this dangerous foreignness ought to be carefully domesticated (Tobin 1992a).

Before we move forward, I would also like to clarify my use of the terms "domesticity," "homemaking," "domestic management," "caretaking," and "motherhood," all of which appear throughout the next few chapters. They are interrelated and sometimes overlapping and therefore can be quite confusing. Japanese women with whom I worked were not particularly concerned about the distinctions among these (and other similar) ideas and often used them interchangeably or in connection with one another. Furthermore, middle-class Japanese women's categorization may not translate exactly to common English usage of these phrases. Yet, I find myself wanting to establish an analytical vocabulary for the time being, if only to be deconstructed and reworked later on.

By "domesticity," I mean the orientation or tendency to focus on the private home as a space of reproduction, as well as concrete activities in and around that space. Japanese women's responsibilities as wives and mothers are subsumed under the category of "domestic work," while "homemaking" refers specifically to the work and activities that are necessary to construct the domestic space, as well as the intention of doing so. "Domestic management" is similar to "homemaking," but emphasis is on the actor's decision-making power and active agency in the construction of the domestic space and selective deployment of her labor. In turn, "caretaking" means the activities that are directly related to the maintenance of the physical and psychological well-being of family members. Caretaking of children is the essential component of motherhood. "Motherhood," however, suggests more metaphorical and ideological significance. It is often extended to the members of the household or elsewhere who become dependent on the care of the woman (e.g., Kondo 1990). Domesticity and motherhood also carry a heavy moral connotation and ideological importance in modern Japan and constitute a major aspect of an adult woman's social identity. It is impossible to speak of a home without referring to the woman who makes it, or of a woman's own self without referring to her as a wife/mother/caregiver.

UCHI AS A PHYSICAL SPACE

Like many other aspects of life during kaigai chuuzai, the housing choices for Japanese corporate families are framed and, in many ways, limited by a number of factors related to their transnational mobility. Factors ranging from the real estate market in the particular locale to the expected length of stay, family size, and financial support from the corporate employer determine the range of housing options (an apartment, a rented house, or a purchased condominium or single-family home). Housing subsidies vary greatly from one company to another. I am aware of a few companies that fully cover rental cost; many others reimburse up to a predetermined limit. Some corporations offer a low-interest mortgage; a subsidiary of a large automobile manufacturer promises to buy employees' houses when they return to Japan (which they turn around and sell to arriving employees). Assistance for utilities is also common in areas where winter heating or summer air-conditioning bills are exceptionally high. Houses and apartments in move-in condition are infinitely preferable to fixer-uppers. The convenience of commuting for the husband is always taken into consideration, and becomes a critical factor if he tends to work particularly early or late hours. Children, depending on their ages, need access to good public schools and the Japanese Saturday school, making certain areas of the city or suburban communities more desirable. The presence of other expatriate Japanese families and the proximity to businesses that cater to Japanese clientele are often considered measures of livability as well. These considerations often combine to create—to different degrees—a "Japanese village" effect in many U.S. cities, where one finds a high concentration of Japanese families in particular neighborhoods and subdivisions in and around the city.

Actual housing selection is often made by the husband, who tends to arrive in the assigned location a few months earlier than the rest of the family. However, he usually has very limited time and resources for house hunting while at the same time getting acclimated to his new work environment. Thus, the decision is narrowed to a few options: sometimes corporate employers have properties available for their expatriate families, or a departing colleague may be looking for a buyer for his home. In places like New York and Los Angeles, there are Japanese-speaking real estate agents who specialize in working with expatriate Japanese clients. The company may also assign or recommend a realtor, who then comes up with properties particularly suitable for the needs of expatriate Japanese families. As a result of these pragmatic constraints, the wives, upon their arrival in the United States, find that they must make do with whatever their husband chose in a hurry and without the benefit of the wife's feedback. Women often complain about their husband's choices: the house may be too big or too old (requiring more maintenance and higher heating bills), or the kitchen may need updating; it may be convenient for commuting but too far from a Japanese grocery store for a daily trip. To make things a little more bleak for an arriving wife, she may find that her husband had no time to do things around the house, and that her new home is in complete disarray, with no furniture, dust and grime everywhere, and even a heap of trash accumulating in the garage. So the very day she arrives in the United States, even before she unpacks her and her children's luggage, she is on her hands and knees scrubbing the floor. Then, before she has had a chance to convince herself that she can somehow manage in this strange house, boxes, dozens of boxes that she shipped right before she left Japan, begin to arrive. The first two or three months come and go while she struggles with those cardboard boxes. Many of my female informants recalled their arrival experience as the toughest part of kaigai chuuzai. One said, "I felt like crying every day, because I was stuck at home trying to get rid of those never-ending piles of boxes."

From the outside, most expatriate Japanese homes in the United States are indistinguishable from other homes in the middle- to upper-middle-class neighborhoods. This is considered a good thing, because of these Japanese families' desire to blend into the landscape of American suburbia, to not attract attention to their foreignness and minimize possibilities of trouble. Besides, they will have to sell the house in several years when they return to Japan, and a customized Japanese home would be much harder to put on the market. The home of Kawagoe-san in Centerville, where I spent many afternoons with a group of Japanese women and their children, was a good example. A nondescript, three-bedroom tract home, it was located on a quiet dead-end street in a relatively new suburban subdivision. Kawagoe-san was fond of the house, particularly the vaulted ceiling in the living room, the large family room downstairs where her children could play in bad weather (which was important in this Midwestern city where winter is long and harsh), and the attached two-car garage (so that she could load and unload her children without stepping outside). At the same time, she complained about the work and cost involved in maintaining the front lawn, which she weeded and trimmed by herself, and the long driveway that she had to clear in the morning after heavy snow so that her husband could drive to work without trouble.

Once inside, however, Kawagoe-san's and other women's homes were marked with distinctively Japanese aesthetics and conventions to reproduce the familiar space of a Japanese home within the foreign physical structure (Cieraad 1999). For example, taking off shoes as one enters is an act of recognition of and respect for the uchi-soto boundary, which *dosoku* (dirty outdoor shoes) must not cross. As transient Japanese families in the United States usually buy homes with standard American features, one finds no structural marker at the entrance (Japanese homes have a raised floor approximately one foot above the foyer level). Some expatriate wives place a small carpet in the foyer to create the boundary; in some homes, children's shoes scattered about the entrance area become an inadvertent yet effective signal.

One also finds that these Japanese families have their own ideas about how to utilize space in an American-style home. For example, the formal dining room and parlor by the front entrance are often left empty, without furniture, for the children's play area. The master bedroom, intended as a private space for a couple, often becomes the sleeping room for all family members if children are still young, or the husband's quiet personal space in other cases. Mothers almost invariably sleep next to their young children, and it is not particularly unusual for a husband and wife to sleep in separate rooms, maybe because the husband snores too loud or the wife is afraid of waking her husband early in the morning when she gets up to prepare breakfast. In the living room, most families have a couch, chairs, and a coffee table (often bought from an expatriate Japanese family who is leaving to go back to Japan), but they usually sit on the floor and use the couch as a back rest.

In the homes of most expatriate Japanese, as well as in my own childhood recollections, uchi is, more than anything else, an experience of comforting chaos. My fieldnote entry on my first visit to Kawagoe-san's home, the regular gathering place for several chuuzaiin wives with young children, includes a fairly detailed description of her home and its physical appearance. I was quite struck by the way Kawagoe-san created, in an American suburban house, the familiarly chaotic, disorganized atmosphere of a Japanese home that I could describe only as cluttered coziness:

> While the living room and dining room were fairly uncluttered, the kitchen and the family room were definitely "lived in." Kawagoe-san's kitchen counter was completely covered with stuff—dirty dishes and pans, towels, food scraps, etc.—as she cooked soup and okowa [sticky rice pilaf] to go with dim sum. It didn't look like she had either enough counter space or storage. . . . The family room . . . was covered with toys. The whole room looked yellow, as many of the plastic toys scattered all over the room were yellow. . . . Adults sat on the floor and on the couch facing the TV, making room by pushing toys aside.

Kawagoe-san's home was sparsely and eclectically furnished; a black leather couch and chair, a peeling wood-veneer coffee table, and a small TV set on an inexpensive TV stand were the only furniture in the living room, most of which she purchased secondhand. A massive dining table, eight chairs, and a matching cupboard dominated the adjacent dining area, which she also bought used from a Japanese family that was departing from Centerville when she arrived. In the family room downstairs, she had just a sagging couch and a TV set, and the rest of the room was taken over by her children's toys. Despite the sparseness of furnishings, her home always seemed cluttered to me, partly because there were so many people in the house. I counted twelve adults and thirteen children in one of the largest gatherings, but normally there were three or four adults and assorted children, with toys and books scattered all over the floor.

This aesthetic incongruity is not simply a matter of Kawagoe-san's personal taste, but a very common scene in many expatriate Japanese homes that I have visited. Japanese tend to pay more attention to the details than to the total effect of home decoration, and this tendency may be even more exaggerated in their temporary homes in the United States. In those expatriate Japanese homes, one often finds an odd combination of sparse and mismatched furniture, little wall decoration, and clashing colors used in upholstery and window treatments. At the same time, there are a lot of uncoordinated knick-knacks, things Japanese and not so Japanese, traditional and modern, placed side by side: a *kimono*-clad doll, a calendar with colorful pictures of Japanese gardens, and plastic cups with Japanese cartoon characters, mixed in with pieces of American folk art, a glossy photograph of Manhattan skyscrapers, and Royal Copenhagen tea cups and saucers. These objects are, in a way, the itinerary of the family's past, present, and future. The kimono doll was a wedding gift from the wife's hometown, and the Japanese garden calendar bears the logo of the company for which one of the husband's brothers works. Plastic cups may be intended for young children, but they also reflect the generational memory of the original *anime* boom that Japanese thirty-somethings often share with one another. Mismatched used furniture, bought haphazardly from Japanese families departing the United States, is the result of a hasty move that the family had to make from Japan to the United States, their cost consciousness; it also reflects the mentality of people on the move who expect to go home to Japan after several years. The American objects in their home also tell a story of movement in recent years: the folk art piece juxtaposed against the New York skyscrapers indicate the different parts of the United States in which the family has lived or at least visited. Fine porcelain from Europe perhaps represents their aspiration toward a more sophisticated taste and a "notch above" way of life that middle-class Japanese coveted throughout the 1990s (see Clammer 1997). These objects both create and represent the hybrid, middle-class identity of the transnational Japanese family who belongs to this domestic space.

The experience of cluttered coziness is not only visual. The constant chattering of Japanese mothers competes with the sound of the video-taped cartoon *Anpanman*, the aroma of soy sauce and *dashi* (fish stock) from the kitchen mingles in the air with the greasy smell of the Mc-Donald's french fries the kids had for lunch. Imagine all of these things —discordant sounds, smells, colors, and designs—thrown together in a cookie-cutter American home, and you have a mental picture of an expatriate Japanese home. In its totality, the general chaos of the domestic space has a strangely calming effect on its occupants: it is a telltale sign of a space in which convenience, informality, and physical comfort have priority over orderliness, the signature of an uchi/home/in-group where no outsiders are expected. This is particularly important to Japanese homemakers abroad, who often contrast their uchi/home against the foreign soto, the strangest of strange places where one always has to be on guard. As they take off their shoes at the entrance and stretch their legs out on the floor, the occupants of this domestic space release a sigh of relief (*hottosuru*). It is the ultimate aim of their domestic work in the United States to make their home a place where their husband and children can relax and recover from a long day in a bicultural workplace and a foreign school.

HOMEMAKING AS SHIGOTO

If you ask a Japanese housewife about her homemaking responsibilities, chances are that she will lead you to believe that she is perfectly willing and content to conform to the expectations of domestic management and caretaking. This was true for almost all of my female informants in the United States. *Shigoto* (work, a job) and *yakume* (a role or responsibility) were the two words that they used most frequently to characterize their responsibility of domestic management and family caregiving. When I commented on the heavy responsibility that they carried, they almost invariably replied, "Demo, korega watashi no shigoto desukara [But this is my job]." The uniformity of the response was uncanny, and it seemed to me almost scripted, as though they thought that it was something they were supposed to say in their role as a dutiful wife and mother. Shigoto in this context implies the obligatory nature of their homemaking, and also their sense of responsibility toward their womanly job. Just as much as the husbands feel responsible for their jobs in their corporate collective, Japanese corporate wives find their domestic labor to be their duty or obligation to the family. Indeed, most of my corporate wife informants understood that their job was to live for others and to fulfill the needs of others. Particularly in the unfamiliar environment of the United States, they felt that their domestic work directly determined the well-being of their family members. Their domestic responsibilities took precedence over any other activities or interests that these women might have, and they had to be prepared to change their schedule at a moment's notice to accommodate the needs of their husband and children.

It takes much work to turn a house into a home, to transform an anonymous physical structure into a space in which people live and to which they belong, which is considered among contemporary middle-class Japanese primarily female work. It is the kind of work that middle-class Japanese women often single-handedly perform as housewives. The language of work and obligation with which expatriate Japanese wives spoke of their domestic labor resonates closely with the ideology of female domesticity that Japanese corporations employ to encourage and coerce these women to create Japanese homes abroad and ensure the reproduction of efficient and loyal labor for their transnational operations. My informants' understanding of domestic labor as a woman's shigoto, then, implies that they bought into the dominant ideology of femaleness, at least on one level of their consciousness. Even as an increasing number of Japanese women, particularly in the past three decades or so, began to seek out a source of satisfaction and identity away from the domestic sphere, domesticity remains at the center of their femaleness (Rosenberger 2000). It is important to keep in mind that my female informants, the middle-class wives of corporate workers and stay-at-home mothers for the most part, are particularly norm-sensitive, conservative women who followed, either consciously or by default, the ascribed path of a Japanese woman to become a "good wife and a wise mother" and acquired the cultural capital associated with this revered woman's place in Japanese society. As one of them put it, being a *shufu* (woman of the house) is a "high-status job" that the majority of middle-class Japanese women find quite attractive. They have much at stake, then, in maintaining the prestige of their wifely/ motherly roles and in keeping up with their responsibilities of domestic management and caretaking.

When Japanese corporate wives go abroad as an extension of their feminine duty, they also become gatekeepers, absorbing the stresses from the outside and restoring the uchi-ness in their family members that was bruised during the day in bicultural workplaces and foreign schools. Fukunaga Katsuko, an ex-chuuzaiin wife and a counselor, wrote a popular kaigai chuuzai how-to book, *Aruhi Kaigai Funin* (One Day, a Foreign Transfer; 1990). She advises prospective chuuzaiin wives to take the news in stride and devote themselves to helping their family abroad, even if it means giving up their career and other interests for the time being. It was as though all of my informants heeded her advice, as they seemed to devote an enormous amount of time and energy to their domestic work during kaigai chuuzai.

WORK ROUTINE

The daily routine of a Japanese corporate wife reflects the fact that she considers homemaking and caretaking the central aspect of her life. While their domestic routines appear similar in general, certain factors—most important, their life cycle stage, family composition, and the location of their foreign assignment—generate variations in the concrete daily routines of these women. I chose two samples (shown on the following pages) from the pool of approximately forty Japanese corporate wives I interviewed and/or interacted with extensively. They share some common features yet show a certain range in the daily routine of expatriate Japanese wives in the United States.

Yokoyama Kazue

Age 36; second year in Westchester, New York

One daughter (age 7, second grade)

Husband, age 38; midlevel manager in trading company; travels often

6:30 A.M.	Get up, prepare breakfast (no lunch box)
7–8:30 A.M.	Get husband and daughter ready for work/school
8:30 A.M.	Drive daughter to school
9–10 A.M.	Housework
10–11 A.M.	Volunteer at daughter's school (twice a week)
11 A.M.–NOON	Grocery shopping and errands
NOON	Lunch (mostly at home; sometimes with friends)
1–2 P.M.	Free (on the day of daughter's ballet lesson, prepare dinner ahead of time)
2 P.M.	Pick up daughter from school; home for a quick snack
3 P.M.	Take daughter to ballet lesson in Manhattan, English tutorial, or play date
4–5 P.M.	Wait for daughter, killing time in Kinokuniya bookstore or shopping
5 P.M.	Go home
6 P.M.	Serve dinner to daughter as soon as they get home
7–8 P.M.	Help daughter with homework (sometimes takes longer)
9 P.M.	Husband returns; serve dinner (sometimes later)
9:30 P.M.	Tuck daughter in (husband helps if he is home)
10 P.M.	Clean up after dinner; talk with husband
11 P.M.	Free, or finish remaining housework (if it was a busy day)
11:30 P.M.	Go to bed

Goto Machiko

late 40s; third year in Centerville

Two sons (15, 17; both in local public high school; older son drives)

Husband: age unknown; upper-level production manager at Maveric; irregular schedule

5:30 A.M.	Get up; prepare breakfast and lunch box for husband
6 A.M.	Husband gets up; serve breakfast
6:30 A.M.	Husband leaves for work
7:30 A.M.	Wake up sons; serve breakfast
8:15 A.M.	Sons leave for school (older son drives)
8:15–9:30 A.M.	Housework
9:30–NOON	Free; prepare for afternoon English classes
NOON	Lunch (almost always at home)
1–3 P.M.	English classes at community college (3–4 times a week)
3 P.M.	Go home
3:30 P.M.	Sons return from school; make snacks for them
4–5 P.M.	Free time for study or hobby
5–6 P.M.	Grocery shopping
6–7 P.M.	Cook dinner
7 P.M.	Dinner with sons
8–9 P.M.	Serve dinner to husband
9–11 P.M.	Free; talk with husband, study or read
11 P.M.	Go to bed (this largely depends on what time husband comes home)

These daily schedules of two Japanese corporate wives demonstrate different and similar constraints that shape their everyday routines. Some differences in their daily activities were determined by the difference in their personal interests. Yokoyama-san liked to go out and spend time with other people, so she tried to find opportunities for social activities, such as volunteer work and luncheons, even when her schedule was already packed with domestic and child care duties. Goto-san was less social than Yokoyama-san and would rather spend her spare time at home reading or studying English. She met most of her good friends through English classes, and their gathering was more of a group study session than purely a social event (I also suspect that her academic interest motivated her, at least in part, to maintain contact with me for a long time). Because her sons were more or less independent and her husband was often late coming home from work, she also participated in a Japanese conversation group once a month, in which a handful of Japanese wives (all in similar family circumstances) helped interested local Americans practice Japanese.

The common feature in both Yokoyama-san's and Goto-san's daily lives is that their schedules are structured around their homemaking and caretaking duties as wives and mothers, and because of that, their days are highly fragmented. Meals are served at the most convenient time for their husband and children; in the late afternoon hours, Goto-san must be home to serve snacks for her teenage sons and Yokoyama-san must take her daughter to a ballet lesson and other afterschool activities. The evening is also a patchwork of different duties for both women, serving dinners at different times, helping with homework, and finishing up housework that was left unfinished during the day. Their family composition and life cycle and their family's specific requirements thus determine the amount of work as well as the degree of fragmentation in these women's schedules. Obviously, Goto-san spent much less time caring for her teenage sons, who were, for the most part, independent and spent much of their time by themselves or with their friends. Yokoyama-san has only one child but her young age made her more care-intensive. It is also evident that their husbands, who are mostly absent from home during the day, determined what time Goto-san's and Yokoyama-san's day began and ended. The few hours of free time that these women had were also scattered throughout the day, making it harder (particularly for Yokoyama-san) to use their free time for "any meaningful activity."

There are two additional factors worth mentioning that are not visible in the summary of their daily schedules. Yokoyama-san's husband often traveled on business. This, in some ways, made Yokoyama-san's day less hectic, as she could sleep in a little later and cook less when he was away. However, when he was gone overnight and on the weekends, the burden, both psychological and physical, of being the sole adult in the household fell on Yokoyama-san, who would not have anyone else in the household to talk to at the end of the day or to fall back on in a pinch. For Goto-san, the independence of her teenage sons was, in fact, a source of much worry. She told me that she did not understand American teenage culture at all, and, though she was happy to see her sons become close friends with American teenagers, she often worried about her sons' whereabouts late at night. The impact of a foreign residence on their future also concerned her a great deal. She contemplated the demeanor of her sons, who seemed overly Americanized to her. She tried in vain to get her older son to study harder for his qualifying exams (which he needed to pass for graduation) and often spent hours with other expatriate Japanese mothers comparing notes about the educational options for their children after kaigai chuuzai.[1]

There are constraints specific to the particular location of expatriate women's residence as well. For instance, New York expatriate wives with more access to Japanese goods and services did not have the same concerns as Centerville wives, who, for instance, had to plan ahead and order Japanese-style bread from a bakery in Chicago. Centerville wives escaped the overcrowding and heavy traffic that annoyed New York wives daily. Expatriate wives in the Research Triangle lamented the lack of information about local schools and educational options for their children back in Japan, while New York wives wondered which Japanese *juku* (cram school) their children should attend while in the United States. At the same time, New York residents spent more time on the road due to traffic congestion and lack of parking and were most vocal about the stress of driving.

Despite these differences, however, the overall requirements of homemaking and the daily routine of Japanese wives are remarkably similar, and there are several constraints at work that produce this uniformity. To begin with, expatriate Japanese families are relatively homogeneous in their socioeconomic origins. Although there is naturally a degree of stratification among Japanese corporate workers, they all enjoy a solidly middle-class status by virtue of their stable employment and relatively high incomes. In the selection process of kaigai chuuzai, the hierarchy is further flattened, as companies send abroad mostly midlevel workers whose operational and management experiences are immediately useful in a foreign subsidiary or branch office, eliminating the top (i.e., top executives at the corporate level whose management experience is not needed at the foreign subsidiary) and the bottom (i.e., non-career-track employees, near-retirement workers, and entry-level workers on the career track) of the corporate organization. The financial reality of kaigai chuuzai in the late 1990s worked to further reduce the differentiation among expatriate Japanese families. As the compensation for kaigai chuuzai continued to shrink across the board, the difference between those in higher versus lower management positions and between those who worked for larger versus smaller companies also shrunk. At the same time, midlevel managers in their forties and fifties had much larger household expenditures due to their children's educational needs and/or the financial and other support that they provided to their aging parents, than, say, a newly married lower-level manager in his late twenties with no children.

The domestic life of expatriate Japanese families is also informed by the corporate vision in which women are positioned as domestic managers and caretakers of the family. This corporate view has two significant consequences: first, it determines the legal status of expatriate Japanese wives as dependents of their husband, making them unable to work legally in the United States. For the majority of Japanese corporate wives, lack of language skills precluded the possibility of employment in the United States in any case. However, some of the wives who had previous work experience and skills and felt that they might be able to find a job in the United States encountered staunch resistance from their husband's employer. Because these women come to the United States on a dependent visa, they need supporting paperwork from the human resources department of their husband's company to apply for a change of visa status. In every case that I recorded, such a request was flatly denied and women were admonished by human resources managers that they should not forget that their first priority was in the home, and not in the pursuit of their own career, while on kaigai chuuzai.

The significance of domestic performance to middle-class Japanese women's gendered selves also acts to reinforce the uniformity of domestic life. For middle-class Japanese women who choose the life of full-time wife and mother, any divergence from the perceived standard of good homemaking and family caretaking directly reflects their shortcoming not only as a wife and a mother, but also as a woman and a person. Among those norm-sensitive middle-class women, corporate wives who follow their husband to his foreign assignment become particularly vulnerable to the pressure to devote themselves entirely to their domestic duty to support their husband and children in the particularly stressful living and working environment of a foreign country.

Yet another source of uniformity is the reification of Japaneseness in the foreign environment. As we will see later in this chapter, the distinctions between what is Japanese and what is not are accentuated in the foreign environment, and, in turn, the variations within what is Japanese become less significant. The job of defining and protecting the boundary around Japaneseness defines the social positioning of Japanese housewives in the tightknit expatriate communities. The assumption that women belong at home permeates not only corporate organization, but also the expatriate community, and has a strong influence on the social networks of women. The perfection of domestic management and the dedication of the woman to her domestic role are valorized to such an extent that women, even those who did not consider themselves particularly "domestic," are caught up in the communitywide vigilance against divergence, an aspect of the transnational life of middle-class Japanese housewives that I explore in more detail in the next chapter.

KAJI, OR THE MAINTENANCE OF PHYSICAL SPACE

Although most Japanese corporate wives do not consciously categorize domestic tasks that they routinely perform, I came to see a sort of consensus emerging regarding the types of work they considered critical in their homemaking away from home: *kaji*, or the maintenance of physical space, cooking Japanese, "being there," learning to get around in a foreign city, and managing the precarious relationship to the soto in a foreign neighborhood. These are not necessarily the categories that my informants used to describe and classify their domestic management, but they are the products of fieldwork interaction, of negotiation between my informants' and my own ideas about housework. For example, the word *kaji* (literally, "housework" or "domestic chore") means to me *all* the work involved in domestic management and family caretaking in their broadest senses. The presumption of a native speaker kept me, for a while, from seeing that many of my informants included only the tasks directly linked to the physical maintenance of the home, such as cleaning, washing, tidying up, yard work, and light maintenance, but not cooking and shopping. On one hand, many of my informants thought of my distinction between homemaking and caretaking as artificial; in their mind, to make a home is to take care of the family and vice versa. On the other hand, they thought it strange to bunch together shopping and chauffeuring children under the category of "getting around." Others laughed and said that all housework melted into one long day of running from here to there, doing a little bit of this or that, and collapsing into their futon at the end of the day. I hope, however, that in the end, my five categories ring true as an ethnographic representation of these women's domestic work. I also hope that they say something about the nature of the uchi that these women strive to create and depict accurately the work demanded of expatriate Japanese wives.

KAJI, OR THE PHYSICAL maintenance of the home, varies somewhat by the chuuzai location, the family composition, and other factors that create different types and degrees of demands on wives and mothers. Women with small children spent more time cleaning and doing laundry than those without; women with sons, compared to women with daughters, spent more time cleaning, washing, straightening up, and sometimes fixing things in and around the house. Women who lived in Centerville, where winter is severe and snow is frequent, often had to shovel snow early in the morning to get their husband's car out of the driveway. In New York suburbs, many Japanese families lived in large, drafty houses built fifty or more years ago, with older appliances, increasing maintenance work for the wives. Nevertheless, when I asked them to compare the amount of kaji that they performed in the United States and Japan, most of my informants said that it became significantly lighter in the United States, and a few responded that it was approximately the same. They explained that better appliances made kaji tasks less time-consuming and that spacious U.S. homes required less straightening up than Japanese ones, thanks to abundant storage space and private rooms for individual family members. For most expatriate Japanese wives, these home maintenance tasks took a total of two to three hours a day. That is about half the time it would take them in Japan.

The physical maintenance of a home away from home also comes with the kind of worries and concerns to which these women are unaccustomed. One of those New York informants who mentioned yard work as part of her daily routine told me that it was important to maintain the outside appearance of the home. In many of those upper-middle-class neighborhoods throughout Westchester County, New York, and Bergen County, New Jersey, the relationship between the local American homeowners and their foreign neighbors became strained through the 1980s and 1990s, when a large number of affluent Asian families, including Japanese corporate families, moved into previously all-white suburbs (Okada 1993; see also Newman 1993). Whereas local resentment toward the foreigners next door rarely resulted in direct confrontation, it often took indirect shape—for example, as complaints about the poor outside appearance of their home. My informant explained that, to avoid such criticism, and to not be told that, after all, foreigners did not belong in nice neighborhoods in the United States, many expatriate Japanese wives in New York and New Jersey suburbs spent hours cutting grass and digging up dandelions in their large front yard for the sake of good neighborhood relations.

Another concern that often came up in discussions of physical space was people coming inside their homes with *dosoku*, "dirty feet," that is, with outdoor shoes on. Soto/outside is associated with dirt(iness), and the act of bringing in this dirt from the outside is a serious infringement of the uchi-soto distinction. Maintaining cleanliness inside is an important part of uchi-making. Their own family members and Japanese visitors would automatically take their shoes off at the entrance area, but most American visitors are oblivious to the invisible uchi-soto boundary. Most Japanese wives, afraid of imposition and wary of having to explain in English, let Americans inside their home with their shoes on and sweep the floor after they leave. This creates not only more work but also a strong sense of intrusion. The word *dosoku* carries a negative connotation of dirtiness and also signifies metaphorically carelessness and lack of respect. It is often used in a phrase such as *dosoku de fuminijiru* ("trample on with the dirty feet"), further accentuating the sense of rude infliction. Even as expatriate Japanese wives permit—or perhaps precisely because they feel they have to permit—outsiders to come into their home with their dirty feet, they resent this intrusion and clean away the dirt with vigor. One afternoon, when I was visiting Kawagoe-san, I witnessed how the dirt from the outside was cleaned up right away, erasing the sign of intrusion. Immediately after she closed the front door behind an electrician who came to fix something in her house, Kawagoe-san was on her knees, wiping the hardwood floor of the hallway and kitchen. All the while, she was explaining to me how she found it easier to let Americans, particularly those who come in just for a quick visit, to keep their shoes on, but she had to clean up after them when they left because she had small children in her house who should not be playing on a dirty floor. "There we go, it's all done," she said as she got up from the floor and put away her rag, once she was satisfied that all the dirt from the outside had been wiped away.

FOOD PREPARATION

One of the things that I noticed very quickly about the homemaking labor of expatriate Japanese wives was that they spent a mind-boggling amount of time on food preparation each day. Regardless of age, family composition, or the place of origin, my corporate wife informants told me that they cooked primarily Japanese food in their home in the United States. What they meant by Japanese food may require clarification. Their repertoire usually included some traditional Japanese fare, such as stewed vegetables in soy sauce, tempura, teriyaki fish, and a variety of sushi. They also incorporated a number of originally foreign recipes, which were modified extensively to accommodate Japanese taste and were particularly popular among children and younger adults, for example, curry and rice, hamburgers, spaghetti with meat sauce, and pot stickers. These Japanized dishes often little resembled their original versions, and Japanese wives distinguished them from truly exotic cooking from India, Europe, and China and regarded them as part of contemporary Japanese cuisine.

Japanese home cooking is, in general, a labor-intensive and time-consuming work. Many small dishes accompany the main dish and a bowl of freshly cooked rice. Many ingredients used in these dishes have to be chopped or cut fine and/or require complicated handling before they can be cooked, such as parboiling, soaking overnight, salting, and marinating. The actual method of cooking may include a combination of boiling, grilling, steaming, sauteeing, frying, and stewing, all of which must be timed correctly.

In Japanese households in the United States, preparation of Japanese food is made even more time-consuming as a result of being in a foreign environment. First, obtaining the proper ingredients for these dishes is a chore in itself. A few large metropolitan areas, including New York, Chicago, and Los Angeles, have large specialty stores that offer a wide array of Japanese and Asian food items, but in most inland cities, Japanese women have to drive a long distance to get to smaller Japanese stores where the selection is often inadequate. Whenever possible, expatriate Japanese wives go grocery shopping at multiple stores every day or every other day, because many of the Japanese dishes that they cook at home require fresh ingredients and specialty food items that they can find only at Japanese grocery stores such as Yaohan (now Mitsuwa Market). Flourishing business at these specialty stores attests to the specificity with which these women purchase food items for household consumption. The great majority of merchandise in such stores is imported from Japan or produced in the United States specifically for Japanese consumers. Even when less expensive substitutes from other countries, like China or Korea, are available, Japanese wives tend to stick with familiar Japanese brands because, they told me, they believe in the higher quality and safety standards of Japanese products. The meat and fish counters feature distinctive Japanese cuts, such as *sukiyaki*-sliced beef or trimmed blocks of tuna of *sashimi* quality. Eggs from a "Japanese" chicken farm in California are labeled "safe when eaten raw," as raw eggs are an essential ingredient in the traditional Japanese breakfast. In fact, the availability of Japanese food often becomes one of the important indicators of how livable a certain chuuzai location is (Taniguchi 1985).

In addition, the majority of expatriate Japanese wives and mothers routinely cook duplicate and triplicate meals to accommodate the irregular schedules of their husband and children. For example, it was not unusual for Ichigaya-san, one of my key informants in Centerville who had a busy engineer husband and two teenage children, to serve breakfast twice and dinner three times on any given day. When I stayed at her home, she started her day at around 5 in the morning to get breakfast and the lunch box ready for her husband, who left home before 7; her children, both high school students, came out to eat their breakfast at around 7:30. In the evening, she prepared the first dinner for her fifteen-year-old son, who usually got hungry at around 6 P.M.; then, she served the second dinner for her seventeen-year-old daughter and her tutor at around 7:30, during the break in their tutorial session. Her husband then came home at a little past 9, and his customary bottle of warm sake and snacks were promptly set on the table, followed by a light meal. If her husband or children were home at midday, Ichigaya-san would also make sure that they had a hot lunch. Although this is a fairly common situation in Japanese households, the increased irregularity of the expatriate family's schedule, and added constraints on the women's own daily routine makes it more burdensome to accommodate an erratic feeding schedule. Someone like Ichigaya-san would spend up to six hours a day in the kitchen and an average of one hour a day for grocery shopping. I knew a few younger Japanese wives with no children who spent only two to three hours a day on food preparation, but the average seemed to be four to five hours, which is in addition to kaji.

Japanese food is in particularly high demand in these families. Many husbands complain that American food is *mazui* (tasteless, poor tasting) or *kuchi ni awanai* (does not suit their taste) and look forward to home-cooked Japanese meals at the end of the day. From the perspective of the wives and mothers, health concerns dominate their choices of food to serve at home. Expatriate Japanese wives often substantiate their preference by pointing out the nutritional benefits of traditional Japanese food, which is rich in minerals and vitamins and incorporates balanced portions of protein, starch, and vegetables. I once stayed at one informant's home after an afternoon-long interview and watched her prepare dinner. Cooking for a busy engineer husband with irregular work hours and two teenage children whose food choices were less than desirable during the day, this informant tried as best she could to serve her family "well-balanced dinners and breakfasts with a lot of variety." Apologizing for an "abbreviated" meal due to her husband's absence, she still cooked two main dishes and four side dishes that night. When I commented on how many dishes she was preparing, she replied, "I think Japanese food is really healthy, because we make a lot of small dishes that let us eat a great variety of food, particularly vegetables." The nutritional soundness of Japanese food is often contrasted to American food's being fattening, empty of nutrients, too salty, too sweet, and generally harmful to one's health. Many middle-aged wives are seriously concerned about the health of their husband, who have no choice but to eat American food at work or during a business trip. "Just think about all the ailments that you can attract by eating all that awful stuff," said an expatriate wife in her forties with a husband who traveled often. "My husband put on a lot of weight since we came to America, and it's really bad [for his health]. It's all because of the American food he's been eating." All the more reason for her to cook and serve strictly "Japanese" food at home.

Uchi-ness is a loaded notion in itself, and the uchi-ness of food is a complex and ever shifting construct. On one level, the uchi-soto dichotomy in food signifies the distinction between recognizably Japanese and foreign recipes, miso soup with tofu versus lobster bisque, for example. On another level, it is domestic versus imported, the food items that are produced inside Japan versus in foreign countries, *naichi-mai* (literally, "rice from inside land," *nai* being the same Chinese character as *uchi*) versus *gaimai* (literally, "rice from soto/outside"). On yet another level, it is home-cooked versus commercially cooked, the food one's mother or wife prepares from scratch versus that of professional chefs and artisans, the simplicity of *imo no nikkorogashi* (stewed taro in dark soy sauce) versus the aesthetics of *takimono* (an assortment of vegetables cooked in light broth to preserve their colors). These inside/outside distinctions are made increasingly ambivalent in contemporary Japanese food culture. For instance, most of the tofu and miso paste consumed in Japan is made from American soy beans. Formerly exotic food, such as Indian curry, becomes a Japanized mainstay of home cooking. In Japan, many wives take out ready-to-serve traditional dishes from department stores or buy boxed "home-style" meals at *konbini* (convenience stores), and men frequent restaurants that specialize in rustic home-style cooking. Thus, in everyday practice, contemporary Japanese in Japan constantly eat the food that is simultaneously "inside" and "outside," while the conceptual difference lingers on as an ideal.

By contrast, these inside versus outside distinctions tend to become exaggerated and reified in expatriate Japanese households as differences between a Japanese home as the bastion of the Japanese self versus the otherness literally at the doorstep of their home. In Japan, one may eat Japanese anywhere—at home, in a restaurant, or at the company cafeteria. In the United States, one often has to eat American away from home and eat almost exclusively Japanese at home. This set of circumstances makes Japanese cooking even more symbolically overdetermined in a foreign environment than within Japan. Thus, food is associated with two spaces or domains between which expatriate Japanese go back and forth daily: uchi and soto, inside and outside, domestic and public, Japanese and foreign. In turn, the particular kind of food that is associated with each domain at once creates and represents the ethos of that domain.

Uchi/inside	Soto/outside
Domestic	Public
Japanese food	American (or foreign) food
Hotto suru (relief, relaxation)	*Kinchoo suru* (tension, stress)

Eating Japanese, then, is synonymous with being home and being Japanese for one's husband and children, who eat American away from home. At the same time, the wives and mothers find it a necessary part of their Japanese homemaking to cook and serve only familiar food from familiar ingredients and recipes. To consume these products of wifely/motherly labor is, in turn, the requirement of Japanese subjects. The late Itami Juzo (1988) shows in his feature film *Tampopo* a mother/wife on her death bed, who, in a coma, jumps up and prepares dinner for her family and then expires. Her husband, crying and shoveling rice into his mouth, orders his children: "Eat! This is the food Mother cooked for us, eat!" The ideological forces of food are written all over Itami's acute, albeit parodic, depiction. Cooking is the requirement of Japanese motherhood, and it is powerful enough to defy the laws of nature and, literally, raise the dead, while the only fitting reciprocity to this motherly love is to eat the meal with gusto. Allison (1995), in her analysis of *obento*, or boxed lunches, points out that the preparation (by mothers) and consumption (by preschoolers) of this elaborate meal at once "produced" mothers and instilled discipline in young children in their everyday routine. Food preparation and consumption are, then, constituents of female Japanese subjectivities, which mediate and represent the ideal relationship between Japanese subjects as well as between the self and the other (Ohnuki-Tierney 1996). In the transnational context of kaigai chuuzai, home-cooked Japanese food becomes the key to the maintenance of cultural identity, reinforcing the importance of cooking and feeding Japanese food as a woman's shigoto/work.

What middle-class Japanese wives had to say about the nutrition and health benefits of Japanese food is probably correct, and their concerns for the physical health of their husband and children were no doubt genuine. But I also see the metaphorical workings of this "scientific" explanation in the context of identity-making. The important principle in this scientific explanation is the connection between matter (i.e., food and body), and its metaphoric extension to the linkage between mind (identity) and matter (food). In the expatriate Japanese wives' language of health and nutrition, you are indeed what you eat. The food one eats is directly linked to one's physical health, and the comparative analysis of nutrients that one incorporates into one's body substantiates this linkage: to eat "unhealthy" American food is to make one's own body unhealthy. At the same time, incorporating the substance that is foreign into one's body stands for a breach of the boundary between Japaneseness and Americanness. The result is an undesirable (Americanized) self residing in an unhealthy (American) body. Forced by circumstance, kaigai chuuzaiin and their children eat American food at work and at school, and expose themselves to foreignness. The effect of food that is simultanenously foreign and commercially prepared—that is, doubly soto—must be offset and reversed by home-cooked Japanese food at the end of the day; thus may the Japaneseness of the self be restored.

As Japan's globalizing economy makes a job transfer to the United States commonplace in Japanese corporate workers' life-long career, Japanese transnational corporations need workers who are international enough to function well in a foreign environment, but not so cosmopolitan that they will lose steadfast loyalty to their company and their country of origin. Women's domestic labor is a key to managing this paradox of globalizing Japanese capitalism. As an extension of their ascribed feminine role of homemaking, Japanese wives are expected to accompany their husband to foreign stations and to reproduce Japanese domestic spaces. Cooking Japanese in their foreign home is one of the ways expatriate Japanese wives mark and maintain conceptual boundaries between the Japanese self and the foreign other and thus protect the cultural identity of their home and family members. In fact, the act of cooking Japanese produces expatriate Japanese wives' subjectivity twice: when they cook Japanese to feed their family they are doing their duty as wives and mothers; then, as they sit down and eat the food they prepared, they also become, along with their family, the consumer of Japaneseness of their own making.

BEING THERE

Japanese women with whom I spoke unanimously agreed that the ultimate aim of domestic management was to maintain the physical and psychological well-being of the family members under their care. This rather formidable and abstract goal was often translated into concrete choices and the daily tasks of the women. In the way Japanese corporate wives spoke of their work of homemaking and caretaking, the distinction between physical and psychological care was constantly blurred in two important ways. First, they shared a notion of well-being that necessarily linked physical health and psychological health. To take care of the body is to take care of the mind, and vice versa. If one's body is not well, it will weaken the mind and sicken the heart; if one's heart is not happy and one's mind is distracted, it will, sooner or later, result in a physical ailment. Thus, in their own descriptions of the day-to-day work of homemaking, women often had difficulty distinguishing (at the urging of the inquisitive anthropologist) the bodily and the mental aspects of caregiving.

Homemaking is their way of providing support to their husband and children, or, as one woman put it, "I just try to keep the house comfortable, serve something good to eat, and have a clean futon to sleep on—there's not much else [to be done for psychological support]." Many others explained that the foundation of psychological well-being is physical health. Fulfilling basic bodily needs, and fulfilling them consistently well, makes their husband and children more resilient under duress and ultimately ensures their happiness and well-being overall. Thus, to expatriate Japanese wives, no clear distinction exists between the work of home management, physical caretaking, and psychological caretaking: doing a good job with concrete day-to-day housework *is* taking good care of one's husband and children; their labor of domestic management also becomes a labor of love and caring for their family.

Another important distinction that becomes blurred in this mind-body connection is that between the women and the domestic space. Women become the important constituent of the restful Japanese home that they themselves create and maintain, and, for "good" wives and mothers, it becomes an imperative to always "be there" for their husband and children. To them, the notion of being there joins different aspects of their homemaking and caretaking work—concrete and mental, physical and emotional, literal and metaphorical. This sentiment is felt most powerfully at the moment when a person returns to his or her uchi/home from the outside. When one announces one's arrival with the customary *"Tadaima* [I just returned]," it is reciprocated by a cheerful *"Okaerinasai* [Welcome home]!" from the mother/wife. This exchange is the same whether one comes home after just a few hours away or after years of absence. It is an acknowledgment of common belonging to an uchi that endured (temporary) physical separation. This scene of homecoming is also gendered: typically, it is a wife/mother who stays at home, maintains it, and greets those (males) who return. Thus, as a concrete practice of the everyday, many Japanese women make sure that they are physically there, at home, when their husband and children return and that they greet them in person with a smile. This seemingly simple and minor act (*kantanna koto, nandemonai koto*) is indeed a key practice in their effort to provide psychological support to their husband and children. The importance of the wife/mother's being there is widespread among Japanese mothers generally. It is considered *kawaiso* (cruel and heartless) for children to have to return to an empty house, without their mother's smiling face greeting them at the door, and Japanese parents tend to believe that a lack of such maternal presence has a long-term negative effect on the child's emotional development. Conversely, mothers who neglect their duty of being there are deemed deficient in their care and affection for children (Uno 2000). Similarly, wives who neglect to "be there" for their husband have to endure outright criticisms and innuendos from others.

Often, I found my interviewees grow restless toward the end of our afternoon meetings, glancing up at the clock and looking out the window. "Oh, I'm sorry," they'd realize that they were distracted and apologize. "My son [or daughter] will be home any minute." I'd apologize in return for taking up so much of their time and begin to leave. Many of my prospective interviewees would simply not schedule a meeting in the afternoon. Sometimes, it was because they needed to pick up their children, which was quite understandable. But some women told me that they had to be home when their children came home, which did not make sense to me at first, as most of my interviews took place at the informant's home. Not wanting to appear pushy, I did not ask these women why we could not meet at their home, where they could see their children when they got home. When I mentioned to Ichigaya-san and other women with teenage and adult children how difficult it was to make appointments with some mothers, they said apologetically that they would have been that way when their children were younger. Ichigaya-san elaborated: "Because I really wanted to be there for my children [*kodomono tameni iteyaritakatta*] when they got home; if I had a guest [when her children arrived], I really couldn't do that."

Being there in this context has the double meaning of both physical presence and mental attentiveness. It means that the mother is at home the moment her children arrive, and is at home for, and only for, them. The presence of an anthropologist, an outsider, in the home interferes not with the former but with the latter aspect of being there. When mothers are picking up their children, the sentiment of being there is quite similar. Many expatriate Japanese mothers make a point of picking up their children by themselves, even when they could have easily taken turns with other Japanese mothers to lessen their chauffeuring duties, or when children could take a school bus, because, many of my informants believed, the first face that children see after school should be that of their mother. To delay that is to delay children's homecoming and their relief from a stressful day at school.

So for a couple of hours after the customary exchange of tadaima and okaerinasai, the mother concentrates her effort and attention on her children, and intensive caretaking activities commence for their comfort, relaxation, and contentment. The mother usually has some snacks ready. After making sure that her children have washed their hands, she sits down with them and attentively listens to them report everything about their day at school. In case the children are not forthcoming with enough details, the mother will have many questions to ask: What did you do in the morning? Did the teacher talk to you? What did she say? Did that bully who made you cry last week bother you today? Do you have any handouts or letters from the teacher? What about homework? Do you want me to help you with it, or do you want to wait for the tutor? When I had a chance to observe these homecoming scenes, I noticed that the interaction between the mother and her children was almost completely one-sided; that is, the mother initiated and did all the emotional work while the children sat passively and simply received what their mother gave them. Children after a certain age—eleven or twelve, perhaps—particularly seemed uninterested in such motherly attention. They often looked down at the plate of sweets on the table or watched TV while their mother was talking to them. They answered her questions briefly and absent-mindedly, and they never asked their mother about her day at home. Nevertheless, the mother never seemed to tire fussing over her children, and the children, however inattentive they might seem, never refused anything that she offered them. This one-sidedness is the ultimate indulgence of children in their mother's care; they are relieved of all responsibilities that come with social inter-action outside the home and can simply bask in the attention of their mother with no obligation to reciprocate or even respond.

The degree to which expatriate Japanese wives and mothers adhere to the ideal of being there is more exaggerated in the United States because, I think, in the transnational context the boundary between the uchi/home and the soto/public space is also the boundary between the uchi/Japan and the soto/America. As Japanese corporate employers often emphasize to the wives of their expatriate workers, transnational work is exceptionally burdensome and stressful. Management of bi-cultural work relations and the demands of the competitive global market directly impact expatriate managers and workers every work-day. In turn, Japanese wives' responsibility of caring for their family's bodies and minds becomes heavier, and the perfection of their domestic management in this difficult circumstance becomes the perfection of their moral virtue as a caring wife and mother.

Ichigaya-san and Kayama-san, two veteran chuuzaiin wives and mothers in their forties and fifties, felt very strongly about their respon-sibility to their children. They told me that their children brought home all the stresses and frustrations of their American school life and that they, as mothers, did their best to lend their support and help them cope. "They [her teenage children] need an outlet for their frustration, a punching bag, so to speak," said Ichigaya-san. "When they come home from school, I try to be as cheerful and positive as I can be, even when I don't feel that way. If a mother is depressed and gloomy, where do children have to go with their problems, to vent their frustration?" Kayama-san, whose children were already in college and away from home, agreed: "My children were pretty much the same way, and I felt that I was the last resort. If I failed [to console them], they had no other place to go." Ichigaya-san and Kayama-san were not certain whether they would have felt quite as strongly about their "punching bag" duty if they had raised their children in Japan. They felt that their children were exposed to an especially stressful environment because of their father's kaigai chuuzai, and that mothers were the only thing standing between their children and an unhappy ending. These perceptions seemed to motivate their extraordinary sense of responsibility to be there for their children, even to the degree that at times seemed almost abusive to an outsider's eyes.

Japanese women's relationship with their husband closely resembles those with their children in many ways, as their primary goal is to make their husband comfortable, relaxed, and "at home." They may not be quite as solicitous as they are with their children; some husbands prefer not to talk or be questioned about work; some use their few hours of freedom at home reading, playing on a computer, or practicing hobby activities of their choice. If this is the case, the wife's job is to let him be and to not bother him—just have a home-cooked meal, hot bath, and clean futon ready whenever her husband calls for them. The same rules of indulgence also apply in the husband-wife relationship. This may be hard to swallow for an American observer whose cultural ideology of marriage privileges the mutual enjoyment and respect of the two equals (even when their roles may differ). Japanese housewives, by and large, assume no such mutual conjugal relationship, but unquestioningly care for their husband as though they were their husband's mother. The relationship is resolutely unequal: between a selfless, indulgent, nurturing mother and a self-absorbed, demanding child who is perfectly willing to let his mother take care of everything (Allison 2000).

GETTING AROUND

Somewhat conflicting with the work of being there is the increased need for expatriate Japanese wives and mothers to be out and about for the purpose of homemaking and caretaking. They know that the effectiveness of their homemaking depends on their pragmatic local knowledge and their ability to get around in a foreign place. For one thing, responsibilities related to child care and education require them to spend a considerable amount of time outside the home and to interact with Americans around them.

Unlike their middle-class American counterparts, driving is not something most Japanese housewives and mothers are accustomed to do on a daily basis. In Japan, children from the first grade on walk to and from school with their friends, and some as young as ten may take public transportation on their own. Particularly in urban areas where traffic congestion is severe and the cost of owning a car is prohibitive, daily shopping and errands are usually done on foot, by bicycle, or on public transportation. Taking the car out is, to many of my female Japanese informants, something cumbersome and tiring. Being in a foreign country aggravates the situation. Complaints about aggressive and ill-mannered local drivers and the high speed of both street and freeway traffic were heard everywhere I conducted field research, but most often in the New York area (and quite understandably). Inadequate language skills and the lack of familiarity of a foreign city are also major factors that add to the stress of driving. Many women fear that they will not find their way back home if they get lost; others worry that they may inadvertently break traffic rules. And what if they get into an accident? How can they even begin to explain the situation to the other involved party and to police officers? What if they misunderstand something and end up being blamed for the accident? Yet, the tasks of home management require them to take the car out many times each day, fight the traffic, and navigate streets and freeways. A considerable number of Japanese women, in fact, categorically refuse to drive on freeways, even in the relatively relaxed driving conditions in Centerville and North Carolina's Research Triangle.

I am not sure how many hours a typical American soccer mom spends driving, but the amount of driving that Japanese wives and mothers in the United States have to put in seems quite excessive. This, in part, has to do with the particular requirements of physically living in a U.S. city yet making their domestic space distinctly Japanese; this duality often doubles women's driving time. For instance, grocery shopping, which many Japanese wives do every day or every other day, has to be done in a regular supermarket for such basic supplies as dairy products, breakfast cereals, children's snacks, and certain common vegetables (onions, potatoes, and the like) and in a Japanese specialty store for imported food items essential for Japanese cooking. Most expatriate Japanese children also attend two schools: a local public school during the week and the supplemental Japanese school on Saturday. Many also go to private tutorials or juku (cram school) in the evening so that they can simultaneously keep up with both U.S. and Japanese curricula. All of these schooling activities require transportation, a responsibility that often falls solely on the mother.

The burden of driving is also increased because of certain limitations that are common to the majority of expatriate Japanese wives. One of those limitations is the fact that most expatriate Japanese families tend to network more within the expatriate community and less in their immediate neighborhood community. This means, for instance, that Japanese mothers have to drive their children across town to play with other Japanese children from the supplemental Saturday school. Similarly, wives and mothers tend to socialize with other Japanese women who are in their own age group and have children of similar ages, rather than American or expatriate Japanese women nearby whose family life has little in common with their own. Another factor is the limited sources through which expatriate Japanese wives and mothers obtain information. With the language barrier being a major issue for the majority of these women, they often rely exclusively on familiar Japanese-language sources, including other Japanese wives, the husband's company, and locally published Japanese periodicals, to find out where, for instance, a good Chinese restaurant is. Once the name of a recommended restaurant gets on the Japanese information circuit, all the expatriate Japanese in the area go to that particular establishment, even when it is on the other side of town. In all three expatriate communities in which I worked, my informants seemed to have an implicit and near blind trust in the information that circulates through expatriate Japanese networks; very few were willing to try out a new restaurant in their neighborhood rather than driving forty-five minutes to the one favored by Japanese patrons.

As a result, Japanese corporate wives in the United States often spend at least a couple of hours a day on the road. The busiest are, by far, the ones who have children in multiple schools or who have to drop off and pick up children at more than one school, at afterschool activities, and at play dates. Each drop-off and pick-up is at a specific time and may be at different ends of a city or involve careful planning to make sure that they are not too late or too early. Somewhere in between, these mothers have to do grocery shopping, run various household errands, do some volunteer work at school, and, if they are lucky, enjoy some leisure activities for themselves, such as visiting a friend, taking craft lessons, or playing sports (see the next chapter for details). Some of the burden can be offset if they can coordinate the driving duty with other mothers during the week or count on their husband to do some of his own errands on the weekend. But too often, this proves too difficult (with other mothers) or unreliable (with their husband), so many mothers spend most of the day driving from one place to another.

The change in the driving routines of Ueda-san, one of the women who used to be one of the regulars at Kawagoe-san's house, illuminates these points. When I met her for the first time in 1996, her older son was in kindergarten and her younger son at age three was still at home. She dropped her older son off at around nine and picked him up at one in the afternoon. Finishing her daily shopping and errands in between left most of the afternoon open for her to schedule activities for herself and her children, which often meant bringing the children to spend the afternoon at Kawagoe-san's house. Two years later, when I went to visit Centerville, Ueda-san was no longer a regular at Kawagoe-san's. When I inquired about her, Kawagoe-san said simply, "Oniichan gakkou ni haittakara [Her older son started school]." This obviously made sense to her and other mothers, but not to me, so she had to explain further: "Until last year, Ueda-san didn't have too many constraints of drop-offs and pick-ups because her sons were still young. This fall, her older one started the first grade, and the younger one got into a nursery school. Now, she has to drop them off at something like eight and nine in the morning and pick them up at noon and two in the afternoon." Furthermore, Kawagoe-san explained patiently, these pick-up and drop-off times could affect a woman's entire day. When she has to drive a child to school at eight, there is not enough time to finish all the regular housework, such as clearing dishes after breakfast, doing the wash, and tidying up. Therefore, after she drops off her children, she has to return home to finish up these chores. Then, by the time she is done at home, there is not enough time to do anything else before the first pick-up in the afternoon. Between two pick-ups, she can perhaps get grocery shopping done, but by the time she gets home and unloads the groceries, she needs to turn around and take the children to soccer practice or to play dates. "So her day's gone, you see? It's only going to get worse as her two boys grow older. There is no more hanging out with us for Ueda-san!"

Kawagoe-san's explanation reveals one of the real problems associated with driving duty: it fragments the day of Japanese wives and mothers into two- to three-hour chunks divided between drop-off and pick-up times, and within such constraints, women tend to sacrifice activities for their own enjoyment. The fact that Ueda-san's husband was in a management position that required him to spend long hours and many weekends at work must also have been a contributing factor to her predicament. Furthermore, many of her close friends were several years younger than she, and their children younger than hers, which meant that Ueda-san had few friends to share driving responsibilities. During my visit to Centerville in 1998, I saw Ueda-san only twice at Kawagoe-san's house. On both occasions, she just came in briefly to drop off something and say hello to everyone, barely taking notice of my greetings. After she left, other women came to me and apologized for her not being able to stay, adding that she had been so preoccupied with her sons lately that they themselves rarely had a chance to sit down and talk with her anymore.

In addition to those errands that require Japanese wives to be physically outside their home, many of their homemaking and child care responsibilities involve interaction with local Americans and communication in English. Going to a doctor's appointment, volunteering at children's schools, attending parent-teacher conferences, supervising homework, finding tutors, and researching educational options are all considered the responsibility of the mothers. In a foreign environment, however, they are often frustrated by their inadequate language skills and lack of information. School is a particularly important local place where expatriate Japanese mothers interact with teachers and American parents. Some mothers manage to meet teachers who truly care about the well-being of their Japanese pupils and American parents who teach them how parents help out in schools in the United States. Some mothers come to appreciate the educational philosophy that at first seemed so strange to them, as I discuss in more detail below. But for the majority of my informants, school was yet another place where they had to struggle to bridge the gap between the Japanese and American systems. For example, even an otherwise simple task of reading about an upcoming school event can take them hours because most of the Japanese mothers have to sit down with a dictionary to make sense of it. They may need to call other mothers or wait for their husband to come home to discuss a particularly confusing passage. If all else fails, they might even have to go to school and speak to their children's teacher face-to-face to make sure they understand the information correctly and know exactly what their children need to do. In addition, navigating the educational systems of Japan and the United States poses a considerable challenge to expatriate Japanese mothers. In most U.S. cities, Japanese children go to local public schools during the week and a supplemental Japanese-language school on Saturday. This results in a double work load for the mothers, on whom the responsibility of supervising their children's dual educational goals usually falls.

GETTING ALONG IN A FOREIGN NEIGHBORHOOD

Another task related to homemaking away from home is to maintain a good, or at least neutral, relationship with foreign neighbors. Husbands, who are rarely home during the day and not so inclined to take time to get to know local Americans, often leave the United States after several years of kaigai chuuzai without ever having a conversation with their neighbors beyond a brief exchange of "Hi, how are you?" on the driveway. Wives, by contrast, have many reasons—some by choice, others by necessity—to interact with their neighbors, and some actively cultivate relationships with their neighbors and try to make friends, particularly when their children are about the same age. But many instances of neighborhood interaction are not so enjoyable. In fact, one of the sources of disappointment that my female informants mentioned about their lives in the United States was that there were few opportunities for them to interact with their American neighbors, who seemed too busy or uninterested to take the time to get to know their foreign neighbors.

Neighborhood relations can also be a source of conflict. Many Japanese families are unaware of both explicit and implicit rules that govern middle-class neighborhoods in the United States, and such ignorance can become the cause of friction. As I mentioned previously, many informants were concerned about their neighbors who would get irritated by an untrimmed front lawn. One complained that some of her neighbors watched her closely, and if she left her children in the house or did anything else that they disapproved of, they would come by afterward and tell her not to do that again. These negative neighborhood experiences were particularly frequent in the Greater New York area, where the large number of expatriate Japanese households have become a source of irritation and resentment among long-time local residents. In Centerville and the Research Triangle, examples of overtly confrontational encounters with neighbors were relatively few, but many women complained of the ignorance and lack of interest that the local Americans indicated for Japan and foreign countries and cultures in general.

Michel de Certeau (1984; de Certeau et al. 1998) situates the neighborhood in the French social context to be a sort of buffer or intermediary zone between the private space of the home and the public space of the larger society. A similar sense of neighborhood and the importance of neighborliness are upheld in many communities in Japan, often in the form of *chonaikai*, or formal neighborhood associations that have not only social but administrative functions (see, e.g., Bestor 1989; Robertson 1991). By contrast, many expatriate Japanese wives were struck by the fact that, while in the United States, the neighborhood right outside their front door became a "foreign country," populated by the "foreigners" whose motivations, thoughts, and sentiments they found difficult to fathom. Men could remain relatively oblivious of this, those women also told me, because they spent most of their time away from home and did not have much direct interaction with their neighbors in their daily routine. The wives and mothers, however, often felt that they had to get along in the neighborhood as part of their responsibility of domestic management, and also to secure a friendly environment for their children. "Besides," one of my outspoken female informants said, "we [the wives] are the ones who have to hear about it if anything goes wrong with the neighbors. Men have workplaces to go to; we are stuck here [in the home and the immediate neighborhood]." Initiating social contact with neighbors is, therefore, no light-hearted matter for women, but most of the men seemed quite surprised to hear their wife speak of such concerns.

To many Japanese women, American suburbia also seems empty and surreal. Kawagoe-san once mused, looking out the window of her living room, "Gosh, when I sit here with you all, it's hard to believe that I'm in *Amerika!*" Outside, beyond the densely parked cars on her driveway, an expanse of well-groomed front lawn reflected the late afternoon sun. "It's so quiet that it seems as though nobody lives in this neighborhood." There are many reasons, both tangible and perceptual, why neighborhood America seems so empty to expatriate Japanese wives. Partly, it is the nature of American suburbia itself, where most Japanese corporate wives build their temporary homes. It is the domain of reproduction, traditionally assigned to middle-class women and disconnected from all other functioning of human society (Chodorow 1989). Through the 1980s and 1990s, an increasing number of American women left their suburban homes behind for wage labor because of their own professional aspirations, economic necessity, or both (e.g., Newman 1993). The most immediate effect of this is the fact that my informants usually saw very few people around the neighborhood. In many of the middle- to upper-middle-class neighborhoods in Centerville and the New York area, my informants told me, few neighbors stayed home during weekdays. Not only the husbands go to their offices elsewhere in town, but most wives also leave for full-time and part-time jobs. In the meantime, children are in schools, day care, or afterschool activities, and if at home, are often prohibited from playing on the street for fear of accident or kidnapping. So the daytime population of these suburban neighborhoods is, to my Japanese informants' surprise, quite low. They also acknowledged that the physical aspects of American suburbs prevented neighborliness, not only for foreign residents but also among local Americans. Attached garages and large front yards are certainly not conducive to neighborhood exchange. In New York and Centerville, severe winter was to blame for diminished neighborhood activities for several months of the year.

More important, Japanese wives find their neighborhood empty and unfamiliar because they are usually unable to form a meaningful relationship with their American neighbors. Expatriate Japanese have a tendency to live in clusters in all three U.S. cities where I conducted research; yet, the density of Japanese households does not usually reach a high enough level to form a "ghetto" environment. Japanese remain ethnic and racial minorities in any given neighborhood, and if an ex-

patriate Japanese resident wishes to develop friends in her neighborhood, then she has to go into the community of Americans and communicate in English. In fact, a lack of communication with American
neighbors was one of the major disappointments among my corporate
wife informants, who fantasized before their kaigai chuuzai about becoming friends with American women. Language was the most obviously and frequently felt barrier, but even those Japanese wives who
spoke English well found it difficult to carry on a conversation with
their American counterparts. One informant made an effort at first to
join the circle of neighborhood women whenever she saw them standing outside and talking. But she soon discovered that she and her
American counterparts had amazingly little to talk about. Another
informant spoke of the emotional gap she felt between herself and
American women she encountered. Beyond the difficulty of a foreign
language, she sensed a vague yet definite difference in the way she and
her American neighbors felt about *futsuu no koto*, or common matters in
their everyday life, such as children's education, household management, and neighborhood activities: "I can't really explain it, but I know
that they [her American neighbors] don't understand where I'm coming from, and that I don't quite know where they are coming from
[about these everyday issues]." As a result, she analyzed, her relationship with her neighbors never progressed beyond a friendly exchange of
"Hi, how are you?" Thus, my female Japanese informants tended to feel
that their differences from their American neighbors were too great to
overcome, and this lack of personal connection became the prime reason
American neighborhoods were "empty" to my informants.

While American neighborhoods generally seemed to Japanese corporate wives an empty place without networks of relationships, there
was a marked difference between the ways expatriate Japanese wives in
Centerville, New York, and North Carolina interpreted the reasons
behind this. In Centerville, expatriate Japanese wives often thought
that Americans around them were good-natured and well-meaning, if
uninterested, unsophisticated, or ignorant in their dealings with their
Japanese neighbors. The sentiments expressed in North Carolina's Research Triangle were generally similar to those in Centerville, but
tinged with the regional stereotype of the old "Jim Crow" South, where
some felt that they were discriminated against as people of color. At the
same time, the great majority found the Research Triangle area to be a

relatively pleasant place to live. In the suburban city of Cary, where many RTP workers and their families live, the neighborhood is more international than southern, with many foreign residents and Americans who have lived in foreign countries, and the expatriate Japanese families seem to feel at ease in this environment.

By contrast, in some New York suburbs, neighborhood relations between expatriate Japanese and local American residents seemed strained, and even hostile. Some of my informants in Westchester County told me that local residents considered expatriate Japanese families unwelcome intruders who exploited their educational resources and returned little to the community; similar comments were made in Bergen County, New Jersey (see Newman 1993). Local hostility was felt everywhere: in the lack of casual greetings, in the discussion of limiting the number of Japanese students in school districts, even in the remarks of neighbors about the poorly maintained yards of Japanese households. In some extreme cases, expatriate wives and mothers constantly felt the watchful eyes of their neighbors on their children and on themselves.

One of my New York informants, Ohnuki-san, told me of her experience with her neighbor. One day, she ran out to a corner store to get a few things before dinner. When she returned home in about twenty minutes, she felt her heart jump as she saw a police car parked on her driveway. Thinking something must have happened to her three children whom she left in the house, she ran inside to find two police officers talking with her children in the foyer. They told her that they received a complaint that the children were left alone without adult supervision and that her oldest daughter, who was twelve at the time, was not considered old enough to baby-sit even for twenty minutes. Later, as she talked with her children about what happened in her absence, Ohnuki-san learned that the next-door neighbor came by right after she left and asked the children where their parents were. This experience taught her that her Japanese common sense could in fact be "illegal" in this country, and also that her neighbors were watching her every move. "I was gone only for twenty minutes. For the police to receive a call and get there before me, [her next-door neighbor] had to have been watching my driveway when I pulled out." This feeling of being watched was so oppressive that she was afraid of going out for a while.

The Japanese uchi in a foreign soto is precious, but also precarious, as the walls that surround these expatriate Japanese homes become overdetermined; that is, they mark not only the physical boundary between indoor and outdoor, but also the ideological boundary between Japan and Amerika and the self and the other. While no domestic space in modern society can exist entirely on its own and resources and services from the outside are always needed to ensure its continued existence (Rapp 1978), the sensitivity about this boundary becomes exaggerated and the external forces are often felt as intrusive in the foreign environment of the United States. To bring in financial resources, men go out to work in a bicultural workplace, where they comingle with American workers and locally hired expatriate Japanese workers whose views of work and career may be radically different from their own. Most expatriate Japanese families also depend on local educational institutions, so the children, too, spend five days a week in a foreign environment, learning to speak English and get along with other children of various ethnic, cultural, and social backgrounds. In turn, people and things from the outside must be brought inside to maintain a household: a plumber who comes in to fix a clogged drain, a UPS delivery man who brings in a large box, an English tutor who comes every Tuesday night, children from next door who come to play. Food items and household supplies must be bought in local supermarkets on a daily basis and, less frequently, clothes, appliances, and furniture from malls and discount stores. Information is another resource critical to settle in and survive in an unfamiliar place: how to enroll in public school, where to find good doctors and dentists, which nursery school is relatively friendly to non-English-speaking children, which restaurants serve food that fits Japanese taste, how to manage bilingual education for their children, how to find a good tutor, which American product can substitute for which Japanese product. Thus, dosoku, or the figurative "dirty feet," are always at the doorstep, waiting to be let in.

One incident that I encountered in Centerville demonstrated how deeply the fragility of a Japanese home permeated the consciousness of Japanese residents there. A Japanese family was found dead in their home in one of Centerville's suburbs, and the local police concluded that it was a family suicide. Expatriate Japanese who knew this family disagreed on the basis of many cultural reasons and their knowledge of the family.[2] In the end, the local police department and the expatriate Japanese community were not able to reconcile their different interpretations of the incident, and four body bags were quietly sent back to Japan for a funeral.

Most of what I heard regarding the death of this family was fragmented and speculative, and there was no way of knowing whether it was indeed a suicide or an accident. What was more intriguing to me, though, was the reaction of the expatriate Japanese wives, who took the local police investigator's "mistake" quite seriously. The gap between the American and the Japanese interpretations of this incident, in my informants' view, was part of the threat that the foreign environment around them posed to the security of their Japanese home life. Aside from the tragedy, expatriate Japanese in Centerville were equally if not more disturbed by the fact that the deaths were scrutinized under foreign eyes. This incident reminded other Japanese families that their own homes and their lives, too, were subject to the probes of cultural outsiders, and that the boundaries around uchi are easily violated by those who do not recognize their significance.

While the maintenance of the uchi-soto boundaries is important for a Japanese domestic space to be an uchi, a place of relaxation, comfort, and belonging where only the members of an in-group are allowed, these boundaries are even more critical and difficult to maintain for Japanese households abroad, surrounded by the foreign soto right outside their doors. Making a Japanese home in the foreign environment of the United States is the outcome of the hard labor of negotiating the boundaries between the self and the other through the everyday practices of domestic management and caregiving. Most important, the critical component of homemaking work is the emotional labor to help fulfill the changing needs of family members so that they remain productive in the foreign environment. Being there and providing support are themes that characterize the nature of domestic work that these women performed, and these concerns permeated their every decision and every task performance of the everyday. These notions are understood to be both metaphoric and literal. For instance, mothers insisted that they had to be there in person when their children returned from school; they also avoided any activities that would keep them from giving their children the fullest attention, including talking with friends on the phone and being interviewed by an anthropologist. Providing support can mean anything and everything that helps their husband and children do well at work and school, from cooking nutritious meals, to making sure that their shirts are pressed, to patiently listening to their gripes. Thus, in every domestic task that they perform, Japanese wives and mothers have to filter out and temper the often inhospitable reality of the foreign environment right outside the door of their home and negotiate the boundary between their Japanese uchi and the foreign soto. In doing so, they themselves become the buffer zone that separates the familiar from the foreign, the self from the other.

CHAPTER FOUR

Playing Her Part

MY AIM IN THIS CHAPTER is to explore how female subjectivity is produced and negotiated among Japanese corporate wives in the context of
kaigai chuuzai. The "relational self" is the anthropological term for
the construction of subjectivity that emphasizes social relationships as
the most significant factor in defining the boundaries around a person.
Past studies have found that Japanese selfhood is relational and role-
oriented, and that the distinction between the "self" and the "other" is
de-emphasized or actively blurred in Japanese social interaction (e.g.,
Hamaguchi 1982; Kondo 1990; Lebra 1984; Smith 1983). Japanese
women are considered to be particularly relational and role-oriented;
that is, they gain the sense of who they are through the fulfillment of
gender-ascribed roles as wives and mothers (De Vos 1973; Lebra 1984;
Rosenberger 2000). The "individualistic" model of personhood, by
contrast, defines a person as the smallest social unit that is characterized
by its essential internal core. A wide range of social theories are based on
the assumption of an individualistic self (an approach often called
"methodological individualism"), yet anthropologists as early as Marcel
Mauss and Bronislaw Malinowski have noted that this is a distinctly
Western and modern idea of personhood and have argued that in other
cultures and historical periods, personhood was defined primarily
through social relationships and interactions (Carrithers et al. 1985;
Dumont 1986).

This dichotomization of relational and individualistic selves is inherently problematic for two obvious reasons. First, some anthropologists have treated them as one-size-fits-all categories, dividing the world into cultures of individuality and cultures of relationality, not dissimilar to the way zoologists create a taxonomy using concrete, observable, and stable characteristics (e.g., this animal has hooves, but that one doesn't). But selfhood is not just a set of concrete, observable, and stable characteristics; selfhood is a "construct" that is flexible and shifting, that can be changed and manipulated. Therefore, the typology of selfhood using the individual-relational criterion is not helpful in the understanding of a particular form of self-construct. In addition, it is troublesome that this dichotomization between individuality and relationality is often conceived of as one of the fundamental differences between the West and the non-West. It results in the exaggerated otherness of those whose sense of self does not conform to the canonized "individual" in largely Western-derived social theory. In fact, this dichotomy is fundamentally misleading. The "individualistic self" is just as much the product of social interaction (e.g., G. H. Mead 1934), and as such, individual self-making is a process as social as any other form of self-construct. Put simply, we all learn to become a particular kind of person through interaction with others around us, and come to perceive our own self in relationship to the model that is upheld by our own social group. Both types of selfhood, one that overtly emphasizes "individuality" and the other "relationality," are thus just two possible models of self-construct, and the process through which we make them our own is equally dependent on social interaction.

Many social thinkers have elaborated on the performative notion of subjectivity that is worked and reworked through social interaction. Erving Goffman (1959), for example, captured the process of self-making with a theatrical metaphor; to him, everyday social life is a stage on which each social actor plays his or her roles and presents his or her self in light of that role. The idea of "presentation" may appear at first to assume that the "self" is internal to the person, which is in turn packaged and "presented" according to social convention. However, Goffman's study also suggests a more dialectical relationship between the self and its presentation. The socially presented self also becomes part of that person, and as a result, the distinction between the self and the presentation is blurred. Pierre Bourdieu (1977) places more emphasis on the actor's agency and views self-making as a more strategic process, in which a person is conceptualized as a social actor who maneuvers around his or her social positioning. To see selfhood as a semi-intentional act of performance and strategic maneuvering does not imply that we can create ourselves in any way we want, however. There are social conventions, unspoken rules, and expectations that govern particular forms of self-performance in a given social context. Self-performance is so ideologically charged and disciplined that transgression may have a devastating effect on the social construction of identity itself (Butler 1990).

The performative construction of identity, in turn, implicates the existence of the "audience" or the social "other," whose responses determine the boundaries around ideal subjectivity and help shape the performance of social actors vis-à-vis this ideal (Althusser 1971; G. H. Mead 1934). If subjectivity is produced through social interaction, then who this "other" is and how social actors relate to this "other" through their everyday performance of identity are key ingredients of the self. Goffman's audience does not reach beyond the immediate local community in which the signs of social selfhood are exchanged, and readily understood, on a daily basis; thus, the political implications of social performance are also limited to the social relationships between individuals who interact with each other face-to-face. By contrast, Butler, Bourdieu, and Althusser see the larger and more generalized social world of the nation-state and modern societies as the playing field for performative identity construction, in which specific and selective forms of discursivity construct normative social identities.

Japanese corporate wives perform their female selves in their everyday life in the United States, and when they do so, they have several audiences in mind: their own husband, their corporate employer, and, perhaps, their American neighbors. However, for most Japanese corporate wives in the United States, the most important and immediate community in which the self is shaped, performed, and reworked is that of fellow expatriate Japanese wives. Given this centrality, what happens in the women's community is fraught with tension and even contradictions; corporate involvement in the context of transnational migration makes it further complicated in many cases.

In general, Japanese women cultivate and maintain many strands of relationships with other women throughout their lives. Their female kin—mother, sisters, female cousins—often form the longest-lasting, most fundamental network of female relationships on which they rely for mutual support at major junctures in their lives (courtship, marriage, and childbirth) as well as solace and advice at times of difficulty, such as the husband's infidelity. If these female relatives live close by, they may also share their labor in child care, domestic chores, and the care of the elderly and exchange information that is useful for their domestic management and children's education. Women also develop other kinds of networks: with other women in the neighborhood and at their children's schools, in classes at the community center or "culture school" (commercial establishments that offer daytime classes in traditional arts, crafts, and some academic subjects), and by making friends with similar interests. If they live in company housing, they will inevitably meet and befriend other wives from their husband's company; otherwise, it is rare to have regular contact with the wives of their husband's colleagues.

These female social networks mean a great deal to Japanese women. Men and women tend to spend much of their waking hours separately, each working and playing in their homosocial spheres. Married Japanese women often find their female relatives and friends to be far more reliable sources of support and mutual aid than their busy husband. Even when the husbands are willing and available, women may prefer other wives and mothers, who need minimal instruction to help with domestic and child care chores. Among younger Japanese couples, husbands tend to be more willing to participate actively in the home life. Nonetheless, their presence at home may be severely limited by the demands of their work and work-related socialization as they progress in their corporate career and begin to take on heavier responsibilities at work. In some households, a husband and a wife may live lives very distant from each other, in a virtual separation within the household (*kateinai rikon*), while maintaining their legal marriage. In such cases, women turn to their own networks of female relatives and friends, entirely circumventing their husband for both emotional support and practical assistance.

Kaigai chuuzai takes women out of social networks with extended family and friends, in which their daily lives were enbedded, and places them in a new and strange place where they will have to develop a new set of human relations in hopes of obtaining support, information, and friendship. Naturally, they make a concerted effort to stay in contact with their family and friends in Japan during kaigai chuuzai; to this end, more and more of these women take full advantage of inexpensive means of long-distance, transnational communication: phone, fax, and, more recently, e-mail. However, as the physical distance and the lack of shared experience make their existing social networks less helpful for immediate support and assistance while in the United States, the primary purpose of their communication seems to be the maintenance of social ties for the future, when they complete their kaigai chuuzai and return to Japan. Yet, Japanese corporate wives find it critically important to have reliable friends locally in times of need and endeavor to establish a network of friends in their kaigai chuuzai locations.

There are several different ways in which women's social networks are organized in any given expatriate Japanese community. First, there are certainly some macro-level economic factors at work, influenced by the types of Japanese subsidiaries in the area, that preselect certain class characteristics of a particular expatriate community. Among the corporate wives, the husband's current job type, rank, and pay are the most direct criteria in determining their class standing within the community, and the women's own socioeconomic and class backgrounds are also significant factors. I found that the educational level of expatriate Japanese wives in Centerville, where many semi-blue-collar technical workers were assigned, was significantly lower than that of their New York and North Carolina counterparts. Fewer than 30 percent of Centerville wives had a bachelor's degree, while 60 percent of New York informants and slightly over 50 percent of North Carolina wives did. Several of the New York informants had postsecondary education; none in Centerville and North Carolina did. The ages of expatriate wives varied more greatly in Centerville, where I met women from their early twenties, who are married to production technicians with no management responsibilities, to women in their fifties whose husbands are the presidents and top executives in charge of U.S. subsidiaries, with correspondingly varied domestic situations and concerns. By contrast, 95 percent of my informants in New York and North Carolina were in their thirties and forties, their husbands typically in the middle-management ranks. These attributes characterize the women's community as a whole, but also further subdivide it by the current economic status of the household and/or by the class consciousness of the women. Like the age of the women, their children's ages also differed, and so their major preoccupations as mothers. For example, in New York, where the educational levels of the parents were relatively high, mothers expressed their concern for their children's educational success more publicly, whereas many Centerville mothers spoke less of educational "success" and more of their children's "surviving" the foreign school system. While younger mothers generally had less immediate worries for their children's schooling than the mothers of teenagers, they were often deeply concerned that their young children tended to quickly pick up English at the expense of their native tongue. In turn, the different ages and life cycle stages often determined relationships among women, so that the mothers of high school students hung out with one another and the mothers of preschool-age children stuck together. This is probably the most common and also preferred way in which Japanese women create a network of friends among themselves.

Various women's social networks serve many functions, both social and political. For example, many women belong to company-sponsored women's groups, which often work as a mechanism of mutual support. One extreme example is the Toyota Fujin-kai, or Toyota Women's Association, for the wives of male Toyota employees (but not their female employees). I did not have any direct contact with Toyota families, but the water-tight solidarity that the Toyota Women's Association demanded was legendary among expatriate Japanese in the United States. Irie-san, who once lived in Louisville, Kentucky, one day gave us an eyewitness account of their "welcome routine." Expatriate wives from the women's association go to the prospective home of an in-coming chuuzaiin family, unpack boxes, completely clean up the place, and stock the pantry and refrigerator. When the newcomer wife arrives in town, she is greeted by the association representatives at the airport, so that the newcomer's husband, who usually arrives at the new chuuzai station a few months before his family, does not have to take time off work. She is then shown to her new home, complete with ready-to-heat meals enough for the entire week, so that she can concentrate on getting settled in without having to inconvenience her family in her first week in the United States. Thomas Rohlen (1989), in his analysis of group conformity in Japanese schools, explains that the discipline of *shuudan seikatsu* (collective life, group living) is made familiar, and even desirable, through participation in various "fixed routines" (also see Tobin 1992b). Toyota women's collective life in their kaigai chuuzai location in the United States appears to be constructed around a similar routinization of mutual aid and dependency, starting with this "welcome ritual" for in-coming chuuzaiin wives. In this setting, the newcomers are taken into the fold of this tightknit expatriate women's community as soon as they set foot on the foreign soil and will never have an opportunity to experience the foreign soto without the mediation of this collectivity (they will, for instance, participate in volunteer activities for the local community *as a group*).

While Irie-san and other women in Centerville envied the ease with which Toyota women seemed to begin their lives in the United States, they also saw its other, more coercive side as well. "It must feel strange to arrive at my own place that other people organized. It seems almost intrusive," Irie-san pondered. Takeda-san pointed out that, though it might be nice on the receiving end, it also meant that they had to reciprocate every time a new family arrived in town—imagine the amount of work involved—and also that they would always have to spend so much time with other wives from their husband's company. "It must become really intolerable after a while," they concluded. These mixed reactions illuminate the double-edged nature of company-based relationships among expatriate Japanese corporate wives: it is certainly helpful to have this more or less formal system of assistance, but it also demands so much of a woman's life to be part of it. Moreover, the corporate hierarchy of which their husband is a part will be reflected in the relationship between the wives as well—the wife of the subsidiary president serving as the president of the women's association, for example—making the relationships between women more hierarchical than need be. As many anthropologists of Japan have pointed out (e.g., Benedict 1974; Kondo 1990; Nakane 1967; Smith 1983), relative hierarchy between two or more persons plays a critical role in Japanese social interactions. This rule applies to informal friendships between corporate wives, who determine seniority among themselves and signal this hierarchy in subtle ways, for instance, slight changes in word choice, use of more formal or informal word endings, and the degree to which they bow to each other. The corporate-based hierarchy of wives is, however, much more visible and definitive, and also carries heavier consequences, because the work relationships between these women's husbands can be affected by the women's relationships. Most women tiptoe around these situations, desperately hoping to avoid all the pitfalls of overdoing or not doing enough, knowing when to open their mouth and when to keep it shut (Mori and Saike 1997; Taniguchi 1985).

More personal, friendship-based relationships among Japanese corporate wives often develop through chance encounters in grocery stores, children's schools, English classes, or hobby lessons, and are possible only with the mutual desire of both parties to develop the friendship. The women usually share many familial and personal characteristics, including age, their children's ages, the length of their kaigai chuuzai, and hobbies and other personal interests. By every female informant's account, belonging to these interest-driven, friendship-based groups was extremely important to make their life abroad livable. Securing connections to such groups often turns out to be a challenging task for some women, however. Some women are reserved; some are too nervous about making social mistakes in the expatriate community to which they are new. Finally, there is the problem of distance. My female informants in Centerville had to be incredibly lucky to find suitable places for escape in the neighborhood, such as a neighborhood friend or a playground, where they can socialize along with their children. For instance, all the women in Kawagoe-san's clique "commuted in" by car from as far as fifteen miles away. Some of the chuuzaiin wives I met in New York suburbs had better luck with the higher density of expatriate Japanese households in this area. Yet, many commented on how easily they could become isolated in their own home, without neighborhood friends with whom they can casually visit without the bother of driving. In North Carolina, the situation seemed similar to Centerville's; public transportation was sparse and expatriate Japanese families were relatively scattered around Raleigh, Durham, and Chapel Hill. In a hobby group that I frequented in Durham, most of the regular participants lived near Raleigh and in Chapel Hill and drove from ten to thirty minutes each way to be there.

The women's communities also offer many opportunities for leisure activities, particularly for those who do not have heavy childcare duties. The most widespread form of social play was *kurafuto* (from the English word "craft"), or participation in hobby groups to practice various handicrafts that they considered quintessentially American. As such, craft hobbies become another way of experiencing this foreign country. Between 1996 and 1997, the list of popular crafts among expatriate Japanese wives included quilting, making stained glass, tole painting, and, above all, making shadow boxes. These popular kurafuto are taught in Japanese venues, including the Maveric Family Center in Centerville, the Yomiuri Culture Club in New York, and the Japan-America Society in Bergen County, New Jersey. In addition, there are numerous private groups that gather regularly to practice the craft of their choice. These groups of four to ten women usually form around a Japanese-speaking instructor, often one of the corporate wives and occasionally a Japanese permanent resident, who is an expert in a particular kind of craft and willing to teach other women for a small or no fee, who is free of young children who would otherwise demand her constant attention, and who is old enough, or has lived in the particular chuuzai location long enough, to be a leader. The group usually gets together once a week at one of the member's homes and spends a few hours practicing various crafts, but more important, the women exchange information and socialize with each other. A number of expatriate Japanese wives also take up sports that are too expensive to practice in Japan, most commonly tennis and golf. These sports are, once again, practiced in Japanese groups, but the instructors are more often American than Japanese. A couple of my informants became avid golfers in the United States, to the point where they were on the course two to three times a week; others went to golf and tennis lessons more casually, as social occasions to hang out with other Japanese wives. Shopping and sampling local restaurants were also popular activities and created similar opportunities to socialize and have fun in the company of women friends.

For women with very young children, like most of the women in Kawagoe-san's clique, many of these activities are simply not practical. Young children are too distracting and also potentially dangerous at craft classes, where people routinely use sharp cutting instruments, glue guns, and some toxic materials. Mothers also find it more exhausting than enjoyable to eat out with young children because they have to keep a close eye on their children the whole time. These constraints leave few child-friendly possibilities available to expatriate Japanese women. They may go to the shopping mall and window-shop for a little while (not for long, though, because children will get bored and start whining), or sit in a park nearby (but only if the weather is nice). The most popular option is a play date at someone's home, which does not depend on the weather (a critical factor in the Midwest and Northeast in winter months) and is relaxing and enjoyable for both mothers and children. For women in their late twenties and early thirties who were mostly mothers of infants and toddlers, Kawagoe-san's *nakama* or clique formed the center of their social world and often the only relief from their constant responsibility of child care. "If we are here [at Kawagoe-san's home], we can let the children play by themselves and we know they are safe," Irie-san explained to me. "So, we can sit here and relax a bit, at least until one of them starts crying."

As the relationships in corporate-based and friendship-based networks greatly differ from each other, most expatriate wives do their best to keep them apart. In many conversations that I had with my informants about this issue, most were adamant that any infringement of the company-related *ningen kankei* (human relations) was sure to ruin their opportunities for fun and friendship, and that their only interests were in maintaining the more carefree, friendship-based circle of women. Yet, the boundary between the corporate and the personal appeared much blurrier in practice, and it seemed to me that the personal was too easily compromised by the corporate. For instance, Irie-san introduced Kawado-san, a younger wife from her husband's company, to Kawagoe-san's group, but when they see each other at Kawagoe-san's, they strictly avoid any "work-related" conversations; in fact, they rarely speak together while at Kawagoe-san's. Irie-san told me later that it was a tough decision for her to involve another wife from her husband's company in her personal network. She did it because Kawado-san was relatively new in Centerville and it seemed to her "very unkind [not to include her]." Behind her words was the implicit assumption that the senior expatriate worker's wife had the responsibility of taking care of the wives of newer, junior workers. Irie-san was spared this responsibility for a very long time, as her husband was the only expatriate worker in the subsidiary. Once she became the more experienced senior wife, she was compelled to do the right thing. Irie-san was constantly "checking" herself, however, making sure that she did not say anything about her husband or his work in front of Kawado-san to avoid any possibility of awkwardness. This need for self-surveillance somewhat diminished the carefree fun Irie-san came to expect at gatherings at Kawagoe-san's.

A need for mutual assistance during kaigai chuuzai tends to infringe on women's ideally carefree friendships. When I looked closely at the nature of relationships in those friendship-based groups, I noticed that their relationships are made more competitive, obligation-driven, hierarchical, and work-like as the group becomes the sole source of mutual aid, labor exchange, and information gathering. In other words, those friendship groups are neither innocent nor arbitrary, and the criteria that bind those women are often more closely connected to their domestic and reproductive responsibilities than the women's own personal interests. They also carefully consider the complicated ningen kankei in the expatriate community that made certain associations more desirable or convenient than others. Precious as it is, the support that expatriate Japanese wives provide one another is not an act of philanthropy but a system of mutual aid, governed by unspoken, informal, yet closely observed rules. Reciprocity is expected among peers, who exchange roughly equivalent services with one another. Senior women are expected to show generosity by giving assistance and advice to junior women without an expectation of compensation. Instead, they receive appropriate reverence from junior women who address them in a more respectful mode of speech. Occasional gifts from junior to senior women are also common. When the junior women came back from a visit to Japan, it was customary for them to bring gifts for senior women who had been particularly kind to them. If a woman fails to respect these rules, or otherwise acts against the wishes of the clique, she may find the display of friendliness and offer of mutual aid quietly withdrawn. Performing impeccable female selves in front of this scrutinizing audience thus becomes the obsession of many Japanese wives, which sometimes overshadows their entire experience overseas.

A MARGINAL WOMAN

Having come from a Japanese family not unlike my informants', with a *sarariiman* father and a stay-at-home mother, I began fieldwork with a certain understanding of femaleness as defined in that particular milieu. Articulating this implicit understanding and using it to interpret the words and actions of Japanese wives in the United States was an unsettling and complex process both for myself and for my informants. I was a marginal woman when I arrived, not quite Japanese, not quite foreign, not quite a woman, but certainly not a man. My marginality in turn solicited comments from some of my female informants and led me to think more critically about the relational, role-oriented selfhood of these women.

What I discovered from my perspective as a marginal woman was the complicated and ambivalent relationship these women have with their gender roles as wives and mothers and the contradictory effects that domesticity and motherhood have on these women's understanding of their selves. I next focus explicitly on the two most important roles these Japanese women played: being a domestic manager and being a mother. This is, in many ways, an arbitrary division, as femaleness, domesticity, and motherhood are all intertwined and entangled in the way these women spoke about them. I arrived at these two constituents of female selves through two key experiences in the field. I begin my discussion of these two constituents with the story of a fieldwork moment when the particular aspect of a female self came to the surface of consciousness, both my own and my informants', and created an opening for inquiry and examination. Then I will elaborate on how that particular aspect of female subjectivity is defined in the normative Japanese discourse and how the particular aspect of femaleness manifests in the context of transnational mobility.

BEING THE "MAIN WOMAN"

When I started my fieldwork in Centerville, I had the hardest time making my potential informants understand that it was an integral part of my fieldwork to "play" (*asobu*) with them. Kawagoe-san, my key informant in Centerville, and her friends understood that I was a graduate student and that I was staying in Centerville for several months for my field research. They also understood that I was interested in them as study subjects, and that I wanted to eventually interview them about their experiences in the United States. But the concept of "participant observation" or "informal interaction" seemed to completely escape them. In the beginning, when I showed up at Kawagoe-san's place for an afternoon of sitting around and talking, they'd ask politely, "How is your study going, Sawa-san? You are getting away from your work to join us this afternoon?"[1]

There were two sources of tension in this initial "misconception," which I no longer think of as a misconception at all. First, my lack of domesticity made me a marginal figure as a woman. Takeda-san, who was working on a second bachelor's degree at a local university, played down the academic side of her life when she was with other Japanese wives for fear of being judged on her inadequacy in domestic duties. Someone like myself, who left her husband behind to pursue her own academic work, was not just being inappropriate; I failed to fit into any social category that these women felt comfortable or familiar with. By asking polite questions about my studies, they were confirming again and again the insurmountable distance that existed between us. Second, what I was claiming (that I was working) violated their sense of space. The gathering at Kawagoe-san was a space for play for these women, and bringing in work to that space of play was unwelcome. Women came together to play, to get away from their domestic work. For me, who did not have domestic work waiting at home, there had to be some other kind of work elsewhere that I was escaping from whenever I joined them.

It was a couple of months later when Irie-san finally got it. After yet another conversation about my fieldwork, she exclaimed, "Sawa-san is an *asobinin*!" An asobinin is literally a person who plays, or a loafer without recognizable and honest means of making a living. They may be gamblers, "wise guys," or someone rich enough to not need a job. The livelihood of an asobinin is play instead of work. One of the most famous asobinin in Japanese popular culture is Asobinin no Kin-san, Mr. Kin, the Loafer, a quasi-historic character popularized in a TV show that has been running more or less perpetually for the past thirty years. The chief judge of Edo, or premodern Tokyo, Toyama Kinshiro, a k a Kin-san, goes about town, mingling with unsuspecting townspeople as a friendly, harmless city loafer, seemingly without a stable occupation or a particular purpose in life, and, at the end of every show, he exposes the wrongdoings of the wealthy and the powerful. Asobinin's marginality also serves as a symbol of resistance against social norms and restrictions, as embodied in Kin-san's slipping in and out of two social milieus. Thus, Irie-san made two moves of signification in one stroke, when she identified me as someone who played professionally and also someone who defied Japanese social conventions in her professional play. My contradictory claim to "work at play" had finally found a familiar cultural category.

The language of asobinin rests on the perceived separation between work and play as dichotomous orientations that dictate their actions in different aspects of their lives and govern their choices at certain times of day. It also summarizes the differences these corporate wives perceived between themselves and me: between housewives who idly spent their daytime hours with each other and a strange anthropologist who wanted to study their lifestyle; between women whose lives centered on home and a woman who left her husband at home to pursue her research interest; between the wives and mothers who found their gathering a moment of reprieve from their domestic work and a graduate student who claimed to "work at play." These differences between me and my female Japanese informants had to be verbalized, in part, because of our similarities, because I was like them and unlike them at the same time. Among anthropologists who conduct their field research among their most distant others, "going native" may be an alluring—if not professionally commendable—prospect, but in other cases, similarity may prove more threatening to the anthropologist's self (Kondo 1990). Now that our paths crossed in a foreign city and chance occurrences put us in the same room in a given afternoon, we found our similarities and differences hard to reconcile.

FOR MIDDLE-CLASS JAPANESE HOUSEWIVES, the home is a place of work. Women as *shufu*, literally "the main woman" of the house, are in charge of all aspects of domestic management, as we have seen. They single-handedly make decisions on major purchases (including large appliances, automobiles, and even houses), take care of short-term and long-term financial planning, supervise children's educational achievement and assist in their career planning, perform household social and ritual activities (funerals, weddings, birth celebrations, major holidays and gift-giving occasions), and care for elderly family members. *Shufugyo*, or the "profession" of shufu, is considered the full-time job of a married adult woman, the job of performing these domestic and caregiving tasks, often with little or no assistance from her husband or other family members. Domestic management gives women at once heavy responsibility and considerable authority within the home.

The historical root of this feminine domesticity is less than pastoral, however, and the authority that comes with the position of shufu is also a double-edged sword. *Ryosai kenbo*, the ideology of "a good wife and wise mother," was part of the modernization agenda of the Japanese national government since the Meiji era and a companion to its *fukoku kyohei* ("enrich the nation and strengthen the army") campaign, which coerced Japanese men to participate in the rapidly expanding state-sponsored capitalist economy and military services (Koyama 1994). The ryosai kenbo ideology helped to establish the ideal of Japanese womanhood as full-time domestic manager and cultural reproducer and to appropriate women's reproductive labor for the national agenda (Muta 1994; Shimizu 1996; Ueno 1987).

Today, it seems, this historical background is all but forgotten among the postwar generations of Japanese women. Ryosai kenbo has become an innocent, if outdated, ideal of womanhood and has no apparent connection with any national agendas; in fact, it is nearly absent from the daily vocabulary and consciousness of younger generations of Japanese men and women. Nevertheless, the identification and idealization of women as wives and mothers remain just as strong a cultural impulse as ever, in the dedicated manager of a sarariiman household, or in a *kyoiku mama* (education mother) who devotes herself to promoting the educational success of her children, particularly her sons (Allison 2000; Imamura 1987). Even to those women who mock, slight, and rebel against the ideal of the good wife and wise mother (e.g., Kelsky 2001; Ueno 1996), there is little doubt that it is the baseline against which their actions are measured.

A look at the genre of popular Japanese magazines that cater exclusively to housewives indicates that the domestic space and its management have become privatized in contemporary Japan as women's personal pursuit, rather than a gender-defined, nationally driven responsibility (see Rosenberger 1995). In the *seikatsu jouhoushi* (living information magazine), or the magazines that specialize in the practical information related to everyday living and home management, the vast majority of articles center on two interrelated points: maximizing household resources and improving the housewife's own quality of life. In the special supplement of *Ohayou Okusan* (Good Morning, Housewives; June 1998) entitled "The

Book of How to Get Money," a housewife's effort to earn a small additional income or to shave off otherwise necessary household expenses is connected to the fulfillment of her own desires and dreams, as the opening paragraph states: "You [the housewife-reader] can freely spend the money that you made by yourself, or save it up to realize your long-term dreams or hopes—it's all up to you. As well as an additional source of income, you may attain a new purpose in life [through these money-making activities]" (4). In *Esse* (1998, 17), a similar money-making article features a housewife who manages to save 50,000 yen (approximately $400) a month by using credit card rewards and other money-saving means. What is she going to do with the money that she saves? "I will save it for something fantastic that I can't do with the regular salary [of her husband]. More specifically, I'm thinking about a trip around the world." The article concludes: "[After all the hard work,] it's your turn to treat yourself and fly away—Bon voyage!"

The mixing of domestic management and personal pleasure cleverly appeals to the wants and needs that full-time housewives feel daily. For instance, being the manager of the household economy puts women in charge of all household income, yet the moral imperative of caring for family members makes it difficult for them to justify spending money on themselves. To redefine penny pinching as money *making* is to redefine domestic money management as a form of productive activity. In doing so, these articles create an alibi for housewives to set the saved money aside for personal use. They also appeal to their housewife-readers with the image of luxury and fun, of realizing desires, such as traveling around the world, that most of the readers have given up as the price of being a shufu.

Most important, these discourses, as they present the image of home as the private space and the housewives as free agents in this space, naturalize the connection between the domestic space and its female managers, and at the same time obscure the connections between the housewives' domestic activities—their contribution to the reproduction of labor and the management of household economy—and the economic and political interests outside their homes (Rapp 1978; Sacks 1975). While the women-as-shufu are authorized to manipulate the household resources by their own choosing for their own purpose, the larger effects of such money-making actions in the household are hard to miss. The rationalization of consumption increases the disposable income of middle-class households and makes them better contributors to the consumption-driven capitalist economy. While every penny is put to good reproductive use (e.g., feeding, sheltering, and caretaking of the productive labor), the "extra" generated by the shufu's diligence and ingenuity can be redirected toward conspicuous consumption, defined in these articles as just the kind of luxury that married middle-class women are supposed to desire (e.g., home renovation/redecoration, foreign travel). Unlike a coercive government body that explicitly regulates the actions of its subjects, the modern power coaxes individuals into internalizing the dominant ideology and becoming his or her own government. Through this mechanism of internalization, "state life [becomes] 'spontaneous,' at one with the individual subject's 'free' identity," without ever referring, and thus calling attention, to itself (Eagleton 1991, 11b). In a way, as long as the government of the Meiji era had to scream out loud to coerce Japanese women into domesticity, there was still an awareness of the home-state connection. When this connection is silenced by the discourse of individual choice and well-being, not in the government propaganda pamphlets but in women's magazines, these women are in grave danger of accepting the "natural" connection between themselves and their home.

Ambiguity, however, is inherent in the workings of the hegemonic, and this conflation of female subjectivity with domesticity is not an exception. What is the possibility for middle-class Japanese housewives to take advantage of the conflation of personal desire and state interest, all the while upholding the ascribed domestic roles? In Japan, they often seek a sense of accomplishment and self-identity through activities not directly related to domestic chores, for instance, friendship with other women, volunteer activities, practicing traditional arts, and part-time jobs, that take them outside the domestic space and get them in touch with the larger social world (Yoshitake 1994). In this formation, female subjectivity appears necessarily dualistic: while the domestic role continues to form the core of these women's social identity, the other, extradomestic activities also provide an important, even necessary, component to their sense of self outside the home (Rosenberger 2000). If they do not overtly contradict their domestic roles, they do actively seek avenues of defining their subjectivities away from them and find their engagement outside the home a formative experience as well.

When kaigai chuuzai happens, being a shufu becomes an even more consuming task for these women, as the requirement of labor reproduction weighs on them much more heavily and immediately than ever before. In the daily lives of expatriate Japanese corporate wives, the flexibility demanded of them by globalizing capitalism manifests in several different ways. For one thing, this flexibility translates to complex mobility practices of the corporate workers and their family members. A good wife and mother has to be there, to be physically present, not only to do all the needed housework but also to become the embodiment of uchi-ness to which her husband and children come home. This ties the woman to the domestic space, to the place in which the physical and psychological needs of her husband and children are taken care of daily. In the context of kaigai chuuzai, however, this means transnational mobility in a physical sense: these women literally have to move to a foreign country so that they can make a home, and be a home, away from home. On the other hand, as we have already seen, they spend a considerable amount of time running around outside the home to be able to manage a Japanese home in a foreign place. One of the common Japanese phrases for a housewife is *okusan*, literally, "someone who stays deep inside" (*oku*). Some of my informants joked about the amount of time they spent away from home during the day, saying that they were *sotosan*, "someone who stays outside." To be a good homemaker and caretaker in the globalizing world takes the kind of nimble-footedness that the previous generations of middle-class Japanese housewives could not have imagined.

Domesticity in the lives of many expatriate Japanese corporate wives can also mean an increased interaction with the world outside the home and outside Japan and going back and forth constantly between their familiar uchi and the foreign soto that surrounds it. In extreme cases, Japanese wives and mothers were constantly traveling between two or even three countries to take care of family members spread around the world. Expatriate wives in their late forties and fifties, whose children are old enough to manage on their own or can be left with relatives in Japan, escape most of these tedious daily activities and educational headaches. However, many of them have different kinds of work that are just as consuming of their time and energy. In this age group, many of the husbands are overworked and stressed managers in a bicultural workplace, prone to many health problems, such as hypertension, diabetes, and weight gain. I encountered several cases in which middle-aged expatriate workers fell seriously ill during their U.S. assignments and their wives had to nurse them back to health in an unfamiliar place, away from family and friends in Japan who would have provided support in such times of need (we will return to these cases later). In addition, their children and aging parents in Japan may also become ill or otherwise require periodic visits, forcing some women to shuttle back and forth between Japan and the United States.

Flexibility is also temporal and results in the fragmentation and unpredictability of their everyday life in the United States, as exemplified by the two sample daily schedules that I presented earlier. Although both Yokoyama-san and Goto-san have some free time (more so for Goto-san) each day, it is scattered throughout the day, in between different domestic chores, and is often cannibalized when the schedules of their children or husband change. In other words, there is very little time that these women can claim as their own. It did not seem to occur to most of my corporate wife informants to manage their time differently so that they could set aside a bigger chunk of time for their own activities. As one of those women put it, they had "no good reason to motivate [themselves] to do that," as their job as an accompanying wife of an international Japanese businessman was to manage their home and to make sure that their husband and children stayed happy and healthy despite the stress of the foreign environment. More important, expatriate Japanese wives feel that their time management strategies must not affect their performance of domestic duties. The perfection to which these women hold themselves is often detrimental to any possibility of carving out any time for themselves. If an expatriate wife/mother has enough time to take a whole afternoon for herself, whether she is taking English classes or practicing golf, the assumption is often automatic and negative: she is not holding herself to the highest standard of domesticity, and she ought to think of how she can spend that time for her family instead.

MOTHER POWER

The fact that I did not have children was perhaps the most significant factor that made my working relationships with Japanese corporate wives awkward. I was Japanese, I was female, and I came from a family background that was very similar to that of many of the women. However, I did not take the typical path of a woman from such a habitus, namely, to work for a few years after college, marry a man with a stable job, quit my job, have a child or two, and become a full-time wife/mother. Instead, I moved to the United States, went on to graduate school, married a foreigner, and postponed having children. If I were, say, an American woman, they could have attributed all our differences to the difference in sociocultural norms; but with me, that was not an option. I was, in a way, a freak of a middle-class Japanese woman, who turned her back on the respectable life that she was supposed to live; that made my character somewhat questionable. The combination of similarities and differences made it difficult for my female informants to relate to my choices and experiences. Among the mothers with young children, there were also more pragmatic issues with having a childless woman around. They were often afraid that their children would do something to offend those who were not used to having children— often crying, whining, and messy children—around. In fact, many of Kawagoe-san's friends apologized to me every time their children tried to get on my knees, or tugged at my clothes, or even looked in my direction. I repeatedly told them that I liked children (which was true) and that their children were not bothering me at all (which was usually true), but I could see that they found it cumbersome as much as I did to have to worry so much about their children all the time. This went on for a couple of months, until the chicken incident.

One day, I was sitting in Kawagoe-san's living room over take-out Chinese lunch with several other women and their children. Although I was becoming a familiar face at Kawagoe-san's, I felt that most of Kawagoe-san's friends were still somewhat unsure about me. They continued to talk to me in polite language, and they rarely initiated a conversation with me. The only exception was Irie-san, who, on a number of occasions, sat next to me and engaged in conversation about my work and my experience in the United States. That day, too, she and her son Yohei were sitting next to me; suddenly, Yohei grabbed a piece of chicken from his plate and handed it to me. The chicken had been pushed around on his plate for a while, and perhaps was even chewed on a couple of times. I took it anyway and immediately threw it into my mouth. I did so partly because I did not want to disappoint the child and also because, somewhere in my mind, I calculated its effect on the mothers. Irie-san was first to speak.

"You know, my husband won't eat the food from Yohei's plate, let alone from his hands," she said. "Men simply can't do that. After all, they are not like women, they are not mothers."

"That's so true," Kawagoe-san chimed in, "but I can't blame them, either. I couldn't have done that before I had my own kids!"

From the way other women chuckled, it seemed to be the same with their husbands. They went on citing instances of men's inability to deal with the filth and dirt (*kitanaimono*) generated by children: half-eaten food, spilled drinks on the floor, runny noses, and dirty diapers.

The chicken incident was a critical turning point in two ways. First, it gave me an invaluable insight into the problem of my marginality; second, it became the beginning of our negotiation to establish me, the childless woman, as mother material (if my true potential was untested). Irie-san and other women distinguished between themselves and their husband by the way they physically related to their children, in particular, through their reaction to the filth and dirt that, in their mind, necessarily came with small children. It suddenly dawned on me that this was, for them, an important criterion of gender categories: those who could handle the filth are (potential) mothers, thus necessarily female. The gender of nonmother females, who could not deal with it, was more ambiguous; it was certainly not the same as that of the mothers. The problem of female academicians, according to these women's stereotype at least, was their lack of motherly ability to take care of the dirty things that children produce and, thus, a fatal flaw in their femininity. The gender category of these (biological) women was left unclear when they could not perform the motherly function. In the eyes of my female Japanese informants, I crossed the threshold into womanhood/motherhood with that gooey piece of chicken in my mouth.

"IS MOTHERHOOD A WOMAN'S badge of honor?" asks Masami Ohinata (1992) in her book on women who, for a variety of reasons, do not have children. In Japanese society, the answer to her question has predominantly been an affirmative, and the women who cannot have children or choose not to have children have encountered criticism and discrimination from people close to them (husband, close kin, friends, coworkers) and also in the court of public opinion. Childless women suffer a critical deficiency as adults, and they are really not women—these are the messages that Ohinata's informants have consistently received in their lives. This intertwined nature of motherhood and femininity is further complicated by the constant slippage between domesticity and motherhood and the homemaking and caretaking labor. It is as though, in the minds of Japanese housewives, being a person, a woman, a mother, and a wife are seamlessly joined together. At the center of this self-construction is women's ability to deal with bodily matters, which in turn nurture dependency in men and children, who soon come to believe that their lives are impossible without the able hands of their wife and mother.[2]

Feminist anthropologists have noted that in the great majority of cultural groups, women are positioned to mediate between the realms of nature and culture, and that in this mediating role they become associated with all matters of bodily function. Taking care of human bodies is often a dirty job, and the association with bodily matters makes woman a lesser being in the realm of culture vis-à-vis man (Ortner 1974). My female informants' attitude toward kitanaimono, however, did not jibe with this characterization. Regardless of their male-centered social values, they did not think of their work of cleaning up after their family, particularly their children, as demeaning. Moreover, there was a certain sense of confidence, even superiority, in the way these women talked about their ability to do the caretaking work, and they seemed to perceive their husband's refusal/inability to deal with the kitanaimono of his own flesh and blood as an evident lack that all men suffered. This difference between women and men becomes the difference in their relationship to their children. For Kawagoe-san and her friends, their connection to their children is immediate, direct, and continuous; the husbands, who are unable to perform the caretaking job like mothers, simply cannot have the same kind of closeness with their children. Motherhood, or at least the sign of motherliness, is made an essential component of femininity, to such an extent that to be a woman and to be a mother is almost indistinguishable. I must have known, somewhere in my mind, the importance of motherliness and, without even recognizing my own thought, exploited my cultural knowledge to establish myself among my female informants.

The ability, desire, and responsibility of caretaking that many Japanese women assume as a natural part of their feminine selves blur the distinctions between their roles as a domestic manager and as a mother. We saw an example of this in the previous chapter in the discussion of being there. As the primary caregiver and the center of uchi, women become mothers to everyone around them. It is telling that as soon as she has her first child, a Japanese woman is called *okaasan* (mother) by everyone around her, including her own husband. As I look at the life cycles of my female informants, I see that the majority of them began to have children within two years of their marriage. In most cases, women took on the responsibility of domestic management for the first time in their lives when they got married and established a new household with their husband; before too long, they found themselves pregnant and being called a mother. Once a woman becomes biologically a mother to her child, her motherhood seems to take over the rest of her personhood: her female sexuality is erased, her heterosexual relationship is recast as a mother-son relationship, and she becomes an okaasan to everybody around her. Thus, domesticity and motherhood virtually go hand-in-hand in a Japanese woman's life, and all caretaking work, regardless of whom she takes care of, becomes "mothering" work. A common Japanese phrase to refer to one's own mother, *uchi no okaasan* ("the mother at the home"), emphasizes the symbolic connection between the okaasan/mother and the uchi/home rather than the biological connection between a woman and her progeny. Furthermore, the motherly role of Japanese women extends beyond domestic relations and, as Takeo Doi (1973) so famously argued, can also become a metaphor for all social relationships in which dependency and indulgence become the key currency. In this sense, motherhood is a metaphor that signifies dominance in a relationship of dependency, the dominance achieved through the act of caretaking and indulgence through nurturing close bonds with the ones who are cared for and making them dependent on the labor of the one who plays the motherly role (see Allison 2000; Kondo 1990).

In this sense, caretaking is power, and the woman as caretaker is at the center of a Japanese uchi whose presence itself is an important component of an uchi. In this domestic arrangement of dependence, the husband-wife relationship takes on the character of a mother-child relationship, based on the total dependency of one on the nurturing of the other. Very few Japanese wives completely forget that the financial contribution of their husband is the foundation of their privileged lifestyle of a middle-class housewife. Yet, the dominance of the wife-mother in the daily interaction within the household betrays the power that Japanese women gain by extending their motherliness. Stories of a husband who cannot even dress himself for work when his wife is away, or a husband who would not eat anything but the food his wife cooked demonstrates the dependency that these adult men develop as they come to take for granted their wife's intervention in their daily life. Men's inability to take care of their children is, then, yet another sign of their own infancy. During kaigai chuuzai, the exaggerated neediness of men and children in an unfamiliar environment generates even more domestic authority for wives and mothers.

The presence of a powerful mother, who turns everyone around her into needy infants, displaces the heterosexual relationship from the construction of her femaleness and gives men only marginal importance in the Japanese household, whose core is the relationship between the mother and her children rather than the heterosexual couple. She is also aware that her bond with her children is much stronger and enduring than that her husband has with them; her husband's physical absence from the home and masculine inability to handle bodily functions make him an unworthy competitor. The close physical and emotional ties between a mother and her children, in turn, feed into the power of the Japanese mother, whose labor of love nurtures both her charge and her own self-identity outside the heterosexual relationship in which women are subordinate.

Mother power is inherently ambivalent and causes anxiety, as dominant mothers and displacement of heteronormative relationships are an affront to the ideology of the modern family and the gendered division of labor that place the male breadwinner at the center of the household with a female domestic manager at his side. As such, the domineering mother figure and her all-encompassing power are a source of anxiety. Anne Allison's (2000) analysis of Japanese popular representations of mothers is particularly revealing of the duality with which Japanese motherhood is constructed and perceived. Mothers are at once the agents of the dominant ideology, who, through their work of caretaking, instill particular values in their children, and a threat to the male-dominant social order whose overpowering presence demasculinizes men. The construction of motherhood in contemporary Japanese culture is an assembly of contradictory formations. I am particularly interested in the relationship between femaleness, female labor of caretaking, and motherhood that comes through in Allison's analysis. While women are eroticized as the object of male desire, mothers are expected to be asexual, and any sign of female sexuality in mothers is treated with contempt and disgust. As a mother, a woman is expected to take care of her children, by making elaborate lunch boxes every school day, for example. But the boundary between good and bad caretaking is slippery, such as when the mother becomes too engrossed in the caretaking of her son in the instance of mother-son incest. The picture of Japanese motherhood that Allison portrays is necessarily ambiguous and contradictory: while Japanese mothers are confident, proud, and capable in their role of caretaking, their femaleness produced through their labor is contested, reworked, delimited, and sometimes rejected within the ideological framework that endows motherhood with its moral authority.

In my own fieldwork, too, I encountered moments when women themselves seemed ambivalent about their own mothering/caretaking roles. The experience of transnational mobility seemed to have provoked reflection on normative femininity and encouraged contemplation on its consequences in their own lives. In some painful instances, as we will see in the next section, the costs and danger that came with domestic roles were exacerbated by the living conditions of a foreign country. In more liberating moments, motherliness created an opening for women to imagine their self apart from the ideology of female domesticity in a globalized world. Yet their thoughts returned, in the end, to the limiting reality of their lives.

BAD WIVES, UNWISE MOTHERS

In the following three stories, I explore the weight of "role orientation" and the cost of failure to perform ascribed female roles in the context of transnational mobility. The first instance demonstrates the significance of being there and the fundamental questions that are raised about women who neglect (or are seen to neglect) this obligation in the eyes of other women, who were by far the harshest critics of one another's performances.[3] The second instance illuminates the built-in danger of domesticity that women constantly have to fight in the particularly unstable social environment of kaigai chuuzai. In the third, we see the ever shifting relationship between the self and gender roles, in which motherhood seems to carry a more intrinsic importance than any other role.

AMONG THE WOMEN I met in Centerville was Kamata-san, an active woman in her early fifties with a successful husband and grown-up children back in Japan. She worked throughout her child-rearing years, despite many difficulties so familiar to working mothers in Japan and elsewhere. Kamata-san recalled her experience of being a working mother as "very difficult," particularly with a hard-working corporate employee for a husband, who did not object to her full-time job but was not home enough to be of any help. When one of her children became ill, she often had to make the gut-wrenching decision to leave him home alone: "I'd put a box lunch, the telephone, and my office number by his futon," she recollected. "It was so hard to leave him like that, and I often worried that he might be too sick to even call me while I was at work." Yet, she persisted through those difficult times to be eventually promoted to a management position, a rarity in the Japanese workforce for women of her generation.

Soon after her promotion, her husband received a transfer order to Centerville to start up and run a U.S. subsidiary of his company. The company urged her to go to Centerville with him, reminding her that her husband would be in a position of heavy responsibility and would need her to take good care of him. Kamata-san, however, could not bear the thought of quitting her job, which she knew she would not get back after five years of absence. Her husband left Japan by himself as a case of *tanshin funin* (single transfer), moving to Centerville to take his position without accompanying family.

After a year of tanshin funin in a foreign city, working in overdrive to get the new company on track, Kamata-san's husband became seriously ill and was hospitalized. Predictably, the blame was put on the fact that he was living alone and had no one to take care of him. Human resources staff from the corporate office of his company in Tokyo asked Kamata-san to go to Centerville immediately, and she finally agreed. She sent in her resignation, and the next day she was by her husband's side in a Centerville hospital.

As I discussed in chapter 3, being there is often taken very literally to mean that the woman should be home whenever her husband and children are home. Virtually all of my informants with school-age children, from first grade all the way up to the senior year in high school, told me that they made a point of personally picking up their children at school or being home when their children came home from school. As to their husband's need for their presence at home, many informants, both male and female, spoke of *wabishisa*, the lonesome feeling of a man coming back to a dark, cold house, eating take-out food that he picked up on the way home. "This is asking for trouble," said a chuuzaiin who himself had an experience of tanshin funin. "You don't eat well; you stay in the office too long to avoid being alone; you feel lonesome all the time. Eventually, you end up in a miserable situation, either by getting [physically] ill, having a nervous breakdown, or destroying the family." By "destroying the family," he meant that men often got involved in extramarital affairs in tanshin funin situations, unable to resist the temptation of female company and all the comfort it promises (Okifuji 1986).

Rather than holding men responsible for their inability to take care of themselves, the breakdown—infidelity, illness, lost productivity—is attributed to the wife's absence. Kamata-san's case was no exception. Despite her ultimate compliance with her wifely duty, the reaction of the women's community in Centerville toward Kamata-san was resigned at best and outright hostile at worst toward their peer who made such an obvious blunder. Very few Japanese women in Centerville seemed friendly with Kamata-san, and I continued to hear passing comments about her current affairs, from her visit to a local Japanese grocery store to her zeal at the annual Japanese festival, that were superficially neutral yet calculated to convey disapproval. Some women who knew of Kamata-san's situation told me that they would not have let their husband go on a tanshin funin, if at all avoidable, implying that Kamata-san's situation *was* avoidable. Some referred to Kamata-san's professional commitment as *tsumetai* (cold-hearted) and *jibunkatte* (self-centered). Others were direct in attributing her husband's breakdown as her fault, stating that it was *saisho kara wakatteita koto* (self-evident from the beginning) that any man in his situation, a single transfer on a very stressful assignment abroad, would sooner or later suffer from a physical or psychological breakdown. No one who discussed Kamata-san with me seemed to agree with my own sentiment that Kamata-san's commitment to her profession was admirable and that her husband's company should not have tried to bully her into quitting her job. "But that's *shikataganai* [inevitable]," they would say. "The company needed him to be there and do the job that he did. By contrast, Kamata-san, who could have done something [to help her husband], chose not to." This one-sided judgment was astonishing, particularly considering that an indirect approach and conflict avoidance are the usual mode of social interaction among expatriate Japanese generally, and women in particular. It seemed to reflect, in turn, the gravity of the offense that Kamata-san committed and the fundamental flaw in her femaleness that such an offense indicates.

WHEN KAWAGOE-SAN HAD a fender-bender in the parking lot of Hinomoto Japanese grocery store, Takeda-san called me to tell me that the accident was quite minor and that neither Kawagoe-san nor her children were injured: "Kawagoe-san is shook up a little bit, but she is in good humor and everything is all right." When she called me back a few days later, her voice had a heavier tone of concern, however. "It looks to me as if Kawagoe-san is quite *nitsumatteru* [stewed and thickened]," she informed me. The repair of her car was taking more time than expected, and in the meantime, Kawagoe-san could not go anywhere without her husband, who came home late in the evening and often worked on weekends. Unfortunately, I was away in Colorado for a brief visit, and her close friends were all busy that week and not able to spend much time with her. Stuck at home all day with her children, her patience was apparently wearing thin. "Irie-san and I were saying that we need you back soon, Sawa-san, to cheer Kawagoe-san up!"

Nitsumaru literally means "to become stewed and thickened." Takeda-san was using this phrase figuratively, of course, to describe Kawagoe-san's frustration at her unexpected home detention with seemingly no end in sight. Kawagoe-san's sense of entrapment and Takeda-san's urgency to intervene show that my female Japanese informants felt domestic isolation as something real and dangerous. According to Takeda-san and other women with whom I spoke, nitsumaru is not a phenomenon specific to the condition of kaigai chuuzai and transiency, but is commonly recognized by Japanese wives and mothers who feel "trapped" in their domestic roles (Ikeda 1984; Ueda 1992). However, the danger of nitsumaru for

Japanese wives and mothers is often increased by the particular living conditions and domestic demands of a foreign place. They recognize that they have a good chance of being isolated in the unfamiliar foreign environment and that some acute cases of domestic isolation have led to a tragic and destructive outcome. Not long before I began my fieldwork in Centerville, for example, a Japanese corporate wife in Detroit threw her infant daughter off her apartment balcony; the baby fell into a creek underneath and died. It was, my female informants explained to me, a typical, albeit extreme, case of *ikuji noiroze* (neurosis or nervous breakdown caused by the stress of child care demands). This woman seemed to be slightly depressed since she followed her husband to his chuuzai location and appeared to have spent much of her time at home alone with her baby. Then, one day, she could not take her crying baby any longer, and, as my informants related the story, all she could think of was to "just get rid of [her crying child]."

My female informants were invariably deeply disturbed by the violent outcome of this story, but they also expressed sympathy for this distraught Detroit wife. Some even said that they could "relate to" the stress of isolation at home that pushed the mother off the edge. Staying home with children could make one extremely tense, they explained, and they had to get away—away from their children, if possible, but more important, away from the closed space called home before they became completely "stewed and thickened" and thus dangerous to themselves and their children. Many veteran expatriate wives recognized domestic isolation as a serious problem, particularly for newcomers, who were yet to develop relationships with other Japanese wives and local Americans in their new place of residence, but also for some long-time residents who, for one reason or another, failed to cultivate and sustain social networks during kaigai chuuzai. In a group interview with half a dozen Maveric wives, everyone agreed that it was a "bad sign" when an expatriate wife stayed home alone "too much." Why was it a bad sign and how much was too much, I asked. It was a bad sign because housewives tended to get depressed and irritable if they did not have a place to go outside their home, to hang out with other women and talk about all sorts of things to let off steam every once in a while. There was no question that everyone needed it; the frequency would depend on each person. Some felt the need to get out of the house every day even for an hour to window-shop at a mall nearby; others went out once a week or less; most went out two or three times a week. Ultimately, it did not matter what they did, they agreed, the point was to be away from their home and be in contact with other women during the day.

In many conversations, Japanese women asked one another how much is enough time to spend with one's children, and how much is too much. The answers to these questions varied greatly from one person to another, but Japanese mothers with children from toddlers to high school age agreed that they spent more time with their children in the United States than they did or would in Japan. They also felt that they were "forced" to spend too much time with their children in the United States because of several constraints of the physical and social environment. One of the physical constraints is the American suburbs, which are spread out with inadequate public transportation. In Japan, they explained, children can become mobile very quickly. First-graders go to school with older children from the neighborhood and eventually go on their own or find friends in the neighborhood to go along with. With bicycles and public transportation, older children travel far from home without parental supervision. In the United States, chauffeuring duties go on forever, through grade school into junior high school and continuing through high school, unless parents allow their children to drive. In addition, a mother's driving duties often increase as her children grow, as their social life and other activities outside the home expand. In Centerville, where there is virtually no public transportation, Japanese parents have to weigh two choices: continuing to drive their teenage children, who are increasingly dissatisfied with their lack of mobility, or giving them permission to drive, which most Japanese parents find unacceptably dangerous. In New York, public transportation is more readily available, but Japanese parents often choose to drive their children anyway, out of their concern for their children's personal safety in this urban environment. The U.S. legal definition of parental negligence is also a major factor in this forced closeness between mother and child. Japanese parents regularly leave their young children, even infants, at home for a short period of time and find it quite reasonable, for example, for a ten-year-old to baby-sit younger siblings for a couple of hours. Many Japanese mothers find out the hard way that this is neither acceptable nor legal in the United States (Fukunaga 1990, 173–174), which exacerbates the sense of enclosure and entrapment within the domestic space.

A lack or insufficiency of supportive networks also can be a serious issue contributing to domestic isolation. When they lived in Japan, the majority of my female informants had either family members or trusted friends whom they could count on for a few hours of child care if they needed or wanted to go out by themselves. In the United States, away from their established networks of family and friends, most of the expatriate wives, particularly in the first phase of their transnational migration, did not have anyone to fall back on. The husband, who is often the only close adult around, may or may not be there, depending on his job responsibility, the employer's policies, and the degree of flexibility that he has in his assignment, to provide the tangible and intangible support these women need.

ONE AFTERNOON, Takeda-san asked Kawagoe-san and Irie-san what they would do if they were "like Sawa-san."

"I wonder all the time," she explained. "What could I do in America, if I could speak English and had a green card like Sawa-san does? I think I would teach Japanese to American students while I worked on a master's degree. What would you do?"

The three of them sat there and fantasized about life in an alternative reality, and each laid out scenarios for exciting careers and lifestyles, which reflected their personal interests and tastes. Kawagoe-san thought that she would start her own business, probably selling children's clothes; Irie-san's interest was in food, so she thought she might start a gourmet grocery store or a restaurant and travel all around the world. We began laughing, however, when we realized that all three of them left their husband out of their dreams, while they kept their children in (or imagined children, in Takeda-san's case, as she had no children at the time).

As I sat there and listened to their dreams, I was struck by the eagerness with which they spoke of a more career-centered life, and also by the marginal importance of marriage and a heterosexual relationship in their scenarios. For Kawagoe-san, it was perhaps not so surprising, as she grew up in a matrifocal family with practically no stable male presence, and it was her oft-stated belief that women could do just fine without men. Takeda-san and Irie-san, however, grew up in more or less normative middle-class families, with parents whose marriage was solid and stable, and there was nothing that suggested that they had any problems in their own marriage. Yet, when they were free to conjure up an image of a good life, they kept the heterosexual relationship and marriage out of it. Ogura Chikako (1998) identifies the pattern in the life course choices of young Japanese women who perceive that the ideal way of life is to *jibun ni shoujiki ni ikiru* (live honestly to oneself). But the ideal remains just that in most cases, and they tend to choose an easier path of settling down with a decent guy and becoming a house-wife. The way my informants separated their married life and their fantasy life seems to follow a similar dichotomy. By contrast, all three women included children, which indicates that motherhood has a quite different significance to them than wifehood. If heterosexual relation-ships are optional to the sense of who they were, their relationships to their children and their motherhood had some innate significance and inalienable value to them.

THE LINE BETWEEN the good and the bad, the wise and the unwise, seems very thin and unevenly drawn, and most women I knew inevitably crossed this line once or twice during their kaigai chuuzai. Most learned quickly what to do and what not to do, figured out how far the envelope can be pushed, and for how long. They modified their outward be-havior, particularly in front of the critical senior wives in their hus-band's company, all the while complaining and joking about the stu-pidity of all this with their close friends. In this sense, they were very pragmatic—so much so that they appeared almost cynical—about the disciplinary ways of the women's community, and they dealt with it matter-of-factly most of the time. There were a few, however, who so clearly violated the standard for good wives and wise mothers of the chuuzai family that they became branded as bad and unwise forever. Sometimes, a deed that seems so minor to an outsider may condemn a Japanese corporate wife to this status in her expatriate women's com-munity and turn her kaigai chuuzai into a living hell. An anecdote in Mori and Saike (1997) tells of the demise of a young newcomer who brought some "inappropriate gifts" to the wives of her husband's supe-riors. The inappropriateness of her gifts quickly "got on the Japanese rumor mill," and this woman was henceforth never mentioned by name, but known only as "that woman who brought strange gifts," even after her husband's U.S. assignment had ended and they had returned to Japan. Being branded during kaigai chuuzai may also carry over to life back in Japan, because the frequent comings and goings of other employees' families can make the expatriate rumor mill a truly transnational affair.

Similar to anthropologists' findings in their analyses of Japanese group dynamics (Allison 1994; Kondo 1990; Rohlen 1989), the institutional authority of Japanese transnational corporations over expatriate wives is displaced and disguised as an informal, and perhaps naturalized, mechanism of equilibrium within the collectivity to keep its members in line without invoking any formal authority in everyday social interaction. In turn, this authority creates diffuseness in the mechanism of surveillance and discipline for chuuzaiin wives, and the women's community, in its most general sense, scrutinizes and regulates expatriate wives' every action. The smallness of the expatriate Japanese women's community is definitely a source of stress, as it is nearly impossible to maintain any degree of privacy in it. Japanese social life routinely allows for a gap between public presentation (*tatemae*) and private reality (*honne*). In fact, managing this duality is a necessary ability for social adults in Japan. Most Japanese corporate wives are well versed in such social finesse and have managed the honne-tatemae duality well enough most of their adult lives. However, when they come to live in a foreign city and join the small and exclusive expatriate community out of necessity, they quickly realize that everybody seems to know everybody else's business, and this lack of privacy can make them endlessly second-guess one another, even in seemingly innocent conversations. As one Centerville wife put it, in the *semai nihonjin shakai* ("small and narrow-minded society of the Japanese") one always has to watch what one says. Despite its cumbersome, even disciplinarian, nature, relationships in this community have to be maintained at all costs, as it is, after all, the source of information and support that are critical to their survival in the unfamiliar place.

If the third story is any indication, Japanese women try to maintain a degree of independence from their ascribed roles and the judgmental attitude of the generalized women's community, as they fantasize about their alternative selves in the company of close and trusted friends. Domesticity and wifeliness are quickly abandoned in their alternative lives, as they each consider their professional interests and disregard the presence of a husband. Motherhood, however, appears as a more essential component of their female subjectivity, without which they are not themselves anymore. One possible interpretation is that role orientation penetrates Japanese female subjectivity so deeply that it can never completely be separated from social roles; thus, the persistence of the motherhood theme in those imaginary lives only demonstrates the false consciousness of middle-class Japanese women. Another interpretation is to consider the multifaceted nature of motherhood as an ascribed role and socially imposed obligation on the one hand, and, on the other, as the most personal and important attachment in these women's lives. There is no doubt that motherhood plays a key role in the ideological construction of femaleness, which in turn ties women closely to the domestic space and constrains their avenues of self-realization, as the nitsumaru story indicates. If we accept the second interpretation, however, we may infer that motherhood is also experienced as a positive and formative aspect of their lives that they choose to retain even in their fantasies. Insightfully distinguishing these two meanings of motherhood, a Japanese woman can play her part in the norm-sensitive community and yet maintain a sense of defiance even in the limiting circumstances of kaigai chuuzai.

THE NEED TO PLAY

It almost never failed that, at around five o'clock, many of the women who had been lounging around in Kawagoe-san's living room began to look at the clock and to think about going home.

"Oh, no, it's getting late already!" Ueno-san exclaims. "I need to stop at Hinomoto store and get some groceries," she explains as she quickly puts jackets on her children.

This is the cue for everyone else that the break is over and that it is time to go home and "work." Other women have their own husband to feed, their own children to bathe and put to bed. Kawagoe-san's house has to be turned over to another function, for the tired husband of our hostess will soon return home, expecting a hot meal and a restful evening.

It was like one of those dramatic scene changes in kabuki theater, in which a whole set would turn upside down and disappear into the basement to make way for the new set that emerges out of the bottom of the stage. In fifteen minutes or less, all traces of the daytime gathering were gone, children's toys and books put away, dirty coffee cups washed, the residue of lunch and afternoon sweets squared away. As they left Kawagoe-san's home and each other's company, the women said to each other, "Mata asondene [Please play with us/me again]," as Japanese children usually do at the end of their day.

THE HOMOSOCIAL COMMUNITY of women is not only a disiciplining mechanism that keeps Japanese women in line, discouraging them from acting outside the roles of good wives and wise mothers. It is also the place where women find friendship, support, and advice. Most important, it is a realm of play away from their domestic responsibilities. The playfulness of women's gathering is perhaps the most important reason Japanese women put up with the more cumbersome side of expatriate human relations. I recall the exaggerated exasperation that some of the women at Kawagoe-san's house expressed over the pending work obligation, "Ahhh, tsumannai [boring, tiresome, or disappointing]. The afternoon is already gone. I've got to think of tonight's dinner, and I have no idea what to make!"

The same work-play dichotomy that my informants applied to me was also at work here: women's networks functioned as the social space in which women expressed their sentiment about their work of domestic management, reflected on themselves and their lives outside of the idealized feminine domesticity, and explored the appropriation of work as an alibi for play. For a Japanese wife and mother whose job is first and foremost to take care of others, doing something, anything, for herself seemed to constitute *asobi* (play) in the broadest sense of the term, and their leisure activities always took a back seat to their responsibilities of homemaking and caregiving. *Asobi* as a catch-all category of everything that was not *shigoto* seemed to make it harder for expatriate Japanese wives to play without fear of offending the standard of domestic duty upheld among expatriate Japanese wives in the community. The bounds of their homemaking and caregiving work were quite vague to begin with and often shifted as the needs of their family members changed. Thus, these women had to be prepared at any moment to sacrifice their play activities, that is, everything that they might do for their own enjoyment or satisfaction. Their play activities also had to be flexible enough to accommodate the unpredictability of their household demands and informal enough so that last-minute cancellation or absence would not inconvenience others too much. Japanese corporate wives had to be creative to get away from home even for a short time and to sneak into their demanding schedule a little time for themselves.

Femaleness that is constructed around domesticity and motherliness is both empowering and disabling. It creates strong connections between women as mothers, but it also divides women who fulfill their homemaking and caretaking roles from those who do not. It oscillates between entrapment and fulfillment; the tie that binds the mother and her children so closely that both of them become immobile is also the tie that fulfills these women's sense of self the most. And in the context of kaigai chuuzai, the influence of the corporate agenda and the foreign environment in which they perform their feminine duty further complicate the matter. Moreover, Japanese mothers have to fulfill their motherly duties in an unfamiliar foreign environment without the supportive network of female kin and long-term friends that they cultivated in Japan. As kaigai chuuzai takes these women out of Japan, away from the network of relationships and familiar resources that they depended on in their process of self-fulfillment, they also find themselves in the "maternal isolation" of Western middle-class women (Chodorow 1989, chap. 4) in which an "almost primal aggression" inherent in the mother-child relationship becomes a dominant theme (85). The mother is all-powerful, particularly in her home away from Japan, because of the child's dependence on her care and lack of alternative sources of support from close kin. At the same time, the mother is totally powerless because the construction of her identity becomes dependent on the presence of her child. When this intertwined and primal relationship becomes isolated and condensed in the foreign environment, motherhood is connected with the potential of death and destruction, as we have seen in the example above.

There is an irony in the danger of uchi, since it is supposed to be a safe haven, whereas soto is associated with danger. Why is domestic space so dangerous in the view of these corporate wives? It seems that the ambivalent position of Japanese women in the uchi-soto construct plays a role here. I stated earlier that Japanese women are marginalized in many social contexts, including the corporate world of work, as "others" to male "selves." Upon marriage and motherhood, they become primary agents of cultural reproduction at home. But despite this transformation, the original soto-ness of women lingers on, because even in their own home they cannot seem to truly relax or be themselves. In fact, for Japanese wives and mothers, uchi is a place of hard and continuous labor, not a place for relaxation and rest. Entrapment in this domestic space means all work and no play.

While the ideology of female domesticity frames the experience of transnational mobility among Japanese corporate wives, we can see that, in their daily actions and choices, they often struggle with the ideal of their domestic selves and seek out, even within the confines of the naturalized roles as wives and mothers and of the small expatriate women's community, avenues through which to express their own personal sentiments, explore social connections and friendships, and resist the implications of all work and no play in the life of a good wife and wise mother. The picture of middle-class Japanese women that emerges from the analysis of these seemingly trivial practices of everyday life is complex and ambiguous. Not one thing that they do routinely in their home-centered lives comes across as simply domestic or duty-driven; at the same time, not one thing is purely for fun or personal satisfaction. Japanese women's understanding of what makes their lives meaningful and enjoyable does not easily lend itself to any conceptualization that, implicitly or explicitly, relies on the self-other dichotomy. Instead, every act carries multiple meanings, is often fraught with contradiction, and is limiting and liberating at once.

Given the stress of living in a foreign place and the increased demands of domesticity, it is more important than ever for Japanese women to play during kaigai chuuzai. Yet I have found that their ambivalence about play is as profound as their feelings about work. I was often struck by two contradictory messages that my corporate wife informants seemed to be sending out: their earnest need to play versus their ambivalence about their play. As the discourse of nitsumaru (to be stewed and thickened) represents, there is a sense among chuuzaiin wives that staying home alone threatened their psychological well-being and affected their performance as good mothers and wives, and that they needed to get away, to be with other women in similar circumstances. At the same time, they appeared to place play very low on their list of priorities, after their domestic work, their family's needs and convenience, and other obligatory social activities, such as getting together with other wives from their husband's company. Nevertheless, expatriate Japanese wives play, and play often, and it is with a sense of necessity that they do so.

The alibi of work in their play is, in fact, a convenient feature of social gatherings among expatriate Japanese housewives. As we have seen, women's friendship-based groups often function as a kind of mutual aid network; thus, their play is justified as an extension of their domestic management. Their fragmented daily schedule also allows them to intermix their play activities with work throughout the day, rather than setting play aside as a separate and distinct domain from work (Nippert-Eng 1996). In other words, as Kawagoe-san once told me, housewives can "play as much as they please," as long as they can connect their play with the realm of their housework and as long as their leisure activities do not conflict with their domestic duties. This intermixing of work and play, and the legitimization of play that is embedded in the context of work, is a familiar strategy in Japanese society, as exemplified in the widely practiced after-work socialization of Japanese corporate workers (Allison 1994). So the wives of corporate workers also find play in their work at home, while their husband goes to work in hostess clubs and golf courses. Given all the work of making a home away from home, Japanese corporate wives have to get creative and find ways to play at work, if they are to play at all. Their insistence on playing perhaps indicates their struggle between overt resistance and silent acceptance (de Certeau 1984). This interpretation of the work-play ambiguity takes us in an opposite direction from my earlier assertions that women's social relationships are taken over by work-driven concerns. We can as easily say that expatriate Japanese wives are subverting the regimen of work by inserting play activities right in the middle of it.

Or perhaps we should think about why my female informants insisted that their work was "insignificant": instead of interpreting this insistence as a sort of false consciousness, we may consider it a strategy to subvert the mechanism of power. De Certeau (1984, chap. 4), in his critique of Foucault, suggests that some technologies, apparatuses, or procedures seem to be favored as instruments of power, and that the practice of making everyday life is not one of them. The practice of everyday life is, in other words, potentially subversive precisely because it is insignificant. Japanese wives may have much to gain by effacing their own domestic work and maintaining a low profile, so that the influence of power may pass them over, because, whether at work or play, whatever women do in their domestic capacities is not that critical anyway. This certainly echoes male discourses, and male ignorance, of women's domestic life (Allison 1994). In other words, they may be using the normative/male image of Japanese housewives as *himajin* (people with much leisure time at hand) to dodge further incorporation of their labor into the world of work, where, as they can see in their own husband's life, both work and play equally become instruments of power.

CHAPTER FIVE

On Vacation

IN THE FIRST CHAPTER, I suggested that tension exists in the theorization of traveling and dwelling. While the move to emphasize the overlaps and ambiguities between them makes it possible to understand fluid mobility practices, distinctions between traveling and dwelling, and between different ways of moving, may also hold meaning among the very people who practice them. This tension offers an alluring conceptual opening for the exploration of corporate-driven mobility practices among middle-class Japanese, particularly of the experience of women whose job centers on dwelling while traveling. The juxtaposing, mixing, and overlapping between dwelling and traveling practices are the theme that runs through this book. In this chapter, I will shift my focus to their narratives of movement and change, to bring out a different view of kaigai chuuzai from previous chapters.

Japanese corporate families are "sojourners," traveling to a specific location to accomplish an explicit task and anticipating a return home at its completion. In this, they are different from tourists, whose purpose is pleasure, wanderers, who have no specific destination, and immigrants, who do not intend to return to their point of origin.[1] This observation resonates with the ways Japanese corporations and individual participants formally define kaigai chuuzai. Along with uchi and soto, traveling and living are another binary with which Japanese corporate families overseas think about their own transnational mobility and their relationship to their national home during kaigai chuuzai. Yet, as in every aspect of social life among Japanese, there is a distinction between the tatemae of kaigai chuuzai, or the formal definition that is publicly acknowledged, and the honne, or the actual, lived experience that is honestly told only in private. Although very little of the daily life of expatriate Japanese wives escapes the concerns of dwelling, filled as it is with the tedious work of homemaking in an unfamiliar place, the theme of travel, and more specifically of "vacation," appeared repeatedly in the conversations that I had with them. All the traveling words they used to describe themselves in the United States connoted temporariness and exclusion, being outsiders, being treated as intruders, being not quite welcome, not having the full rights of true residents. Behind this categorization of their stay in the United States as travel is the uchi-soto binary. If uchi is the place where one belongs and lives, then soto is the place to which one travels. The third binary between Japan and the United States is overlaid as well to create a three-way link: Japan/uchi/ living and Amerika/soto/traveling.

The difference between various forms of travel also has tangible consequences in the women's immediate experience of transnational mobility. Being a corporate-sponsored sojourner provides certain material resources and promises social and cultural privileges. It also gives direction to the sojourner's movement, assigns him or her tasks, and sets a time limit to his or her travel. The daily life of Japanese corporate wives in the United States showcases many of these privileges and limitations. The majority would have never even imagined living abroad unless it was because of their husband's job assignment. The corporate subsidy makes possible their affluent lifestyle in the United States. Thus, only in their duty to create a home for their family members do they become privileged middle-class sojourners in the globalizing world. They seem aware, in fact, that they are a particular kind of transnational sojourner whose mobility is dictated by the interests of Japanese capitalism and whose life has little to do with the foreign place in which they end up for the time being beyond the interest of short-term survival.

Five years, however, does demand a measure of livability, and, as we have seen, Japanese corporate wives work hard at making a home for themselves and their family in a strange and unfamiliar place. In their daily practice, traveling is almost invisible, overshadowed by the concerns of living and dwelling. Knowing that this home is only temporary and has to be abandoned in several years, engagement in the concrete work of homemaking predominates their everyday life during kaigai chuuzai. However, even in the domestic tasks that these women perform in the United States, we find a great deal more ambiguity and flexibility than is initially apparent, where homemaking necessarily involves traveling outside their comfort zones. As we will see in this chapter, the formal distinction between traveling and dwelling becomes complicated for two reasons. First, the definition of uchi often becomes ambiguous during kaigai chuuzai, making it difficult to know where one belongs and where one is only a traveler. Second, there is a seeming inconsistency between the words and actions of Japanese corporate wives, who have many responsibilities and concerns during kaigai chuuzai yet speak of themselves as "vacationers." Another important element in their mobility trope is the notion of Amerika, or the specific ways in which contemporary middle-class Japanese imagine, experience, and talk about the United States, the ultimate cultural other since the beginning of Japan's modern history. As such, it may significantly differ from the ontological state of U.S. society, and from Americans' own experience of it. Some components of what contemporary Japanese consider part of Amerika may seem exaggerated, even upsetting. Nonetheless, Amerika constitutes a significant part of the Japanese worldview and plays a significant part in their travel narratives.

The distinctions between sojourning and vacationing, dwelling and traveling, uchi and soto, and Japan and Amerika will never completely dissolve in the minds and actions of Japanese families overseas. They will always remain sojourners somewhere in their mind and will keep waiting for the day when they return to Japan. At the same time, for the wives and mothers who have to ensure the well-being of their family members through the years of sojourning and upon their homecoming at the end of the journey, the questions of living loom large. In the end, it is not the question of whether to live or to travel. They must be able, simultaneously, to travel and to live, from the very first day of their kaigai chuuzai. So, in this chapter, I explore how, in the daily life of Japanese corporate wives in the United States, the boundaries between traveling and living become less certain and more permeable. There are many ways in which this blurring takes place: transiency in homemaking itself, temporary visits to Japan, and a simultaneous affinity and fear that many feel toward Amerika. Along the way, I also hope to clarify the significance of a "long vacation" and why this notion is central to the Japanese women's understanding of their transnational homemaking.

TRANSIENT HOMEMAKERS

Kaigai chuuzai's duration and purposefulness clearly mark it as an experience much different from a one-week group tour to the United States, and the fact that they will be making a home in this transient situation causes some anxiety. Mori Rie, who lived in Los Angeles for five years in the early 1990s and published her experience in a manga-essay, describes in a consciously comedic tone the shift in her thinking about kaigai chuuzai. At first, it seemed like an extension of an overseas trip that she was used to taking as a single woman. All she thought about was "I can live in a big house, I can buy brand-name goods at a lower price, I can go to Disneyland many times, I can play golf inexpensively, etc." However, a new awareness eventually kicks in as a *chuuzaiin fujin*, or the wife of a kaigai chuuzai appointee, who embodies "an international woman who supports her world-trotting businessman husband" (Mori and Saike 1997, 10–13).

One of the ways this shift manifested was in her preparation for life in the United States. She confesses to her "mistake" in shipping a two-year supply of shampoo from Japan, which "took up all the storage space in the bathroom [in her home in the United States]." She recalls, "I over-reacted to the word *chuuzai*. . . . I used to purchase and bring home shampoos of different brands from different countries. Silly me!" (Mori and Saike 1997, 15). Mori is not alone in making the error of overpreparing. Most expatriate Japanese families I know brought a two-year supply of everything: shampoo and conditioner, toothbrush and toothpaste, soy sauce and miso paste, MSG and powdered fish stock, underwear and socks. Two years later, they plan on replenishing their supply during a company-paid visit back to Japan as part of their kaigai chuuzai benefit. As Mori reflects, there is a significant concern among the outgoing kaigai chuuzai wives of not finding familiar and appropriate products overseas that suit their particular needs: shampoo and conditioner because Japanese hair is different from Western hair; toothpaste because they may not like the taste of a foreign brand; essential seasonings for Japanese cooking just in case these are hard to come by; underwear and socks because foreign sizes may be too large. Once they arrive in the United States, many of these concerns turn out to be unfounded, and, as Mori did, many Japanese wives regret the expense involved in hauling unnecessary goods all the way from Japan. The adventurousness of a traveler, whose aim is to experience and rebel in the unknown, is hereby replaced with the caution of a temporary dweller, whose concern is now to conserve the familiar, expressed most vividly in her everyday consumption behavior.

As life in the United States becomes their everyday, the shift away from the temporary dweller's conservatism is also visible in changing consumption choices, as some Japanese women begin experimenting with local products and eventually find such experiments interesting and even enriching.

"It's acorn squash," Ichigaya-san said definitively. "I thought all this time it was pumpkin, but the closest thing that comes to *kabocha* is really called 'squash.' It looks a little different, but if you cook it right, it is really not bad at all."

We were talking over a cup of green tea about food substitutions. For Ichigaya-san, on her second Amerika chuuzai, it became a challenge to use local products in her everyday routine, including cooking. She tried to cook pumpkins the Japanese way, stewed with soy sauce and a little sugar, many times with dismal results. She had all but given up on American pumpkins when she noticed acorn squash that looked much more like the familiar kabocha. This is partly a difficulty of translation. A Japanese-English dictionary defines "pumpkin" as *kabocha.* In a grocery store, a shopper sees a large, bright orange orb called "pumpkin" and assumes it is the American version of *kabocha.* Ichigaya-san was feeling at once proud and silly that she was adventurous enough to try something new, yet she was silly enough not to try for so long. In these minor adventures, I see the subtle shift in expatriate Japanese wives' attitudes toward their lives in the United States. As long as they are looking to Japan for the source of everything consumed at home, their kaigai chuuzai remains a prolonged travel. When they begin to look for ways of using locally available goods to suit their needs and tastes, they are finally beginning to live here.

This realization also brings out an important distinction between living in America and becoming American. The chuuzai families, however long they may remain in the United States, are keenly aware of their Japaneseness, if only as their place of origin and not so much as their place of permanent dwelling. They may assume some American manners and customs in public, while retaining the most familiar and thus comfortable routines in their intimate life inside the home. Living in the United States as Japanese is a hybrid practice, like acorn squash stewed with soy sauce and sugar. It is also a creative process in which one must trust one's own senses and resourcefulness over the dictionary definition and unexamined common sense. As such, it also signifies a departure from the practice of international tourism in which one consumes whatever the paid intermediary, such as the tour guide, puts in front of him or her.

As we have seen in chapter 3, Japanese households in the United States cannot exist without interaction with the outside world. Wives have to know how to get around in a foreign city, let service people into their home, and navigate through neighborhood relations. This being a foreign country, each of these occasions becomes another experience of crossing the boundaries around uchi/Japan to a foreign soto. To put it another way, in their homemaking, the women travel to a foreign place every day. Anxiety always accompanies such crossings, no matter how short the trip, how familiar the destination, how simple the task. The ways expatriate Japanese wives navigate through the streets of American cities resemble the ways Japanese tourists visit foreign places. The women find strength in numbers, prefer to follow a knowledgeable leader rather than find their own way, and take seemingly inconvenient steps and routes without question, as long as the leader is familiar with them. On most foreign tours, the leaders are paid professionals, such as tour conductors and travel agents. Japanese corporate wives usually find an informal leader among themselves, as in the case of Kawagoe-san, or in one of the Japanese-speaking local residents, usually, Japanese women who are married to American husbands, or Japanese-speaking American women, in some cases.

Much of Kawagoe-san's local geographic knowledge came from *senpai*, or senior corporate wives with long experience in Centerville whom she befriended when she initially arrived. Those senpai wives, too, learned many of their navigation tricks from their own senpai when they arrived as *kohai*, or junior wives. This mechanism was very similar in all three expatriate Japanese communities in which I conducted research, while the size, composition, and history of each community affected specific ways in which local knowledge was passed down. More experienced senior women, who usually know their way around the local area, would show newly arriving junior women around the city, pointing out where to shop; how to get to schools, doctor's offices, and important government offices; and where to find good restaurants. Some of the senior women get to be in that position of respect by their husband's rank; he is in a supervisory position himself and looks to his wife to take care of his underlings' families. Others, like Kawagoe-san, become a senpai by virtue of the length of their kaigai chuuzai experience and/or their willingness to organize social activities and help take care of others.

This social mechanism has a distinct effect on the amount and types of information on local geography available to Japanese corporate wives. It is common for them to ignore a nearby store in favor of another store of the same kind further away but frequented by senpai wives. Similarly, everyone went to "Kawagoe-san's" Mr. Wok, a chain restaurant that had several locations around Centerville, even when there was another one near her own home. They rarely ventured to other, unfamiliar Chinese restaurants for fear of miscommunication, embarrassment, or disappointment. If a particularly adventurous woman cultivates a new restaurant, a fancy bakery, or a cute coffee shop, word spreads through her social network very quickly, and everyone heads out to the same shop in the next few days, often running into each other, joking and complaining about the Japanization of yet another attractive local business.

There is another way in which homemaking turns into traveling. For various reasons, many Japanese couples choose to live apart for a time when the husband receives a kaigai chuuzai order: the wife remains in Japan while the husband goes abroad alone. Children's educational concerns are the most common reason for this decision. In other cases, the wife is the primary caretaker of the elderly parents. Any other reasons, including the wife's professional commitment, are not considered "good enough" to warrant such a decision. The couple may decide, instead, to go together to the husband's kaigai chuuzai location and leave children and other family members behind. Whatever they decide, the wives and mothers find themselves split between two, or even more, places where their caretaking work is needed.

The story of Matsuda-san, a well-groomed and sociable woman in her late forties whom I met in North Carolina's Research Triangle, is a good example of homemaking on the move. Ever since her husband, who worked for a major electronics company, was assigned to North Carolina, Matsuda-san was in constant motion, traveling back and forth between Japan and North Carolina every month. She and her husband had two children, a second-year college student and a high school senior who was preparing for the college entrance examinations. When her husband received the corporate order to go to North Carolina, Matsuda-san asked him to go by himself so that she could stay in Japan with her children, who could not possibly leave Japan at these critical stages in their education. Her husband, however, did not like the idea of tanshin funin (single transfer) and tried to convince Matsuda-san that their nearly grown-up children would do fine by themselves. Matsuda-san came up with a compromise: she would split her time between Japan and the United States, taking care of her children in Japan for two months, then being with her husband in the United States for two months. "If that arrangement had worked, it would have been all right," Matsuda-san sighed. "But my husband started complaining that he couldn't manage by himself for two months at a time." So Matsuda-san was flying back and forth every month between her husband and her children. At each home, she would clean, take care of all household matters, and cook up a storm to stock her family's refrigerator with a month's worth of dinners. When she was done with all the cooking, it would be time for her to hop on the plane again, go to the other home, and repeat the process. After almost a year of this grueling routine, "I'm beginning to be very tired," said Matsuda-san, which seemed to me a gross understatement.

There are similar stories of itinerant housewives in any given expatriate Japanese community. Many of them in the United States would periodically travel back to Japan to check on their children or elderly parents. Those in Japan would come to spend time with their husband in a tanshin funin situation. In a rare case, family members were split on three different continents: the wife/mother, who lived in Japan with a son in college entrance preparation, regularly traveled to Europe to see her daughter in a boarding school and to the United States to see her husband. In every situation, their travel is defined as part of their domestic responsibilities, and their time away is consumed by piled-up household work. Although these cases are not common, it is telling of the impact that repeated kaigai chuuzai can have on family life, particularly on the wives and mothers who must carry on their caretaking tasks simultaneously in multiple locations.

SHIKATAGANAI KOTO, OR INEVITABLE MATTERS

The traveling life is a hard life, and even on those relatively privileged middle-class sojourners, transiency takes its toll. Their life here in the United States, however temporary, poses limitations in certain areas while demanding women's immediate attention in others. This limiting nature of transiency is one of the meanings of "travel" for Japanese corporate wives. Or perhaps they employed the language of travel to convince themselves that whatever difficulty or dissatisfaction their kaigai chuuzai life presented was inevitable. While expatriate Japanese wives' sense of duty comes through clear and strong in their words and daily activities, there is a sense of burden in their exaggerated domesticity during kaigai chuuzai. Although they derive a great deal of pleasure from seeing that the product of their labor makes their family happy, they also resent and resist the imposition of domesticity as the sole purpose of their life abroad. The latter sentiment resonates with Nancy Rosenberger's (2000) observation that activities outside the home, such as paid labor, volunteering, and learning traditional art, have become increasingly important to the self-construct of Japanese housewives in the past two decades. To most Japanese corporate wives, kaigai chuuzai means disruption or difficulty in this process of self-fulfillment outside the home. Also, transiency, domestic demands, and separation from their social network in Japan force them into domestic isolation. The irony hardly escaped my female informants that more (geographic) mobility meant more (domestic) fixity.

When Japanese corporate wives leave Japan to accompany their husband to various places in the United States, they also leave behind much more than a familiar place to live. They leave the female-centered social networks—female family members, long-term friends, other mothers/wives from the neighborhood—through which they received, and provided to others, both tangible and intangible support in domestic management and child care. For instance, if a new mother is unsure of the cause of incessant crying of her infant, the first person she goes to for advice and support may be her mother or her older sister. If she needs to get information about a good preschool in the area, she might talk to another mother with an older child in the apartment complex. If she wants to complain about her husband's late nights, she might call up her sister or get together with her neighbors. If she desperately needs to get away for a day, she can meet up with her friend in the city for lunch. When she comes to the United States, she will no doubt stay in touch with these people; however, the physical distance between Japan and the United States makes the maintenance of social networks expensive and difficult. When she needs someone here and now, for example, to baby-sit for a couple of hours so she can go to a doctor's appointment, it is impossible to tap into the resources of her relatives and friends in Japan.

Many Japanese corporate wives also leave behind careers and other activities outside the home in which they had invested much time. Approximately 20 percent of my female informants said that they quit their long-term work (full-time or part-time) to come to the United States. I encountered only one case in which the wife did not have to choose between her own career and her husband's; they both worked for a large company as specialists in information technology and were assigned together to the company's Research Triangle facility. In several other cases in which the husband and wife each had professional careers (as in Kamata-san's case in chapter 4), the woman was encouraged, or even expected, to quit her job and accompany her husband, even though she would not be able to get her career back on track after kaigai chuuzai.

The sense of loss is not limited to those women who left professional careers behind. Another Centerville informant, Goto-san, was also frustrated that she had "nothing to do" in the United States. Although she did not have a professional career prior to kaigai chuuzai, she found a variety of part-time jobs and volunteer opportunities as a teacher, and continued her language study after she married and became a mother of two. Her two sons were in high school and did not require much of her attention any longer; her engineer husband came home tired and left for work early. But what was there for her to do? "Since I came to America, I have become a housemaid. All I do is cook and clean," she told me. Goto-san found that there were few learning resources that suited her needs in the United States, and she was frustrated that her progress in English was much slower than she hoped. She tried some language classes at a local community college, but they did not give her the sense of purpose that she seemed to be looking for: "So what if I took an English class or two? Nobody cares if my English is better, and I don't think I've gotten any better in the last three years in Centerville. I just go through the motions, so that I feel like I'm doing something."

A younger Japanese wife, Kato-san, expressed a similar sense of loss more broadly in terms of self-improvement. She was another active, self-motivated woman who continued her language study on her own after college, volunteered at a food co-op, and participated in an environmental movement in Japan. She seemed to be well-adjusted to her expatriate life and was active in a Centerville volunteer organization. So I was surprised to hear that, after three years, she was eager to go home. When I asked her why, she said that she was "falling behind" her friends in Japan, who continued to study, volunteer, and better themselves, while she was idling in a sleepy Midwestern U.S. city. "I was a lot more mobile and resourceful when I lived in Japan," she explained. "I had friends, I knew where to get the information I needed, I belonged to groups and organizations where I could network [with other women]. Here, I have lost all those things that I worked on, and instead, I have a few friends who feel as idle as I do. I had fun [in the United States] for a few years, but now I want to go home and get back to those things that mean something to me."

As these individual cases demonstrate, the avenues for social participation suddenly drop out of these women's lives, and domesticity is inflated as the essence of their feminine selves during kaigai chuuzai. As a result, Japanese corporate wives' sense of self often becomes flattened, lopsided, and incomplete. But their relationship to their womanly work is complicated, because shigoto is both the source of fulfillment and pride and the cause of frustration. If they simply find their homemaking tasks oppressive, they can just abandon them. But the labor of maintaining a Japanese domestic space, cooking Japanese food, and being there for the family is, undoubtedly, a necessary condition of their feminine identity, without which they cannot be a complete person. Domesticity is, in other words, a necessary component but not the efficient cause of their gendered selfhood. They need to do domestic management to be *a person*, but that alone cannot constitute a full and complete person.

While they are cut off from socially engaging activities in Japan, finding alternative activities in the United States proves extremely difficult due to legal and linguistic limitations. Paid employment during kaigai chuuzai is nearly impossible for Japanese corporate wives, who have a dependent visa status and usually are not qualified to work. Women who wish to become contributing members of the local community also quickly realize that their lack of communication skills precludes most volunteering and other socially engaging activities that they hoped to participate in while in the United States. Similarly, many other women's groups and political activism are not viable options for them. In desperation to find "something to do" that is not housework, many expatriate wives resort to leisure activities: hobby groups, sports, shopping, gourmet luncheons. In each of my field sites, particularly in New York, many recreational activities were readily available, and it seemed quite easy for a Japanese wife to distract herself with an assortment of these activities. But for women who worked full time or had other activities that they found meaningful before kaigai chuuzai, such diversions simply did not fill the loss they felt in their transient life.

Children's future also becomes more precarious than ever during the prolonged foreign residence, yet many mothers find themselves ill-equipped to help them. I will not provide detailed accounts of the trials that the children of expatriate Japanese corporate workers go through; these are found in several published works in both English and Japanese (e.g., Farcus and Kohno 1987; Okada 1993; Osawa 1986; White 1992). Instead, I focus on how they affect the mothers. Once again, their challenge is that of in-betweenness. While their children need quickly to learn to communicate in English (which most of them do not speak at all when they arrive in the United States) to catch up with the curriculum in the local school, make friends, and take part in extracurricular activities, they are also expected to keep up with the Japanese curriculum as well, by attending a supplementary Japanese school on Saturdays, a juku in the evening, or sometimes both. Mothers, often conscious that they were asking too much of their children, still have to encourage, coax, and scold their children to balance their double duty, to keep their options open both in the United States and Japan.

As the frequency, duration, and unpredictability of kaigai chuuzai appointments increase, the difficulty for mothers increases as well. Their children may have to survive in the U.S. school system for years to come, or they may be transferring back to Japan in a year. Mothers were often aware of the incongruity of these requirements that made their children's lives in the United States seem like one long homework session. "I wish I could tell my children to just go and enjoy their experience in America," many mothers would say. "But when I think of their future, when they go back to Japan and compete for college entrance, I have to keep taking away more and more time from them and keep a close eye on their progress in the Japanese curriculum."

At the same time, many Japanese mothers were frustrated and upset that they were ill equipped to help their children. Even grade school homework assignments are sometimes too complicated for the mothers to oversee, let alone those at the high school level. Asking an American teacher a question about their children's grades, filling out a simple school form, or reading a handout on the next week's school event becomes an arduous task involving dictionaries and hours of labor. Complicated procedures involved in transferring school records, fulfilling graduation requirements, and translating credits across national boundaries are mostly the responsibility of the mothers, who are often completely lost in the bureaucratic maze of two separate school systems. They collect tips from other, more experienced Japanese mothers to help their children's transition between Japan and the United States, but are often frustrated, unable to find answers to the specific problems of their own children.

Japanese wives often seemed fatalistic about these difficulties that they encounter during kaigai chuuzai and would shrug them off, saying, "Shikataganai," which roughly means that there was nothing they could do, that it was inevitable. Traveling is hard, but what else can they do, knowing that their residence in the United States will end one day as abruptly and impersonally as it began? The language of travel allows expatriate Japanese wives to articulate their predicament without explicitly blaming their husband or their corporate employer for the difficulties that they experience during kaigai chuuzai. They often explain the issues related to the foreign assignment, such as financial burdens, children's educational concerns, and their personal dissatisfaction, as the result of their traveling, or the inconveniences inherent in

long-distance movement and prolonged transiency. The more important kaigai chuuzai is in their husband's work life, the more strongly
these women consider domestic management abroad as their duty, and
the less likely they are to directly express their discontent and criticize
their husband's company. Generally, engineer husbands in Centerville
were themselves reluctant expatriates who regarded foreign assignments as neither enjoyable nor beneficial to their career, whereas many
of the New York and North Carolina expatriate workers defined their
foreign assignment as an integral part of their corporate work life. Thus,
I found the wives of semi-blue-collar workers in Centerville to be more
vocal critics of company policies than well-educated wives of white-
collar managers in New York and "globalized" high-tech workers in
North Carolina.

Beyond these differences, however, it is a common and fundamental
assumption of the expatriate corporate Japanese that they will sooner or
later go home to Japan, and that their real life there, which they left
suspended during kaigai chuuzai, will have to resume without interruption on their return. However, they find out, even before the end of
their kaigai chuuzai, that their sense of home/uchi is no longer beyond
question. That realization often occurs as a result of a corporate-paid
visit to Japan, intended as an opportunity for expatriate families to
recuperate from the rigors of living abroad and return refreshed to their
kaigai chuuzai locations.

ICHIJI KIKOKU: TEMPORARY RETURN AS TRAVEL

Every two years, most Japanese corporations pay airfare for their
kaigai chuuzai families to go home to Japan for a visit. This practice is
called *ichiji kikoku*, or "temporary return." Many male kaigai chuuzaiin
take frequent business trips back to Japan, but the great majority of
family members anxiously wait for this opportunity to go back to Japan
for a couple of weeks, to shed the stress of living in a foreign place, to see
their extended family and close friends, and to shop. More than anything else, many Japanese wives say, they feel the enormous relief of not
having to speak English, knowing where to go and what to say, being
able to understand the signs without thinking hard, being at home and
confident again, after two years of feeling lost, awkward, and unsure in
almost every public place in the United States.

Ichiji kikoku is not just a recreational trip, however. There are many things to be done during their brief stay, usually between two and four weeks, in Japan, and even before they commence their trip, preparation leading to it can be extensive and tiresome. Many families have homes, bank accounts, and other financial and material concerns to be taken care of; many others must pay obligatory visits to relatives, who would be upset if they left Japan without seeing them. They may have family members who are left behind in Japan, elderly parents or children during the "examination hell," whose affairs need to be attended to. If they have a child in junior high school or high school, they may plan on visiting prospective universities and high schools and meeting with admission counselors about their anticipated return to the Japanese educational system a few years later. Some families even time their ichiji kikoku during the entrance examination season in winter and early spring, so that the mother can stay with the child to render support during the time of trial.

Preparation to maximize their time in Japan often begins weeks earlier. Buying gifts for family and friends is a big headache for departing Japanese wives. In one of the group interviews, my informants diverged from the focus of our discussion on their homemaking activities in the United States and began to talk about the responsibility of gift giving when they went back to Japan. The gist of the conversation was that it was extremely hard to come up with good souvenirs in the United States, and that every time they went home, they spent agonizing weeks (let alone a large sum of money) shopping for suitable gift items for their relatives, friends, neighbors, and their husband's colleagues in Japan. Similar comments were repeated to me time after time by different groups of Japanese visitors/residents in the United States. The difficulty of bringing *omiyage* home was discussed openly and frequently. Women, more often than men, appeared to be in charge of omiyage purchase and distribution, which made sense as an extension of the household division of labor that puts women in charge of most domestic affairs and social activities in and around the home.

Ichiji kikoku can also be an unsettling experience for many. The discomfort of home, or the places and spaces in Japan where my informants thought they belonged, was a salient, and perhaps the most disturbing, feature of ichiji kikoku. For example, Ichigaya-san reflected, "I guess I became 'Americanized' without knowing it. My in-laws pointed out very quickly how outspoken I had become, and it wasn't a compliment." She also felt the constraints from people outside the family closing in on her in a way that never occurred to her before kaigai chuuzai.

"In our neighborhood [in the small town where the Ichigayas lived in Japan], everyone hangs out wash by eight o'clock in the morning. If you don't have your laundry out by nine, you can expect someone to drop in, to see if you are sick." This seemed intrusive to her after her experience in an American suburb, where she could do whatever she pleased when she wanted without remarks from her neighbors. Whereas some of her counterparts in New York were conscious of their watchful neighbors, Ichigaya-san's neighbors in Centerville seemed to keep a polite distance, thus giving her this sense of freedom.

Many others discovered the discrepancies between their images of home and the reality of homecoming during these visits to Japan. A few years of foreign experience had somehow made them "less Japanese" in the eyes of other Japanese, and their old uchi was no longer a completely relaxing or familiar place. Shimura-san, one of my New York informants, was not particularly excited about her kaigai chuuzai, and her choices of friends, children's schools, and leisure activities all indicated that she would rather remain within the expatriate Japanese community for the duration of her husband's foreign assignment. Yet, she told me that her last visit to Japan was very tiring. She found that Japanese in public places acted "rude and unkind" to one another, letting the door shut in front of others, never making eye contact, and never offering a hand to an elderly person or a mother with small children. These are the kinds of actions that she became accustomed to in the New York suburbs and came to expect from others without realizing it. When she arrived back at JFK Airport, she felt *hotto shita* (relieved). Earlier, I described how Japanese wives defined their homes as *hotto dekiru basho* ("the place where you can let out a sigh of relief"). Shimura-san, to her own surprise, discovered that Amerika had become her "home" of a sort: "I really didn't know this until then [after her ichiji kikoku], but this must mean that New York is where I live now."

Amerika is not just a Japanized pronunciation of the English word. It is a complex historical formation of the cultural and political other, a mirror against which Japan came to imagine its own totality as a modern nation-state. When this other becomes an everyday reality, the reactions of contemporary Japanese are decidedly mixed and contradictory. The Japanese vision of Amerika is at once frightening and utopian. I next explore how these conflicting images of the United States simultaneously influence the sojourning experience of chuuzai families and provide a space in which to reflect on their lives in Japan.

THE STORY OF A KIDNAPPED JAPANESE WIFE

The fact that Amerika becomes more familiar to Japanese families as time passes does not erase its foreignness. In fact, living outside Japan in a country that Japanese consider significantly less orderly and more violent deepens their ambivalence through their everyday engagement with it. In the perception of Japanese residents, Amerika is a *kowai tokoro* (scary or intimidating place), and corporate wives, many of whom do not speak English well and have no point of entry into American social life, particularly feel this as a negative aspect of living in a foreign country. Public spaces, where they have to interact with an indefinite number of strangers, are particularly "scary." In stores, shopping malls, doctors' offices, and children's schools, on trains and buses, or wherever these women consider American and "outside" of their familiar territory, they often feel left out and unsure, surrounded by American strangers who occupy the same physical space but share little else. Both Japanese news media and the entertainment industry often portray the United States as a dangerous country, with gunslingers, drug dealers, and psychopaths on the loose, and these images of Amerika color the Japanese perception of American society as a whole as dangerous, violent, and lawless. Even after Japanese arrive in their new American home in the quiet middle-class suburbs, this perception never completely leaves their mind. And surely, there are just enough cautionary tales around to keep them in a constant state of alarm about their foreign surroundings.

One such tale is the story of a kidnapped Japanese wife. It is a simple little story, an urban legend, if you like. A group of Japanese wives from the suburbs go shopping in Manhattan. While they are walking around on Fifth Avenue, one of them gets separated from the group. The rest of the group goes looking for her, but eventually they head back home, thinking their friend must have found her way home on her own. When they return home, however, they are shocked to find out that their friend never made it home. A few days later, she finally comes home in a disheveled state. She was kidnapped off the street by a group of black men armed with handguns, drugged, and raped. In her state of shock, she cannot say where she was held and what the perpetrators look like. In many versions, there is no mention of what happens to her after the incident; in others, she is sent back to Japan or she committed suicide out of shame.

I first heard this story in 1996 from a Centerville informant who had recently arrived from Japan and seemed quite concerned about personal safety issues in the United States. As an example, she mentioned "the kidnapped Japanese wife in New York." I later encountered other informants in Centerville, and then in New York, who also knew of this story. I was astonished to find the same story in the memoir of Tetsuo Yamazaki (1984), who served in the Japanese consulate general's office in New York for three years starting in April 1977. Yamazaki and other consulate personnel conducted a thorough investigation and concluded that the story was a complete fabrication. Regardless, as I found out in 1996, the story was still circulating in the expatriate Japanese communities around the United States as a factual story of a recent event, without losing its captivating and horrifying quality nearly three decades later.

In the analysis of folk tales and oral tradition, repetition and variations are important clues. Repetition signals which features are essential to the message of the story that is often disguised; variation, too, can give us clues about underlying themes that peek out somewhat unexpectedly (Dundes 1980). We can take a close look at the story of the kidnapped Japanese wife in a similar way—not just as a wild and unfounded rumor (which it most likely is), but as a reflection of something that is otherwise unspeakable, conveying meanings that are perhaps so ambiguous, contradictory, and disquieting that they can be told only in disguise.

Following are the components that appeared persistently in all the versions of the story that I know of:

1. Guns and drugs are always involved in the process of kidnapping.
2. Kidnapping happens in a public place that is, or ought to be, safe.
3. The victim is not only away from home, but also leaves her group.
4. The perpetrators are always black.

5. Rape always takes place.
6. The victim always returns home.
7. Japanese men are never part of the story.

It is immediately clear that, at one level, the story of a kidnapped Japanese wife reflects the widespread understanding of the United States as a dangerous country and the fear and concern of corporate Japanese migrants. Even before their residence in the United States, my informants told me, they were "well aware" of such problems in American society as the laxness of gun control, the pervasive use of illegal drugs, and the association between certain ethnoracial groups and violent crimes. These "factual" components about American society lends the tale a sense of reality (component 1). The crime statistics of Japan and the United States certainly validate their perception of danger; Tokyo, for instance, remains one of the safest cities in the world despite a recent rise in violent crimes. Japanese media have also been eager to portray the United States as a crime-ridden, violent society in which gun-toting criminals freely walk down the street, drug dealers haunt every neighborhood, and even ordinary citizens keep guns in their home. All these known elements of danger in American society are faithfully represented in the story, and two other aspects of the story further exacerbate the sense of danger: urban decay and the unpredictability that makes every person a potential target of violent street crimes. The kidnapping happens somewhere in New York City—I have heard Fifth Avenue, near Macy's, and the Port Authority bus station— in broad daylight, suggesting that there is no safe place in the urban public space in the United States (component 2).

The story also points to anxiety about the constantly changing urban environment, where a woman can be raped in a once reputable department store during its business hours (this was an actual incident), and where police presence does not guarantee even minimum security in a transportation center. The incident occurs while expatriate Japanese wives are on a shopping trip, again juxtaposing an innocuous commonplace activity and the unpredictable nature of street crime. Thus, the story of the kidnapped Japanese wife closely reflects the image of the United States as a kowai tokoro and appeals to expatriate Japanese residents with the terrifyingly immediate sense of danger thirty years after its original telling.

Component 3 is a clear caution against going soto and the disastrous outcome of going solo. Fear has its own ecology, as Mike Davis (1990) would have it, and produces its own material reality. It transforms the built environment of a city, generates physical boundaries, changes people's patterns of behavior and their interactions with others. Similarly, the story of the kidnapped Japanese wife has had an effect on the daily routines of Japanese residents in the United States, particularly on Japanese corporate wives in or near large urban centers, to whom the danger represented in the tale seemed immediate and real. When the story was initially spread in the late 1970s, Yamazaki (1984, 108) reports, many Japanese housewives stopped going into Manhattan altogether. But it had a more diffuse and broader impact on the actions of Japanese residents in U.S. cities. Even in places such as Centerville and North Carolina's Research Triangle, where violent crime rates were much lower than in New York, expatriate Japanese stuck together ever more closely to one another, went out to public places only in large groups, shunned public transportation, and kept their children in full-time Japanese schools, if possible. Fear, then, had the effect of keeping the boundaries tight around these Japanese communities and keeping women close to home.

On one hand, the fear of Amerika is generalized and broadly applied to anything non-Japanese that surrounds these expatriates. On the other hand, a closer look at the story tells us that the sentiment of *kowai* is racialized, and different *jinshu*, or "races," pose different degrees of threat to expatriate Japanese in the United States (component 4).[2] In their understanding of social hierarchy in the United States, expatriate Japanese seem to accept the moral authority and symbolic superiority of white Americans over Americans of color with little reservation. My Japanese informants in all three cities readily recognized African Americans (*kokujin*, or black people) and Spanish speakers with dark complexion (*hisupanikku*, or Hispanics) at the other end of the ethnic spectrum. Blacks and Hispanics are often categorically given a dangerous low-life status, depicted as people who infest the streets and steal from and harm innocent people. Most of my Japanese informants knew no one in particular from these ethnic groups, and they seemed to have no desire to get to know one. In Centerville and North Carolina, where ethnic/racial minorities other than African Americans are either small in number or socially invisible, expatriate Japanese understood race in the black-white dichotomy and tended to position themselves as privileged outsiders to the racial division, who, with their corporate affiliation and financial means, could afford to buy into the middle-class white enclaves, although they were not an integrated part of the local power structure.

In New York, where they encountered much more complex and fluid ethnoracial distinctions, the category of whiteness was further divided between "true" whites (*honto no hakujin*) and other, presumably less true whites. True whites had a stereotypical Northern European physical appearance (light complexion, blue eyes, blond hair), were middle-class, Christian, and English speaking, pretty much equivalent to WASPs. Other, lesser whites included those of Southern and Eastern European origins, Spanish speakers with lighter complexion, and Jews. While many informants in New York found that lesser whites were friendlier to Japanese than true whites, association with these lesser whites was not considered as desirable as with true whites.

The top and the bottom of the racial hierarchy were clear in the minds of most expatriate Japanese I spoke with, but they generally had very complicated and even contradictory relationships with Asian minority groups. Many Japanese informants expressed a sense of familiarity and cultural affinity with Japanese Americans and non-Japanese Asians. At the same time, they also seemed to find irreconcilable differences, and sometimes inferior qualities, in them. In northern New Jersey, where a large number of Koreans and Korean Americans live side by side with expatriate Japanese, the tension ran high at times in the neighborhoods and schools. The expatriate Japanese also seemed to have strained relationships with Japanese Americans and the long-term U.S. residents of Japanese origin as well. In interpreting the Japanese notion of racial difference, I find particularly instructive the work of Homi Bhabha (1994), who extends the "Freudian parable of fetishism" to understand the workings of racial stereotypes in colonial situations. Both a sexual fetish and a racial stereotype substitute for a lack/difference and give an appearance of presence/completeness; yet the presence of fetish itself is a reminder of the lack/difference that needed to be substituted to begin with. The split between knowledge and disavowal, similarity and difference, and wholeness and absence makes the stereotype ambiguous and unsettling and causes a pathological obsession and repetition. Thus, "the same old stories of the Negro's animality or the inscrutability of the coolie must be told (compulsively) again and afresh, and are differently gratifying and terrifying each time" (77). However, unlike the sexual fetish that must remain secret, the stereotype is made visible and public by the "epidermal" representation of difference, the dark skin. In this instance, the power operates skin-deep, by making and marking the racial difference on the surface, by "authorizing" discrimination by the darkness of the skin.

Many scholars have pointed out that the Japanese concept of race closely resembles that in the West, in which light/white skin is the symbol of superiority, high moral character, and progress, and dark/black skin signifies inferiority, low moral character, and backwardness (Creighton 1997). Whether this notion of racial difference is borrowed from the views of the white Western colonizers or has much deeper cultural/historical roots is not a question I am prepared to address at the present moment. I would like to point out, however, that most Japanese welcomed and even took pride in the "honorary white" status that their national economic power afforded them in apartheid South Africa, which seems to suggest the acceptance of colonialist racial hierarchy. This racial binary also appears to inform contemporary Japanese encounters with the foreign, both actual and imaginary. Japanese media are at once the reflection and the source of this racial ideology in which white faces and bodies are often idealized in Japanese TV programs, movies, magazines, and other popular representations, while non-Japanese with darker complexion rarely appear, and when they do, only as a grossly caricatured and comedic stereotype (Clammer 1997; Russell 1996).

The lived experience in the United States appears to confirm this worldview that expatriate Japanese bring with them: their encounter with the "foreign" in this "dangerous" country is always already racialized, in which criminal elements are darker, poorer, and/or non-English-speaking. In the story of the kidnapped Japanese wife, too, the danger of American society is visibly racialized and quickly naturalized by the dark skin of the criminal perpetrators, who represent the most foreign of foreigners. The relationship between danger (difference) and dark skin (metonymy of difference) runs bidirectionally: the dark skin condenses and makes visible the dangerous nature of this foreign country, and at the same time it explains away and normalizes that danger by the darkness of the skin as the signifier of low morality, criminal behavior, and danger. Thus, the difference is as soon dismissed as recognized, and the implicit connection between dark skin, foreignness, and danger accepted without ever being spoken of.

The most haunting and racially charged element of the story is perhaps the fear of miscegenation as represented in the sexual violation of middle-class Japanese women by American men of color (component 5). Earlier instances of sexual relations between Japanese women and foreign men had a decidedly Orientalist overtone, particularly during the postwar U.S. occupation period (Dower 1999). More recently, the cultural and economic dynamics of interracial sex appear to have changed dramatically. Karen Kelsky (1996) analyzes the connection between Japanese neonationalist ideology and the "yellow cab" phenomenon, the media obsession over Japanese women who seek out sexual relationships with foreign, particularly black, men. Essentialized cultural singularity is the main tenet of *nihonjinron*, the quasi-academic nativist discourse of Japaneseness (Minami 1994). Yellow cabs challenge this construction of Japanese national identity with their sexual relations with non-Japanese and elicit a fear of breached boundaries. At the same time, there is also an undeniable sense of fascination in the interracial sexual exploits of yellow cabs, which are made possible by the newly achieved wealth and power of the nation-state, whose citizens, even young female ones, can afford foreign lovers.

The story of the kidnapped Japanese wife certainly contains the same fear and fascination of interracial sex, but differs from the yellow cab phenomenon because its victim is a married middle-class woman who is kidnapped and raped against her will. In fact, it seems to resonate more strongly with the discourse of sexual violence in another time and place: the European colonial enterprise in Asia in the late nineteenth and early twentieth century (Stoler 1997). Commonalities between these two "colonial" discourses are uncanny. For instance, the sexual assault of European women by colonized men of color was perceived to be a real and immanent danger, though there was no evidence that sexual assaults actually took place in any kind of regularity to warrant such alarm (Stoler 1997). The fear of sexual assaults on European women stemmed from anxiety about the "degeneracy" that European colonials were believed to suffer for being outside of their own social and physical environment too long, and resulted in strict policing over European women who were, as agents of cultural reproduction, to safeguard the boundaries around Europeanness (Stoler 1997). It is not at all surprising that control over European women's bodies tightened at times of political uncertainty in the colonies.

The story of the kidnapped Japanese wife is likewise an unsubstantiated rumor that embodies Japanese anxieties about contamination and degeneration as a result of prolonged contact with otherness. Japanese have often postulated increased racial mixing as the root cause of the demise of U.S. power, as exemplified in the much criticized public statement of Prime Minister Nakasone in the 1980s that the IQ level of the American people was lower than that of Japanese largely because the lower intellectual levels of black and Hispanic Americans brought down the overall average. In turn, this "mixedness" of the United States is perceived as a threat to the "purity" of Japaneseness and becomes the source of danger that, eventually, gets to the expatriate Japanese and "creolizes" them. Here, a historical irony is hard to miss: in postwar Japan, the United States served as the model for Japan's modernization, and Japanese often measured their own progress by the number of years that they were "behind" American society. When Japan caught up with, and even arguably surpassed, the United States in the 1970s and 1980s, the decline of this formerly dominant other began to suggest the demise of Japan's own future self: the paved road toward hybridity and, by definition, degeneracy.

The convergence of race and sex is at the heart of the nativist construction of Japaneseness, in which "Japanese blood" is—both literally and metaphorically—the essence of Japanese cultural-national identity (Yoshino 1992). The maintenance of Japaneseness, symbolized by blood, depends on control over the bodies of women, who are themselves "other" to male selves that are native and authentic (Kelsky 1996, 185). What makes the story of a kidnapped Japanese wife particularly gripping is the sexual transgression over the maternal bodies of the good wives and wise mothers of the nation, designated exclusively for reproduction and nurturing (Allison 2000). Furthermore, the circulation of this story coincided with the time of Japan's transnational economic expansion and major power shifts between Japan and the United States and had the effect of limiting expatriate Japanese women's physical movement and urging them to concentrate on their domestic duties. The possibility of sexual assault scared expatriate Japanese wives into staying close to home (Yamazaki 1984), and many in the expatriate

Japanese community interpreted this story as a moral tale that the wives and mothers ought to dedicate themselves to their domestic responsibilities, and those who neglected their motherly and wifely duties deserved severe punishment.

There is, however, an inherent ambivalence in the telling and retelling of this "stereotype," a sense of uncertainty about the Japanese cultural-national self and its relation to racial others. This anxiety appears most poignantly in the misogynist ending of the story. After the devastating assault, the wife and mother "comes home," bringing that sexualized body and racial contamination to uchi/home, the locus of Japanese identity making (component 6). The only possible way to deal with this contamination is the erasure of the body: by dismissal or suicide. Racial and sexual differences thus articulate in the woman's reproductive-turned-sexual body, revealing the precarious foundation on which Japan's national identity is based. We, at least I, never hear about what happens to the female victim, except in those versions in which she commits suicide. The indeterminacy of the ending leaves room for speculation about what takes place after the interracial contact.

I also find curious the conspicuous absence of male Japanese figures in the story of the kidnapped Japanese wife (component 7). In the versions that I heard and read, there are no angry Japanese men looking for those black criminals, pressuring the local police authorities to crack the case or demanding apologies from the *New York Times*. This lack sharply contrasts with the aggressive, masculinist tone that nationalistic discourses in Japan often take on (e.g., Morita and Ishihara 1989) and suggests the impotence of the masculine-nativist self to assert its own agency either in the form of protection (of the threatened self) or punishment (of the intrusive other) in the context of interracial/transnational encounters.

Yoshimoto Mitsuhiro (1989) has argued that the impetus for *kokusaika* ("internationalization") does not oppose neonationalist ideology, but together, they make up yet another version of the Japanocentric worldview. Yoshimoto's words aptly summarize the discourse of Japanese national identity that was predominant at the time of Japan's unprecedented economic prosperity and publicly expressed sentiment of pride, and perhaps arrogance. But as I look at the story of the kidnapped Japanese wife at the end of the millennium, the ideology of

Japaneseness does not seem quite so tidily self-contained. If the stereo-type is a "suture," as Bhabha calls it, and discloses as much as it conceals the inherent ambiguity in authoritarian knowledge and identity, then every time the story of the kidnapped Japanese wife is repeated, it intimates the uncertainty of Japaneseness in the brave new world of global capitalism and, perhaps, creates a rupture in which social trans-formation becomes possible, if only a little bit at a time.

"A LONG VACATION"

A phenomenally popular Japanese TV show, *Rongu Bakeeshon* (A Long Vacation), evolves around a talented but painfully self-conscious young man, Sena-kun.[3] Struggling to make a living as a piano teacher, he ends up sharing an apartment with the neglected fiancée of his former room-mate, an attractive, wild, and honest woman getting "too old" at age twenty-nine to be a fashion model. In the end, Sena-kun finally over-comes his reserve, wins a national piano contest, and departs for Europe with his roommate-turned-fiancée. The last scene shows the two run-ning hand-in-hand toward a church in an unknown European city, late for their own wedding.

When I began my fieldwork in Centerville, Japanese women were still talking about this show, although its final season ended before my arrival. Every woman in her twenties or thirties whom I knew there had seen at least some of the episodes; a few were self-acknowledged "fa-natics," who rented the videos of the show to see it again and again. There are many reasons this romantic drama was so popular among female viewers in their twenties and thirties. The androgynous charm of the leading actor, Kimura Takuya, is the obvious one, the portrayal of a "trendy lifestyle" yet another. While trendiness itself may have proved too removed from the day-to-day reality of working women and house-wives, fantasy is cleverly interspersed with common real-life issues such as age discrimination against women, which in turn makes the story line easy for ordinary viewers to relate to. The predictable formula of romance and the happy ending are yet another source of attraction, which is more "assuring" and "comfortable" to watch, according to my informants. The most poignant theme in the drama is, however, the sense of in-betweenness that Sena-kun calls "a long vacation." From after college until the time when they have to stop chasing their youthful dreams, the twenty-somethings are on a sort of "vacation," in which they are allowed to take it easy and float around a little while before the reality of adult life kicks in. Sena-kun's initial failure to launch a successful musical career, his indecision about his future, and his painful insecurity about his own abilities as a musician and as an adult are all familiar themes of young adult life.

At first, lives of Japanese corporate wives abroad seemed to have little in common with that of Sena-kun, and I took the *Ronbake* craze among them to be an escapist activity. Yet, after a while, I began to wonder about the resonance between *Ronbake* and the kaigai chuuzai experience, both of which revolved around the odd sensation of being neither here nor there, of being in between, of being liminal. Like Sena-kun, who felt he had no choice but to float around in an extended period of idleness and console himself by thinking of it as a vacation, kaigai chuuzai forces Japanese corporate wives into an extended period of in-betweenness and a sort of liminality, a temporary existence removed from their "normal" life (i.e., the life they left suspended in Japan), neither here nor there (i.e., being Japanese but living in the United States), challenging and difficult, yet, in some novel ways, carefree and exhilarating. Sitting in their home away from home and hearing their own words coming out of the mouth of this fictional character, Japanese corporate wives, who frequently called kaigai chuuzai a form of travel and sometimes a prolonged vacation, seemed to identify this uncanny similarity. This is how the language of travel and vacation, with all its ambiguity and flexibility, became a compelling frame for me to tell the story of transnational mobility among middle-class Japanese wives.

THE WORD "VACATION" suggests a possibility of pleasure, of breaking away from the mundane, of rejuvenation and change. The language of vacation insists on allowing room for playfulness even in the task-driven traveling life. There is, for one thing, an escapist connotation in vacation and kaigai chuuzai that temporarily removes the traveler from her everyday life and allows her to indulge in pleasures otherwise impermissible (Crick 1989; Harkin 1995; MacCannell 1976, 1992). To some, a break from the part-time work that they hated but found necessary to make ends meet in Japan was a welcome change during kaigai chuuzai, made possible, in part, by increased benefits during the foreign residence. It also offered a temporary relief from heavy familial and social responsibilities. Some of the women were obligated to live with and take care of relatives while in Japan, and being away in the United States to them was indeed a vacation from the stress of having in-laws in their life. Some had quarrelsome relatives or nosy neighbors and felt it burdensome that they had to pretend to get along with them. When they left Japan for kaigai chuuzai, they were relieved that they did not have to deal with them for a while, at least not on a daily basis. This "freedom" for five years was a gift to those who expected to live with such social obligations their entire life. They refused to be encumbered by the temporariness of this freedom and sought to take full advantage of this time away from burdensome *ningen kankei* (human relations). In the words of one informant, "I enjoy [the freedom] while I can, and worry about the in-laws when [my husband] is called back to Japan!" Freedom from relatives encouraged some women to plan family vacations every time their husband could get away. Some redecorated their home exactly the way they wanted. With no one else around the house during the day, others rejoiced that they could take a nap whenever they wanted![4]

"Vacation" in Amerika also brings the pure pleasure of material abundance and conspicuous consumption to many Japanese housewives. Most expatriate Japanese families can afford to live in much larger homes and take many more vacations while in the United States. Many wives enjoy shopping for brand-name clothes and accessories, playing golf and tennis, and frequenting theaters and concerts, all made possible by additional income and benefits during kaigai chuuzai, relatively affordable leisure activities, and a higher standard of living that is beyond the means of an ordinary middle-class family in Japan. They also find foreign travel much more accessible and affordable from the United States, and many families take full advantage of this to take frequent trips within the United States as well as to Europe and Latin America. In this environment of affluence, they indulge in the "feeling of richness" (*ricchi na kibun*), even though it is theirs for a limited time.

These materialistic aspects of vacationing are practically interchangeable with vague yet persistent notions of "freedom," "democracy," and "happiness," that Japanese consider the essence of the American way of life. This understanding of "the American way" is often translated into consumption behavior. Living in Amerika and experiencing firsthand the material affluence of American society often leads

Japanese corporate families to affirm this "myth of the American way of life" (Clammer 1997, 96; also see Watson 1997). Japanese have their own reasons for thinking that taking part in the material life of the American middle class is also about experiencing the values and ideals that they have historically constructed and associated with the United States. Since Commodore Perry's "black ships" rattled Japan out of isolationism in the mid-nineteenth century, the place of Amerika in Japan's modern history was sealed as the salient symbol of what was to come forcefully from outside, that is, the powerful West and its message of modernization. This symbolic association was further reinforced during the postwar occupation period, when America's military and economic forces overwhelmed Japanese (Hosoya and Homma 1991). The effectiveness with which American hegemony permeated postwar Japan was, however, mainly due to the United States' ability to suggest an alternative, better way of life to the Japanese masses, who were in a state of material and psychological devastation. The well-behaved conqueror's lavish display of wealth seemed to quickly convince the great majority of postwar Japanese that their ultimate goal was to mimic Amerika, the utopian symbol of modernity, democracy, and affluence rolled into one (Dower 1999). From then on, Amerika became not just a common Japanese term for the United States of America, but also an imaginary place where the benefits of modern society, such as equal opportunity, personal freedom, and material comfort, are made accessible and affordable to the masses (see Watson 1997).

Amerika was the utopian other of postwar Japan, and if democracy and freedom were nifty political ideals that filled the postimperial ideological vacuum, ordinary Japanese also desperately needed something to fill their empty stomachs and their hallowed future. Amerika not only provided for the empty stomach (in the form of food and other material aids) to remedy the situation in an immediate and physical sense; it also presented the blueprint for Japan's future society in which material wealth for the masses is an assumption rather than an exception. To become Amerika, and to achieve its particularly materialistic version of modernity, is to consume all the happiness that money can buy.[5]

At the same time, a near obsession with luxury consumer goods (i.e., relative to the economic condition of most Japanese at that time) also betrays the anxiety that lurked behind Japan's "economic miracle": no matter how wealthy Japan-as-a-nation has become, it has failed to achieve the kind of democracy and happiness for "ordinary people," as implicated in Japan's postwar modernization agenda. The symbolic value of Amerika remained largely intact, despite the radical economic and social changes that took place in Japan in the late twentieth and early twenty-first century, because, in the minds of middle-class Japanese, their lives somehow could never truly match those of their American counterparts.

Whenever my female informants spoke of material wealth, their thoughts turned quickly to a more psychological "wealth" (*yutakasa*) and "leisureliness" (*yutori*) of middle-class America vis-à-vis the "poverty" (*mazushisa*) of their Japanese lifestyle. Amerika, my informants often told me, is the country of freedom, wealth, and individual happiness, where they and their family members could have a more human-like or humane lifestyle (*ningen rashii ikikata*). Such a ready opposition between the self and the other is overly simplistic, and I also suspect that my informants' utopian notion of Amerika is tied to the role of the United States in postwar Japan as the purveyor of democracy and modernity (Dower 1999). Yet, the expatriate Japanese interpretation of the life of "ordinary Americans" as "more human-like" is often based on their own daily observations in this foreign country. Irie-san, who lived in a middle-class neighborhood in Centerville, told me about her next-door neighbor who came home from work promptly at 5:30 P.M. every day, played with his kids, mowed the lawn, and lit up the grill to cook dinner for the whole family. "How is it possible," she asked, "for a man to have a full-time job to support his family, *and* come home early to do all that?"

If the transient life of a kaigai chuuzai family forces Japanese corporate wives to accommodate its difficulties and resign themselves to the mentality of shikataganai, a "long vacation" signifies an opportunity in which to escape from the trappings of everyday life in Japan, to reflect on their life-as-usual vis-à-vis foreign others next door, to consider different kinds of life that exist outside the bounds of their Japanese middle-class lifestyle, and to revel in the realization that there is a possibility for a better way of living than they were led to believe. It opens up a discursive space in which women can relieve themselves from the all-consuming duty of homemaking and caretaking, allow themselves to forget, at least for a little while, constraining realities that await them back in Japan, and reflect on more humane choices that they can potentially make for themselves and their family. Such openness, I argue, does not simply remain a convenient rhetorical device. During their long vacation, Japanese corporate wives also experience several profound changes in their lives that, in some cases, permanently change their relation to their domesticity, their family, and to Japan. Although the vacation will come to an end sooner or later, its transformative potential goes far beyond wishful thinking in some critical instances.

MATERNAL LOVE AS A TRANSFORMATIVE FORCE

Ruth Benedict's (1974) *The Chrysanthemum and the Sword* is a truly outrageous text. In this study of Japanese national character "at a distance," she misses so many points and makes so many overgeneralized remarks, yet, just when you are ready to abandon the book, she mentions something in passing that fascinates you. In one of those moments, Benedict analyzes the concept of *on*, or the indebtedness (on the part of a receiver) incurred by an act of kindness (of another person). She cites the famous story of Hachi, the loyal dog, who religiously went to the train station every day to find his master, even years after the master had passed away. She concludes: "The moral of this little tale is loyalty which is only another name for love. A son who cares deeply for his mother can speak of not forgetting the *on* he has received from his mother and mean that he has for her Hachi's single-minded devotion to his master. . . . It implies a return upon this indebtedness and therefore it means love" (100–101). If Hachi and a proverbial son are at the receiving end of this *on*, Hachi's master and a proverbial mother are the givers of this indebtedness, who are, in turn, obligated to care for their charge with similar devotion. To them, then, obligation and duty become another name for love.

The notion of obligation and duty as another name for love raises an important epistemological question for the anthropologists of Japan: When their Japanese informants speak of their yakume or shigoto, as so many of my female informants did, are they speaking of "obligation," or are they speaking of "love," as we understand the word in English? When anthropologists found Japanese women to be particularly role-oriented and dutiful to their responsibilities as wives and mothers, did they miss the point by taking their informants too literally? The story of Kayama-san made me wonder how, as an anthropologist, I could interpret and write about the unspoken love of a mother who, whether she came out and said it or not, deeply cared about her children, and how I could convey that motherly love can be a transformative force.

KAYAMA-SAN'S OLDER CHILD, a son, was in the eighth grade when he first came to Centerville and had a very difficult time in a local middle school there. After three years of confusion and discouragement, he decided to take entrance examinations at some Japanese high schools. The results were disastrous, and he became severely depressed and, according to Kayama-san, "did not speak a word" for the next four months. In the meantime, Kayama-san, as devoted a mother as she was, did everything in her power to help her son, from gathering information about Japanese schools, to regularly meeting with her son's teachers, to cooking his favorite food, to just being there for him. Once he recovered from the depression, he went back to his high school in Centerville, and his grades began to improve. Eventually, he entered a university in the United States and had a very fruitful college life. His college graduation was a proud moment for Kayama-san and her husband, who for a long time had no idea what would become of their son. After the ceremony, the son thanked his father and said that, after all, it was a good experience to come to America. At this point in her story, both Kayama-san and I began to cry. Ichigaya-san, who overheard us from the kitchen, brought over a box of Kleenex for us. If I am not mistaken, her eyes were turning red, too.

Kayama-san told the story of her son without ever directly referring to her feelings for him; instead, she talked in a calm, even manner (until she broke down at the end), mostly about her *yakume* (role) as a mother. Yet, all three of us knew that she was, indeed, talking about love. In turn, her son thanked his *father*, but not directly his mother, as though the silent devotion of his mother could be acknowledged only in this awkward, roundabout way. From her emotional outburst after relating her son's words, I believe Kayama-san understood her son's appreciation as a reward for *her* as well as for her husband. Japanese sensibilities demand that love and devotion never be mentioned, as they are conditioned to respond strongly to unspoken emotions. There was a sudden mutual understanding between Kayama-san, Ichigaya-san, and me that, despite different choices and experiences in our lives, we were coming from the same place at least on this issue of silent love.

In turn, the practice of verbalizing love in American families was a constant source of amazement among my Japanese informants. I was married to an American at the time of fieldwork, and many women asked me whether we had to verbally confirm our love all the time. When I replied, "Just occasionally," my informants would smile knowingly and say that, after all, some things had to remain Japanese in my otherwise American life. David Schneider (1968) suggests that love, in the middle-class American context, translates to a specific kind of relationship based on "enduring, diffuse solidarity," or a set of supportive and cooperative relationships that "does not have a specific goal or a specific limited time in mind" (52). Thus, love is to be constantly spoken of, because it functions as a signifier that stands in for something else: the promise of enduring, diffuse solidarity. When Japanese women talked about the daily expression of love between American couples, their tone ranged from benign curiosity and incredulity to ethnocentric smugness. In every conversation that I had about love and its verbal expression, my informants assumed that frequent verbalization somehow robbed this profound emotion of its precious meanings. To them, love should not stand for anything. Instead, every task, large or small, that they perform as a wife and a mother stands for their love. Perhaps the frequent reference to obligation and duty in their discourses of transnational homemaking indicates their affection for their family that became intensified through the experience of kaigai chuuzai.

This is not to say that love somehow makes everything okay. Love *is*, or at least can be, blind, defining women's work and its product, the home, as a source of personal satisfaction and masking the exploitive side of domesticity and motherliness. In the name of unspoken love, patriotic wives and mothers during World War II were expected to send their husband and sons to their military duties without tears, with pride and confidence. Today, in the name of unspoken love, corporate wives and mothers are expected to abandon their career, sacrifice personal interests, and take care of their husband and children away from their familiar environment, at remote stations in Japan and in foreign countries. Despite that, there is a subversive possibility in the obligation/love of a Japanese mother. For one thing, it provides a culturally sanctioned way for Japanese women to speak out against the hegemonic, which coerces them into the domestic roles to begin with. A family psychologist in Centerville whose Japanese background attracted many expatriate clients told me that Japanese wives tended to feel that it was immodest and unfeminine for them to complain about their own predicament, but often expressed their own adjustment problems in terms of their children's difficulties. So, she would often begin her work with her female Japanese clients by discussing "children's issues."

Children's hardship during kaigai chuuzai also gives Japanese mothers reason to complain to their husband's corporate employer, at times in a forceful, even obnoxious, way (Mori and Saike 1997). Obligation and duty in these contexts represent not only love, but the agency of Japanese women who may otherwise feel that the expression of such negative feelings is inappropriate. Being a mother of children growing up in a bicultural environment, with all its difficulties and rewards, was often a life-changing experience for my informants. Many of them had to reconsider what their roles should be in the lives of their children, and confront their own values that defined "wise" mothers and their "successful" children. In Kayama-san's story, the true reward was her son's recognition of his parent's love and the mere fact that she and her son made it through the difficult times.

Many other expatriate Japanese mothers found that their children came to them for advice and support more often than they would in Japan, and that their relationships with their children were closer and more personal. It may sound contradictory to a general understanding about the closeness of Japanese mothers and their children, but many of my female Japanese informants told me that Japanese teenage children normally "left" their parents and ceased to tell their parents about their daily lives outside of home. But in the United States, they had to learn to open up to their parents, since they had few alternatives outside the family.

"Teenagers [in Japan] rarely speak to their parents about anything," a mother of two teenagers told me. "Here [in the United States], they are sort of stuck with me, because they don't have as many friends to whom they can really open up, and also because they can't go anywhere without me [driving them]. This is an unexpected benefit of kaigai chuuzai for me. I'm so much closer to my children than any mother can ever be."

Many answers on the survey questionnaires I circulated also commented on the mother's improved understanding of her children, because the isolation and difficulty in a foreign country made a child and a parent more "friend-like," more like partners who work together to get through the tough times.

Motherly concerns for the children's well-being are often the avenue through which Japanese women become involved in volunteer activities and political movements in Japan (Motoyama 1995; Yoshitake 1994). Some of my informants found the means of social participation through children, by helping in school events or by volunteering at the school library. The children's school was also one of the most common places where these women met other Japanese mothers, and also one of the few places where they had direct and substantial interactions with American parents and teachers. Motherhood, in these cases, was the constructive force that connected women to the larger world outside of their home and that motivated their actions toward change.

HUSBAND AND WIFE

I was sitting stiffly in the living room of Yamagata-san, precariously navigating through one of my first semistructured interviews for my pilot study in Denver, Colorado. The phone rang halfway into the interview, and she got up to take the call in the kitchen. From the tone of her voice and the bits and pieces I made out from the living room, I guessed that it was from her husband. Soon, she returned to her seat, apologizing for the interruption. "It was my husband," she said, confirming my speculation. "He's been away on a business trip, and he was just checking in on me." I hesitated here, debating if it was wise to get into the topic of her husband, which, I was afraid, could be taken as intrusive. "Does your husband travel a lot?" I asked, finally deciding that this would be an innocuous enough question. She nodded. "Quite a bit, in fact. His clients are all over the United States." Then, with a shy smile on her face, she added, "When he is out of town, he calls me every day to make sure that everything is fine at home. It's been his habit for all these [over twenty] years, since we came to America. He would have never done that in Japan."

The point that I wish to make here is quite humble: It is the small things, the trivial things, that really matter in life. A beautiful new building, designed by the most coveted architect and loaded with the newest innovations in architectural technology, fails miserably when a visitor cannot find the button to flush the toilet. Or, imagine climbing into a shiny new SUV, only to realize that the cup holder doesn't accommodate your favorite coffee mug. This simple wisdom, when applied to the question of globalization, can be easily overwhelmed by high-minded, sophisticated theory, like that by Michael Hardt and Antonio Negri (2000), who conceptualize the novel world order that they call "Empire" as the manifestation of decentered, all-encompassing power. The only possibility of resistance or subversion resides in the multivalent nature of Empire itself, and ultimately, they imagine, the revolutionary movement will percolate through the use of technologically sophisticated methods of communication that eradicate distance and unite those around the world who act against Empire. Rather than arguing about the possibility of such a global revolution, my point is that, quite aside from such a large-scale change, the global, which increasingly affects life's most trivial details in all corners of the world, is also undermined precisely at the same location in which it intervenes with the minute, most mundane details of daily life. Our analytical attention to globalization must have a dual focus: while keeping the global reach of this new world order firmly in mind, we also need to pay attention, very close attention, to those small, minor, uninteresting facts of life.

After a few years in the United States, many things, large and small, can change in the life of an expatriate Japanese wife. She learns to get around in the local area with little trouble, celebrates Halloween, Thanksgiving, and Christmas at her own home or the homes of her husband's American colleagues, and exchanges cooking recipes with her neighbor. Domestic management and child care require interaction with the world outside her home, and she has created many points of connection with her foreign surroundings. While networking with other expatriate Japanese wives is critical, she has also found American neighbors to whom she can go with questions about local schools and neighborhood rules, and has hired an American woman as her English tutor, who can also give her advice about local customs and cultural events. At her children's school she has become friends with American mothers through volunteer work. Communicating with these foreigners through the barriers of language and cultural differences is hard, yet there are also delightful moments—when she finally gathered the courage to join the group of women from the neighborhood for a sidewalk chat, when she managed to negotiate prices with American customers at her garage sale, and when she found out that her *origami* lessons were very popular with her children's classmates. These community-based contacts can lead to other activities outside the domestic space, as the experiences of some of my informants indicate.

If these are all part of the constantly changing lives of expatriate corporate families, the biggest and most fundamental changes happen in their domestic life and in their family relations, particularly in the relationship between a husband and a wife. In Japan, both men and women assume that everybody's husband comes home late at night and everybody's wife takes care of all the family matters. Once in the United States, they realize that what they thought was ordinary (*atarimae*) is not so in another cultural context. By the end of their kaigai chuuzai, many changes, large and small, may become an integral part of life for these sojourning Japanese families, something that they carry with them no matter where they go next. For instance, who would imagine that the subversion of gender ideology that serves the interest of globalizing capitalism begins with the argument over who takes out the garbage on Monday morning? One of my female informants was tickled to tell me how she convinced her husband to help out around the house. She told her husband that American husbands in their suburban neighborhood took out the garbage, and should their American neighbors see her doing it, they would think of him as a "very bad husband." Her husband has not complained since about taking out and bringing in the trash bin.

And who ought to tend the barbecue grill in the backyard? Another Japanese housewife bought a charcoal grill for her backyard after seeing her neighbor's husband cook dinner nearly every night during the summer months. With two small children, it could be a real chore for her to prepare dinner every night and to occasionally entertain her husband's colleagues at home. "My husband will never help in the kitchen," she explained to me. "But now, I can railroad him into cooking, telling him that it's the 'American' custom for men to do the barbecue, without him thinking that he's really doing the cooking."

These are trivial details, indeed, and the Japanese women who told me these stories were more than aware of it. Their full-time occupation while in the United States is to create a Japanese home in a foreign place, in which the productivity of those expatriate workers and the boundaries around their Japanese identity are protected and maintained. In other words, these women become the conservative agents of cultural reproduction in the context of transnational mobility, which in turn constructs their middle-class femininity through the fulfillment of their ascribed gender roles as wives and mothers. As homemakers and family caregivers, the mundane becomes their domain, and the detailed and mind-numbing routine of domestic tasks takes up nearly all of their time and energy. They claimed that their lives in the United States were "boring" and often trivialized their own comments with disclaimers, such as "Oh, this is just silly stuff, but . . ." or "I'm sure you are completely bored to hear about this." Surely, the battle over a trash bin, the negotiation around a barbecue grill, and other such domestic trivialities do not have the tell-tale signature of earth-shattering, revolution-causing acts of resistance. In fact, there is little chance that these domestic decisions of the everyday will start a full-scale uprising among middle-class Japanese housewives. So why do they matter?

Kaigai chuuzai can result in serious marital difficulties and even divorce, because some wives begin to question normative gender roles (*Yomiuri Shimbun* 1998b). In my own fieldwork experience, divorce between expatriate Japanese wives and husbands was extremely rare. Many women instead became more outspoken about the burden of domestic responsibilities. It was often through everyday practices in and around their home that they began to renegotiate their domestic relationships. In addition to the instances above, many husbands/ fathers also become more involved in financial management and educational decisions for their children. Japanese wives, who are used to making household purchasing decisions and supervising children's education, may find it desirable to involve their husband in the United States, particularly in the beginning, because their communication skills and local knowledge are insufficient to do these tasks alone. Domestic tasks are shared in many households and become a more or less permanent practice, even after the wives become more familiar with the local surroundings. These practical changes have a subtle yet definite impact on the Japanese wives' perception of their relationship with their husband. Domestic management, previously the sole responsibility of the wife, becomes a joint responsibility of both the husband and the wife, and many of my informants commented that they welcomed the increased presence of their husband at home and enjoyed the sense of closeness and egalitarian partnership as a result of shared family responsibilities.

THE WORK-HOME CONNECTION

My questions about husbands most often drew hesitant responses, and at times outright refusal to answer, from my female Japanese informants. Their hesitation reflects the clear division of labor between men and women in middle-class Japanese households and the women's general ignorance of, and lack of interest in, their husband's daily work routine (see chapter 3; Allison 1994; Imamura 1987). On the other hand, an average Japanese middle-class wife during kaigai chuuzai has more direct connection with the corporate world of work and becomes a more engaged member of a corporate community than she ever did in Japan, through *attendo* (entertaining corporate guests at home), through corporate-sponsored women's organizations, or in company-held social events (such as a Christmas party) that include employees' families. Wives can also become more involved in their husband's work and begin to understand the corporate world of work better than they could ever imagine in Japan. Corporate entertaining, for example, is an added burden to the expatriate Japanese wife's domestic work load; yet it also gives the wives an opportunity to meet their husband's colleagues and clients, to overhear business-related discussions, and to feel a sense of connection to his work. At times, the organization of work at the chuuzai location also makes it necessary for the wife to stand in as a secretary for her husband. As the separation of work and home is more complete in Japan (due to the distance between business centers and suburbs and the organization of work that rarely spills over to domestic spaces), these women might not have found out anything about their husband's work, even after years of marriage and coresidence.

Through these experiences, the connection between corporate interests and women's homemaking labor also becomes clearer than ever. This realization often brings wives and husbands close as partners. As the anecdote about Yamagata-san and her husband indicates, the bond that develops between a husband and a wife during kaigai chuuzai, when they have only each other to rely on, is experienced as qualitatively different from that in Japan, where the husband and the wife have many other social relationships and many safety nets other than marriage. An important factor in the changing husband-wife relationship is the distance from the interpersonal networks and social activities in Japan that keep married couples apart from each other for most of their waking hours. The social lives of married Japanese men and women are largely gender-segregated, and a husband and a wife (perhaps with the exception of the honeymoon period) rarely spend their leisure time together as a couple. In times of need, they often turn first to their homosocial networks outside the marriage—extended families, corporate socialization groups, and long-term friends—for support, encouragement, and advice. Kaigai chuuzai pulls a Japanese husband and wife out of their respective, and largely independent, webs of human relationships and puts them together in a strange place with little external support. I heard a practically identical line from different informants in different chuuzai circumstances: "Kokodeha, otagaishika tayoreru aitega inai [Here in the United States, we only have each other to rely on]." In other words, expatriate Japanese husbands and wives in the United States not only depend on each other to share the responsibility of work, but also seek personal support and camaraderie in each other—in many cases, for the first time in their marriage. Once established, this sense of partnership seems to last, even after the husband and wife develop new personal networks in the chuuzai location. To many of my informants, this is "the best thing" that happened to them during kaigai chuuzai.

At the same time, some women begin to speak up against their husband's corporate employer, often through their husband but sometimes more directly. Some of my informants laid a guilt trip on their husband, using the hardship of homemaking in an unfamiliar place as a way of gaining more assistance in household matters. At a large Japanese-owned company, the Japanese Wives Association was vastly unpopular among the wives of their expatriate employees, who found this corporate-sponsored organization "stuffy." In the end, the Japanese managers, who got tired of listening to the wives' complaints about the association, abolished the organization altogether. In another case, a group of wives whose husbands all worked in the same Japanese-owned company went directly to the corporate management and demanded that their corporate entertainment duty be reduced. The critique of kaigai chuuzai practices may also be publicly voiced under the guise of a personal narrative. Many of the published memoirs of former corporate wives reveal, through the details of everyday life both abroad and back in Japan, the negative effects of displacement and the difficulty of homecoming after kaigai chuuzai. Written from the personal view of an ordinary wife and mother, these memoirs often contain both implicit and explicit criticism of the corporate dominance over middle-class Japanese families and the narrow definition of Japaneseness that does not tolerate difference.

It is also important that these domestic changes come with some significant modifications in the male world of work. Leniency toward male workers' absence for family-related reasons is a common occurrence in foreign subsidiaries of Japanese companies, as the wives of their expatriate Japanese workers do not have anyone else to turn to for support and assistance in household matters. Japanese corporations are also forced to compromise their strict work regimen and reduce work-based socialization in response to the reaction of American employees and/or to avoid confirming the negative perception that Japanese corporations work their employees to the detriment of their private life. As male Japanese workers spend more time at home with their family, they often find themselves enjoying their expanded roles at home and depending more on their wife's support than ever before. While corporations make these modifications in the name of economic interest, they inadvertently blur the boundaries between work and home, and between male and female work.

TRAVELING AS CRITICAL PRACTICE

These three moments of change—maternal love, the relationship between husband and wife, and the work-home connection—combine to suggest an even more fundamental and perhaps the most significant change caused by transnational mobility. That is the increasingly unstable definition of the "everyday." In the working of power that Antonio Gramsci has called "hegemony," ideology is diffused in social practices and naturalized customs, blended into our everyday life as "normal," "natural," and "mundane." Everydayness masks the ideological functions of the activities that take place in the home, such as eating, keeping clean and healthy, sleeping, making love, and being able to get up and go to work the next day. These activities nourish us as individual persons, but also make us productive workers and useful citizens, ideal subjects of modern power, and allow us to reproduce more people like ourselves who will continue to perpetuate the cycle. Dislocation, it seems, can trigger critical awareness of this everydayness and call its insignificance into question. When the mundane homemaking activities are dislodged from their naturalized social and cultural contexts and are relocated to an unfamiliar place, suddenly a crack appears on the otherwise smooth surface of ordinariness. Simple daily acts that one used to take for granted, such as running to a nearby grocery store or exchanging greetings with a neighbor, are no longer so simple or mundane when they involve speaking in a foreign language or becoming confused and embarrassed. Domestic routines are no longer routine when one sees a neighbor with a different routine.

Corporations, though unwittingly, participate in this destabilization of the mundane. They make explicit the connection between masculinized work and female domesticity as they urge the wives of their male expatriate workers to perform their duty as the accompanying wives. At the same time, the work routine at their overseas subsidiaries is modified to accommodate the bicultural workforce and to allow some flexibility for their expatriate workers to spend more time with their family, which further reveals the arbitrariness of the strict work regimen required in most of their Japanese facilities. The revelation that work and home are, after all, not two separate domains but are interconnected and interdependent comes as the result of the conscious appropriation of women's domestic and reproductive labor by transnational companies. Because the function of uchi as the location of subjectivity making is made more visible, unexpected change and subversion can also take place and cause fundamental transformations in the personal relationship at the core of the nuclear family, the reproductive unit of industrialized society. The majority of Japanese corporate wives were able only partly to recognize and articulate to me this potentially transformative moment; in most cases, their awareness was incomplete, inarticulate, and fleeting. Particularly as these women approach the end of their kaigai chuuzai, they often turn away from these possibilities of change, if unwillingly, and instead shift their attention to the question of homecoming.

Japanese wives and mothers begin to worry as they approach permanent return to Japan, and understandably so, given the often jarring experience reported by their predecessors. They know that a few years of foreign experience make returnees from foreign assignments "less Japanese" than other Japanese, and that the return to their old lives in Japan may prove even more complicated than adjustment required in a foreign country. While they have to undo the effects of transnational experiences on themselves and their family, they themselves have little to return to, having quit their jobs and dropped out of other extra-domestic activities to go abroad. Then return to Japan becomes another experience of displacement and discontinuity, as they bury the memories of their foreign home and deny the value of their own labor that created that home.

CHAPTER SIX

Home Again

IN NOVEMBER 1996, during my fieldwork in the Greater New York area, I returned to Centerville to visit Kawagoe-san, who was preparing to move back to Japan in a few weeks. When I arrived, her home was in an appropriately chaotic state: furniture all out of place, clothes scattered about waiting to be organized and packed, stacks of boxes in the corner. Irie-san took me aside and told me that the transfer decision came at the last minute and that Kawagoe-san had been running around since to get everything ready for the move. Kawagoe-san's husband was in Japan, seeing people in the Tokyo office in preparation for his transfer and, because they did not own a house in Japan, looking for a place to live.

Kawagoe-san was visibly nervous as she waited for her husband's call. He had already been out apartment hunting for a couple of days and was finding out that most of the desirable properties close to his work were out of their reach. He started to work his way down a train line that would take him to his new office, further and further away from the city center. The call came when Irie-san and Takeda-san came over for dinner and the four of us were eating, talking, and having a good old time. Kawagoe-san jumped up, walked into another room with the phone, and did not return for a good half-hour. When she came back to the table, we learned that she and her husband were split on their preferences on two apartments. Kawagoe-san wanted the place that was more convenient for grocery shopping, was close to an elementary school for Miho, and promised more privacy for the growing family. Kawagoe-san's husband, on the other hand, wanted the other apartment, which was closer to the train station.

"Which one is he going to decide on?" Takeda-san ventured to ask, to which Kawagoe-san grunted in reply.

"I'm sure he'll think of what's good for you," Irie-san guessed.

"That's what *your* husband would do, since he is a kind person," snapped Kawagoe-san. "But I'm not so sure about mine."

"Did you tell him what you wanted?" I asked.

"Sort of."

I was a bit irritated at her indecisive answer. "What do you mean by 'sort of'?"

Irie-san winced, and Takeda-san was signaling me to back off. But to me, this seemed like a big decision, and she was the one who had to take the brunt of it if they moved into a place that would make her miserable. As far as I was concerned, Kawagoe-san's husband was being unreasonable, and it did not make sense that Kawagoe-san, usually outspoken and pragmatic, seemed hesitant to express her opinion to him. Sheepishly, Kawagoe-san began to explain how she had a hard time asking her husband to accept her choice because she could tell that he really liked the other place. Then, suddenly regaining her usual sense of sarcasm, she added, "Besides, I don't really have much faith in him. I have a feeling that that selfish screwball is going to do what he likes anyway."

FOR THE MOST PART, Kawagoe-san handled the moving arrangements with her usual pragmatism; nonetheless, she did seem irritable sometimes and she revealed her anxieties to some of her close friends. This anxiety of homecoming is by no means unique to Kawagoe-san, who had three young children and many reasons to be unsure about her family's future in Japan (see chapter 2). Her indecision about apartment selection reflected how divided she felt between her own worries about reestablishing a home in Japan and her concerns for her husband's difficult situation at work. It is the combination of many pressures such as these that makes everyone anxious at the end of their "long vacation." Organizing and executing the move falls primarily on the wife, and there are many factors that can go wrong or become complicated. In addition, it is the time for the wives to "unmake" the home away from home, the time to take apart the product of their work, and the time to think about, often with a considerable amount of self-doubt, what they have accomplished in the past several years as the wife of a kaigai chuuzaiin.

On one occasion, Kawagoe-san talked to me about her disappointment with the fact that the only thing she had to show for her five years of work was a couple of children. "Not that there is anything wrong with having children, but just giving birth to children left and right in itself can't be considered a real accomplishment."

She was referring to the tendency of expatriate Japanese wives to start having children soon after their arrival in the United States, out of their need to create "something to do." "Just giving birth" did not fulfill Kawagoe-san, because she recognized it as the endeavor of the Kawagoe family as a whole, and not her own. She felt that she needed an individual project, aside from the collective undertaking of raising a family. She went on to tell me her plans to learn how to access the Internet and to start her own business when she went back to Japan. She was going to collect used children's clothes while she was in the United States and sell them to Japanese mothers who found recycled American clothes to be a novelty. It seemed like a very clever business idea that could only come from an expatriate corporate wife and a mother of two (soon to be three) young children, who shopped frequently at resale shops and garage sales and also regularly hosted her own garage sales. She was trying to take advantage of the lower prices of children's clothes in the United States, and of the fact that many Japanese have a taste for things American and will pay a premium for, for example, used Levis from the United States. She was also calculating that, if her business took off, it would give her opportunities to regularly go back and forth between Japan and the United States.

Kawagoe-san's life back in Japan did not fulfill these expectations. She did start a small business of used children's clothes, but it never became profitable. She and her husband bought a house a year after they returned to Japan, and her daily routine centered around the home, punctuated by grocery shopping, chatting with other housewives in the neighborhood, and, once her children started going to preschool and elementary school, occasional afternoon outings with friends.

"It was like a dream," Kawagoe-san said of her five years in Centerville. "It was almost like it never happened now that we are back in Japan."

Kawagoe-san herself enjoyed living in the United States and saw no particular reason to return to Japan. In fact, four years after kaigai chuuzai, she often finds herself "wanting to go back" (*kaeritai*) to the United States, and she laughs at herself for such a "confused" state of mind. At the same time, she says, she knew it was best for her family to return to Japan, and as a member of this family unit, it was also the best decision for *her*. Kawagoe-san's choice resonates with those of many other Japanese corporate wives who return to Japan regardless of their own desire.

At the end of a "long vacation," each Japanese corporate wife is compelled to look back at her life in the United States, figure out what kaigai chuuzai really meant for her, and get ready to plunge into the post–kaigai chuuzai phase of her life. In this chapter, I consider the process through which corporate wives prepare themselves and their family for homecoming and examine different conclusions that Japanese families make at the end of their "vacation."

UNMAKING A HOME

If homemaking in a foreign place is made possible by continuous, tedious work of the everyday, the *unmaking* of that home requires equally hard and mundane labor, accompanied by a considerable amount of anxiety and worry. The husbands are preoccupied with their professional concerns related to transfer; they may have already begun to get involved in a new project in Japan. The wives are usually the only adult member of the family who takes care of all the familial and household demands of the move. For them, the homecoming after chuuzai will be a complicated event, as they will not only have to reinitiate their homemaking project back home, but they will have to undo the effects of transnational experiences on themselves and their family. The end of Kaigai chuuzai, for many of them, proves its most stressful phase.

It often seemed as though Japanese wives and mothers began preparing for the eventual return to Japan as soon as they settled into their new life in the United States. Almost every decision that they made upon arrival, from housing to furniture purchase to children's schooling to networking with other women, was contingent on how long they imagined they might stay at that particular location. This mentality was particularly strong among the mothers of school-age children whose long-term educational future was threatened by the transnational move. Goto-san, for instance, imagined that her husband would be in Centerville for five years, given precedence and the length of his working visa. When they arrived, her sons were in the seventh and ninth grades. In two years, she would have to decide whether to send her younger son back to Japan for high school (which starts in the ninth grade in Japan) or keep him in the United States until graduation from high school. The latter option was somewhat risky, because in Centerville, a student had to pass several comprehensive subject tests to receive a high school diploma. If he did not pass them by the time his father was due back in Japan, he would have to remain in Centerville by himself or return to Japan without a diploma. Her older son was in an even more precarious position. He would have to get a high school diploma in Centerville to go to college either in Japan or the United States, yet he was finding it difficult to keep up in a foreign language. These kinds of considerations were very common, and in most cases, each family had to make the best choice available without knowing exactly how long they were going to be overseas.

There are usually about three months between the corporate order and the actual report date at the new assignment. However, in many cases, there are earlier, informal indications of upcoming transfer, giving families up to a year to make preparations; they may start packing and shipping items, shorten their apartment lease, get their children to spend more time on Japanese than English, and so on. They have to be careful, though, because the date of reassignment may be pushed back at the last moment. Takeda-san's husband's reassignment was postponed twice, for six months each time, after they sold their Centerville home and sent off all off-season clothes. As a result, many moving tasks have to wait until the transfer is certain, and the last three months of kaigai chuuzai tend to be a very busy, stressful time for the women. If the family owns a house, they have to sell it; if they rent, they have to sublet or break the lease and pay penalties. They have to decide which pieces of furniture to take back to Japan, to sell, or to abandon. They have to sort all the family belongings and send them back to Japan in stages, starting with the large surface shipping six weeks before the departure date, a much smaller shipment by air a week before, and then the luggage they carry with them on their flight. If their children are in school, they have to arrange to have school records transferred. If any family member has long-term medical needs, his or her medical records have to be transferred as well. At the same time, they have to make arrangements to restart their life back in Japan, finding a place to live, reopening bank accounts, filing paperwork for children's transfer to a Japanese school. Few of these tasks can be managed long-distance, so either the husband or the wife (or both) have to go to Japan at least once to take care of them. I witnessed several of my informants going through this process of disassembling and repacking to go back to Japan, and all of them felt overworked, out of control, frustrated, and exhausted. They are working all the time, calling people, driving to offices and schools and back, and so on and so forth. They all had long and complicated checklists, and many of the items could not be checked off until the last minute. The pressure to get everything done in the limited time and in the right sequence is enormous.

In addition, moving back to Japan involves intangible sources of stress that are of equal, if not greater, importance to this whole process. For one thing, they have to disassemble the place that was, however temporary, their home. What used to be their living room, kitchen, and bedrooms become strange spaces with stacks of boxes; what used to be familiar and comforting becomes empty and strange; the home, the place where they lived, reverts back to its earlier state, a piece of real estate on the market. For women, it is also the undoing of all the work that went into turning an anonymous physical space into the family home. That has to be an unsettling experience for anyone. Whether they enjoyed living in the United States or not, it takes time to prepare for *kikoku*, the return to Japan. Many women told me they have to make a psychological switch, gradually distancing themselves from life in the United States and starting to plan for their lives back home. Three months are much too short for this process to take place before they plunge into the more tangible tasks of moving.

When Japanese corporate families go home to Japan at the end of their kaigai chuuzai in the United States, they are expected to slip back into their old niche in the world of middle-class Japanese as quickly and smoothly as possible, and this is no easy task. The husband will have to return to the rigidity of the corporate work regimen and complicated human relationships at the corporate headquarters. The wife will have to take on heavy family obligations, such as taking care of elderly parents. Mounting educational pressure will affect the mother as well as her children. Extensive tutorials or cram school that these returnee children often require to catch up with the Japanese curriculum may cause considerable financial strain, and the mother may have to take a part-time job or find piecework. Returning corporate families also expect that their experience of the "more human" way of life in the United States will slowly fade to the background. I found most of my female informants to be pragmatic and resigned about all this when faced with an imminent return to Japan. After all, their life in Amerika was a long vacation, and all vacations had to come to an end. Everyone expected to get busy unpacking, setting up a new home, getting adjusted to small living quarters and nosy neighbors, attending to problems their children might encounter in Japanese schools. The phrase *shikataganai* ("there is nothing they can do") enters their narratives once again, as they try to convince themselves to go with the flow.

SELF/OTHER

Confronting the foreigner whom I reject and with whom at the same time I identify, I lose my boundaries, I no longer have a container . . . I lose my composure. I feel "lost," "indistinct," "hazy."

—JULIA KRISTEVA, *Strangers to Ourselves*

The foreigner without, to paraphrase Julia Kristeva, is only the reminder of foreignness within, and at the recognition of this, the distinctness of the self becomes fleeting. Expatriate life—used here in the broadest meaning of the term, that is, life away from home and not by personal choice—forces this confrontation with foreignness despite all the mechanisms of protection, as daily exposure to something and someone foreign at once familiarizes the extraordinary and de-familiarizes the ordinary. This outcome is often shocking for these protected travelers who did not anticipate such an experience and are unable to respond flexibly. If Japanese women are supposed to uphold and protect the boundaries around their Japanese home, and by extension their family's Japanese selves, an extended stay in a foreign place has an unsettling effect on what they once thought stable and unquestionable. The discomfort of home, or the places and spaces in Japan where my informants thought they belonged, was a salient, and perhaps the most disturbing, feature of transnational experience for Japanese corporate wives. Most of these changes take place gradually and quietly over the course of kaigai chuuzai. Mothers and wives, who tend to be very insightful about the changes in their husband and children, are often quite unaware of changes within themselves, or at least so they claimed to me. There are indications, however, that they had thought about their own changes well before the end.

Many of my female informants, for instance, had a glimpse of their future homecoming when they went back to Japan for a brief visit (as described in chapter 5). They were quick to point out the tolerance and civility with which their American counterparts conducted themselves and treated others, in contrast to the narrow-mindedness that they perceived to be common among Japanese both overseas and at home. A strong sense of admiration and affinity, and even identification, also developed between my Japanese informants and the allegedly foreign American lifestyles and values, as they were apparently able to relate to the American way of life and criticized their own Japanese ways. Granted, my female Japanese informants' views of middle-class American life were partial and idealized. But in their understanding, there is a real and uncanny resemblance between their ideals of happy family life and the family life of the Americans they saw throughout their kaigai chuuzai.

The construction of Japanese uchi/self depends on the contrast against the foreign soto/other—in the particular situation of my informants, Amerika. If this soto/other is no longer so distant and strange, what becomes of their uchi/self? This is precisely the question that the naturalized conception of uchi/home/self avoids and silences. In Japan, everybody's husband is too busy to spend any time with the family, and women think of it as *atarimae*, or ordinary and natural. Nearly every Japanese wife I knew talked extensively about the differences between Japanese and American family life, while assuring me that they had very little to do with local Americans and that they understood very little about their customs and lifestyles. Once in the United States, they realize that what they thought was atarimae was not so in another social context: unlike their own husband, American husbands create time for their family on weekends. As they see different forms of family or husband-wife relationships, a question begins to take shape in the minds of expatriate Japanese wives: Why doesn't my husband care about his family?

When asked, these women were also quite clear about their own cultural affinity to Japan. They called themselves Japanese and were conscious that they were more comfortable communicating in Japanese, that they could never assimilate enough to pass as an American by any means. At the same time, they were aware that they could potentially be seen as *henna nihonjin* ("strange Japanese"), those who are originally from Japan but become influenced by foreign culture. Their reflexivity comes not from their acculturated status; they speak instead from a unique vantage point, somewhere in between two places and two sets of cultural assumptions, both of which they consider their own in some respects and alienating in others. They identified themselves as Japanese and thought that they would die Japanese, no matter how long they lived outside Japan. Yet, their knowledge of what's outside makes them strange inside.

I knew that the same women watched their American neighbors carefully and tried to imitate in their own household what they found desirable about middle-class American life. They celebrated major American holidays in their home away from home, took every opportunity to travel around the United States, practiced American folk art, ate American food, and eagerly looked for different ways of incorporating the pieces of this cultural other into their life. Through these everyday acts of homemaking abroad, and through their seemingly trivial decisions to incorporate something foreign into their home, they are making indelible marks of foreignness on their uchi/home/self although they rarely take due credit for their creativity in using and consuming foreign images, ideas, and customs to refashion everyday life for themselves and their families.

The familiarity of things foreign and the strangeness of things Japanese suggest a possibility of an entirely new way of constructing the self. Those moments when Japan seemed strange and Amerika more familiar registered for these women as a jarring, even frightening experience, and they panicked at the confusion of not knowing where they belonged. This is perhaps why the majority of Japanese women felt conflicted about their own experience of self-other ambiguity and often dismissed the importance of such an experience. Many expatriate wives wonder, in fact, whether they and their family can truly go home after the realization that there are different opportunities outside Japan and that the lifestyles that they always assumed to be a given inside Japan no longer are desirable or even tolerable (Goodman 1990; White 1992).

As long-term and multiple foreign assignments become more common with increasing globalization, the expatriate family's senses of in-betweenness and homelessness grows stronger. Expatriate Japanese families have to, and very often want to, learn the ways of the locals in the United States in order to make their lives there more meaningful and enjoyable. At the same time, they fear the loss of belonging and cling to Japan as their cultural home even as they, if unwittingly, begin to see Japan from a distance. Or, as one of my male informants in New York pointed out, expatriate Japanese families live in a "double structure," with their consciousness split between the ideology of uchi and the newly emerging hybridity of their family life away from Japan.

Anticipating the potentially difficult homecoming after kaigai chuuzai, 10 percent of about 120 Japanese corporate wives whom I met for interviews and/or informal interaction chose to shut out as much foreign influence as possible from their lives in the United States.[1] Particularly in the New York area, it was quite possible to remain culturally "as Japanese as in Japan," or even "more Japanese than in Japan" (Flory 1989). With full-time Japanese schools and day care centers, stores and other businesses with Japanese-speaking attendants, and various expatriate organizations, it was not difficult for Japanese wives to live in the Greater New York suburbs without speaking much English for the duration of their chuuzai assignment. Although these are relatively rare cases among my informants, I suspect that this is an underrepresented segment of the expatriate Japanese population in my data, because they are more conservative and thus much less likely to participate in my research.

At the other extreme are those who decide to make the United States their permanent home, whose stories follow in the next section. Approximately 80 percent of the women between these extremes are torn between their own conflicting needs and desires and that of their family. They see many positive aspects to their life in the United States, such as a more leisurely pace of life, warmth and friendliness in the local community, civility and equality extended even to foreign residents, and closer ties among family members. Some wish they could stay, but in the end, they determine that, all things considered, it is best to return to Japan when the foreign assignment is over. I heard from Kawagoe-san and many other women that if it was just about them, they would prefer to stay in the United States. However, they almost invariably continued, their children would be better off with a Japanese education, their aging parents and in-laws would soon need their assistance on a regular basis, and their husband's career opportunities would be better in Japan.

Nevertheless, many of these women also hoped to retain some of the positive changes that had taken place in their life while in the United States. They wondered, for example, whether their marital relationship could remain close and egalitarian even though their husband would no longer be able to share domestic responsibilities. Some thought about continuing their English studies, or the possibility of turning their newly acquired language skills into a new work opportunity back in Japan. Five of my key informants from Centerville and New York went back to school during their stay in the United States with their husband's support and planned to teach English or American culture when they returned, once they saw their family members readjusted to life back in Japan. They want to go home, in other words, with a piece of the other that they learned to enjoy and admire. But for the time being, their own needs and hopes will have to take a back seat.

While these individual choices and preferences played a significant part in how Japanese corporate wives managed the end of kaigai chuuzai and the transition back to Japan, there were also larger social and economic forces that were far beyond their control. For those kaigai chuuzai families who were abroad in the 1990s, the even larger force of the global economy affected their homecoming outlook: the collapse of the so-called *baburu ekonomi* (the bubble economic boom) in 1991 and ensuing *Heisei Fukyo* (the economic recession of the Heisei era). An increasing number of chuuzai families are also exploring alternatives to going back to Japan, and I will discuss several cases to illuminate these alternative choices.

RETURNING HOME AFTER THE BUBBLE

The collapse of the bubble economy in the early 1990s had a decisive impact on the pattern of kaigai chuuzai.[2] Further tightening of already shrinking chuuzai benefits and subsidies was immediate, and in the following years Japanese corporations, no longer flush with excess capital, began to scale down their overseas investments. As a result, many kaigai chuuzaiin were called back to Japan or reassigned to different locations and tasks that were more economically prudent. In the mid-1990s, the number of expatriate Japanese residing in the United States dropped for the first time since the end of World War II (MITI 1996). In this climate, homecoming began to take on a whole new meaning. For one thing, Japan's sagging economy made the prospect of return less attractive than ever before. Those who owned a house in Japan lost much of their investment and were returning to negative equity. Corporations expected no growth in the near future, lessening career opportunities for husbands; the possibility of layoffs were becoming a reality, making the largely single-income middle-class family's financial future more precarious than ever.

In the minds of middle-class Japanese at this juncture, something more than a company was destroyed when Yamaichi Securities, one of the giants in Japanese stock trading, went bankrupt. In 1996, in the midst of Heisei Fukyo and the slow and inconsistent effort by the Japanese government and the private sector to restructure the economy, Yamaichi became the omen of the changing times that most middle-class Japanese were slow to acknowledge.[3] Yamaichi's end began when its unethical and illegal trading practices became public. Typical scenes in such cases of corporate scandal in Japan followed: initial denial, the revelation of irrefutable evidence, and the public apology by the management team, who got down on their knees and bowed their heads to the floor. Yet, the final outcome was unexpected: going against precedence, the Ministry of Finance imposed official sanctions and let Yamaichi take the fall. Hundreds of elite white-collar employees were let loose to fend for themselves in the job market that traditionally shunned midcareer job change.[4] It was still relatively easy for younger traders, particularly if they were good at what they did, to find another job. Those in their forties and older weren't so lucky. They had been making a living by managing other people's work for too many years and had little expertise or skill that could be transferred easily to other companies.

The shock wave of Yamaichi's bankruptcy reached across the Pacific and hit expatriate Japanese communities in the United States, particularly in New York, where Yamaichi had a large subsidiary. The fortunes of its former employees were similarly divided here as well: those who excelled in dealing in Wall Street could find a job with the New York subsidiary of another Japanese securities company or could even go to work for an American counterpart, but those who had no job prospects in the United States had to go back to Tokyo, which was swarming with job-seeking stock dealers. Corporate subsidies were running out quickly and the severance package was minuscule, forcing ex-employees to pay for their move back to Japan. A panicked exodus ensued. Japanese-owned moving companies were quickly booked up, and at a Japanese-owned travel agency that used to have Yamaichi's corporate account agents apologized all day to ex-Yamaichi families that they could not extend the same credit to noncorporate customers. Throughout these frenzied activities, these ex-Yamaichi families kept asking themselves, "Back to what?" Staying was not an option, yet they knew that very little was waiting for them at home.

This was, by far, the gloomiest homecoming scenario that I encountered during fieldwork, and relatively few returnees were impacted so directly by Heisei Fukyo. However, the impact of this incident went much further. When it happened, I was in the middle of my project in New York, and for the weeks following Yamaichi's demise, the subject came up in almost every conversation I had with Japanese residents, even the ones who did not work for Japanese companies. It seemed to signal to those Japanese overseas that something critical yet unfathomable was taking place in Japan, eroding the foundation of their middle-class life for the first time in postwar history: no more corporate largesse and no more guarantee of lifetime employment. This shift had occurred in corporate America decades earlier, and perhaps the Japanese should have seen it coming. But they didn't. At least in part, their obliviousness had to do with their belief in Japanese uniqueness. Somehow, they thought, Japanese companies are different from American companies, and their relationship with their corporate employers stronger, more personal, more interdependent. American companies might pay lip service to employees' well-being, but Japanese companies really meant it. Japanese companies, they believed, would stick with their employees through thick and thin in the way that American companies did not.

Then, the bottom fell out.

This betrayal of security did not remain at the level of corporations.

Japanese corporate families overseas also began to wonder about their country as a whole. One informant in New York who did not expect to return to Japan for a few more years said to me, as though to represent the sentiment in the expatriate community, "I'm really scared to think that, by the time we are ready to go back [to Japan], there may be no country for us to go back to." These Japanese citizens overseas were beginning to think, perhaps for the first time in their lives, of the fragility of their way of life and of the privilege of being a middle-class sojourner, a member of the corporate family, and a Japanese citizen, privileges that may be taken away from them, literally overnight. To most corporate Japanese, their own future seemed to be connected directly to the future of their corporate employer; their corporate employer, in turn, necessarily depended on the protection of the nation-state. Thus, without the country, they, as individual families, had no future either.

Homecoming for Japanese corporate families overseas becomes difficult for many reasons: they may be worried about very concrete, day-to-day problems of fitting back in, for example, in a new neighborhood or a new school; they may be concerned more generally about social acceptance of returnee families; they may have a reason to believe that the husband will be marginalized in the Tokyo office; or they may fear that Japan as they knew it has disappeared. For one reason or another, the feeling of having no place to return to entirely changes the significance of kaigai chuuzai. A vacation is a vacation only so long as there is a home to go back to at its end. The possibility of losing that home threatens to turn these people into perpetual wanderers, emigrés, refugees—a prospect that few corporate Japanese overseas are ready to consider. The Yamaichi incident brought this possibility to the consciousness of reluctant middle-class Japanese, which was always already present, albeit without acknowledgment. Being a sojourner made overseas Japanese families even more sensitive to this possibility, and their sense of uncertainty was magnified as they witnessed the ex-Yamaichi families' exodus.

CHOOSING TO STAY

It is difficult to determine exactly how many Japanese corporate families choose to stay in the United States on a permanent or semipermanent basis after their kaigai chuuzai. The Japanese embassy and consulates around the United States do not differentiate among Japanese citizens residing temporarily or permanently in the United States. In their statistics, corporate workers and their families on kaigai chuuzai are combined with people like myself who have made the United States their permanent home. However, one possible number is suggested by my field data: approximately 10 percent of my informants stated that they had become or were about to become permanent residents in the United States as a result of their kaigai chuuzai. Still, this figure is not statistically significant and is most likely inflated by the fact that (potential) permanent migrants felt that they had something important to tell a researcher and thus were more eager to participate in my research. The difficulty is confounded by some common practices among prospective permanent residents: many of them feel that it is appropriate for them to complete the chuuzai assignment and return to Japan before they can resign from their job with a Japanese company and return to the United States; in such cases, the connection between their kaigai chuuzai and their decision to immigrate may not become apparent. It is also common among this group of Japanese families that the husband stays on the Japanese corporate payroll, either as a long-term chuuzaiin or as a locally hired consultant, while his intention to reside permanently in the United States is understood and accepted, if informally, by his Japanese employer. Some chuuzaiin also come up with flexible, almost guerrilla-like strategies. One of my female informants, Yokota-san, took a calculated risk, for instance, of staying behind in the United States with her children when her husband was assigned back to Tokyo. She and her husband anticipated that he would be reassigned in the United States sooner than later, and the impact of another move between the United States and Japan seemed too great for their teenage children. Their unique decision paid off in just over a year: the husband was sent back to another city in the United States on a long-term assignment, and the family was reunited.

Whenever Japanese corporate families consider making the United States their permanent home, two familial concerns weigh heavily on the decision. Children's educational achievement and future success are obviously a very important factor. To the majority of expatriate Japanese mothers and fathers, this usually means a prompt return to Japan to minimize the impact of foreign residence on their children's progress. Some parents do everything in their power to keep their children in a Japanese educational environment while in the United States. This tendency was more visible in the New York area than in other field sites, where parents were often themselves elites in an occupational system driven by educational pedigree. Another factor is the care of aging parents, which tends to fall heavily on middle-aged couples these days because of ever lengthening life expectancy and shrinking numbers of children in each generation. Given these significant factors, what motivates a small but increasing number of Japanese corporate families to choose to stay in the United States after their kaigai chuuzai?

Beyond the material affluence that made the daily life of middle-class Americans easy and enjoyable, what impressed my informants the most was *yutori*, or the wealth of the mind that seemed to come along with such material conditions. While almost every informant whom I encountered in my field sites referred to the yutori of middle-class Americans as the most positive aspect of life in the United States, the sentiment seemed particularly strong among Japanese wives and mothers who had reason to believe that conservatism and "narrow-mindedness" made Japan a less desirable place to live for themselves and their family members. Some of my informants made the decision, against conventional wisdom, to remain in the United States to give their children the best educational opportunities. One of the reasons that Ono-san, one of my New York informants, cited as contributing to her decision was that frequent dislocation would cause difficulty in her teenage children's education. Although the majority of expatriate Japanese parents think that their children, like themselves, ultimately belong in Japan, some, like Ono-san, determine that their children have become "too American" to be accepted in Japanese schools or find jobs in Japanese corporations. Two other veteran chuuzaiin wives in New York, Kasama-san and Mutoh-san, both raised their children in the United States and felt similarly to Ono-san. Mutoh-san could not say enough about the commitment of the local schools that allocated many resources and did their best to educate foreign children as though they were "one of their own." Kasama-san, too, praised the "fairness" and "flexibility" with which her two sons were treated in their local schools. At the time of our encounters, Mutoh-san's and Kasama-san's children were at various stages of young adulthood as successful "bicultural" individuals. The two mothers felt that their children owed this to

American education, which did not squash their unique cultural backgrounds, while Japanese schools would have treated their Americanness as a sort of abnormality. In each of these cases, there is a distinct familial factor that made these women wary of perceived rigidity in Japanese society that could be directed toward themselves and their family members who exhibited difference, either physical or behavioral.

The material and mental affluence or yutori of the United States also makes this country more livable for individuals with disabilities. In a case that I encountered early in my fieldwork, a Japanese couple decided to remain in the United States because of their son's physical handicap. They felt that his minor difference would make him unwelcome in Japanese schools. By contrast, they found that his handicap was not considered a major learning impediment in the American educational system, and their son was able to live "as a normal child would" with a little extra care provided for him by the school. Adults with disability also find the United States more accommodating. Ishii-san, whose husband suffered from a severe stroke and became partially paralyzed, found that the U.S. society provided people with handicaps a more *ningen rashii ikikata* (human-like or humane lifestyle) than Japan. While her husband's Japanese employer balked at having to keep an incapacitated employee on an expensive chuuzai payroll, the Ishiis persisted and stayed in Centerville while Ishii-san's husband worked on his rehabilitation. When she took her husband to physical therapy in the hospital or out for a walk in the neighborhood, she found local Americans friendly, open, and sympathetic: "Many strangers came to talk to us, and told us to hang in there. They asked us about my husband's condition, and told us about their friends or family members who went through a long period of physical therapy and recovered some of their mobility in the end. If we were in Japan, people would have just looked at us with this disgust in their faces and pushed us around, because we were in their way." For these Japanese families, the yutori of American society, which encourages tolerance and even affirmation of difference, was worth more than anything that Japan promised them, both tangible and intangible—job security, guaranteed promotion, predictability of the future, closeness to extended family and long-term friends, ease of communication, the sense of belonging.

These permanent migrants (and potential permanent migrants) are actively taking advantage of the job opportunities for bilingual and bicultural specialists in many areas of business and industry which the globalizing economy has opened up in recent years. During my field-work, Japanese corporate families choosing to stay in the United States and elsewhere began to be recognized as a new and significant trend, evident in the feature articles in *Yomiuri Shimbun* (1998a). Under the headline "Kyuuyo yori Jiyu wo Sentaku [Choosing freedom over wage]," one article suggests the combination of economic instability in Japan, more exciting career opportunities in the global arena, and the yearning for a sense of fulfillment as the primary motive for kaigai chuuzaiin to stay in the United States. In my understanding, this "trend" has been much more salient in Greater New York than in Centerville. Significant factors for this difference are more numerous and more diverse job opportunities in the New York area. Another obvious difference is the type of chuuzaiin in New York and Centerville. Many New York chuuzaiin are white-collar workers with advanced English-language competency and marketable skills in such hot areas in international business as finance, banking, and trading, whereas most Centerville chuuzaiin, with much less sophisticated English abil-ity and narrow specializations in manufacturing, have less prospect of finding a job with local firms.

These long-term decisions made by expatriate Japanese couples are also indications of the redefined conjugal relationship. Japanese men cannot, and would not, make such a decision without consulting with and securing the support of their wife. In the decision to stay, the wife's interest and willingness is a factor almost as weighty as the husband's professional opportunity. For one thing, even when the husband initi-ates the discussion about permanent migration, the wife's support is necessary for such a drastic change in their family life. It also appears that the wife's central role in the decision to permanently live in the United States is a relatively recent phenomenon. I came across several veteran expatriate Japanese wives who first arrived in the United States prior to 1980. Their decision to stay was made primarily by the husband for his career interests, or jointly by the husband and wife if the main concern was their children's welfare. In these older cases, my female informants often played the self-sacrificing roles of a "good wife and a wise mother." By contrast, interest among contemporary expatriate wives to stay in the United States seems to be motivated more by their own fascination and aspirations than by their concerns for their family members. The wife may even be the one to propose to stay permanently and to convince the husband, initially against or ambivalent about the idea, to go along with it. I came across a few wife-initiated cases of permanent residency in my fieldwork. The Japanese realtor with whom I worked in New Jersey to find my field housing was a former corporate worker who "went local." When I asked him why he decided to stay, he said that it was his wife who refused to go back to Japan after several years in the United States. So he quit his corporate job and became a realtor to accommodate her wishes.

If those who actually remain in the United States are still small in number, a much higher percentage have a latent desire to stay, indicating a much more widespread inclination among today's Japanese to consider living outside Japan as a realistic and desirable alternative. For example, my field data show that a large number of expatriate Japanese wives, ranging from 40 percent to 60 percent depending on the field site, were seriously interested in permanently staying in the United States. There is, however, a clear gap between expressed desire to remain in the United States and the actual choices that they tend to make. In reality, these women knew that they and their husband were not able to choose permanent migration because of pragmatic reasons, including job availability, children's education and cultural identity issues, and aging parents back home. They regard permanent residency in the United States as their personal dream that will never come true. There are some regional differences in this trend. In New York, international financial analysts were said to have many opportunities to move to a U.S. bank or securities company; in North Carolina, workers in the computer industry found themselves in a deterritorialized job market where major multinationals routinely recruited skilled employees from around the world. By contrast, the specificity of manufacturing know-how and inadequate language skills of most expatriate workers in Centerville radically reduced their job prospects outside Japan.

I also wonder how much the expatriate Japanese sense of freedom has to do with the fact that they usually do not have extensive social networks in this country. My own experience of transnational migration tells me that there is a great deal of freedom in being a stranger or a traveler in a foreign land. Many of the constraints that bind you in your own home do not follow you across the ocean, and as a visitor, the constraints that bind local people do not apply to you either. Thus, a transnational migrant lives for a length of time in a vacuum of social control between her home society and host society. Of course, if she gets involved in ningen kankei of an expatriate community, the constraints from home catch up with her very quickly. Or, a transnational migrant may live in an interstitial space between "here" and "there" for quite some time, becoming a "cosmopolitan" in the true sense of the word. By contrast, if she eventually becomes a member of her host society, she will have to live with a different set of demands and limitations. I do not have any meaningful way of estimating how many of my informants belonged to which category, but it seems that most of them would fall somewhere between the first and second types. I wonder whether, once having moved the base of their lives from Japan to the United States, those would-be permanent residents would still feel the sense of freedom that Amerika initially represented to them.

STAYING IN MOTION: MINEMOTO-SAN'S STORY

Minemoto-san's case is worth a close consideration at the end of this ethnography, as her story exemplifies the transformative possiblity of homemaking away from home in important ways. I met her two days before the end of my New York fieldwork, at her *kamishibai* (paper theater) performance at the Japan Center in Manhattan. Kamishibai was a very popular form of entertainment among children in postwar Japan. It is like manga or comics for public showing, each cell of the manga drawn on a large piece of paper, with lines written on the back. For a small fee, kamishibai performers would come around the neighborhoods and tell various stories, from folk tales to pictorial versions of children's literature to superhero stories. Later, after TV took over its niche, it survived for a long time in kindergartens and elementary schools. I went to Minemoto-san's performance because another informant told me that she was once the wife of a kaigai chuuzaiin and began her kamishibai as a school volunteer. An interesting example, I thought, of someone who expanded her horizons as a result of kaigai chuuzai.

Minemoto-san's kamishibai performance was nothing noteworthy. She had a good reading voice but lacked the flare of professional performers. She read well-known folk tales whose plot every school child in Japan has memorized by heart. Yet, there was something in her performance that was appealing and memorable, so I walked up to her afterward and we began to talk. It turned into a long and involved conversation through the rest of the afternoon and into the evening. Here is what I learned about her life.

Minemoto-san was, in her own words, a "typical" wife of an expatriate corporate worker; married to a salaryman who worked for a large trading company, she initially accompanied her husband to Houston for several years, where she raised three children. Worried that her children did not have enough opportunity to learn about their own cultural heritage as Japanese, she started a volunteer group with other Japanese mothers that went to schools and read from Japanese books and told Japanese folk tales to expatriate Japanese children. When her husband was reassigned from Houston to New York, Minemoto-san formed another group of Japanese mothers and continued her storytelling activities at school. Even after all her children grew up and went their own way, she continued her storytelling, eventually becoming a sought-after performer in Japanese communities around the United States.

When Minemoto-san's husband was transferred back to Tokyo in the early 1990s, she wanted to continue her storytelling activity, which by then was requiring her full-time attention. To do so, she had to keep their home in a New York suburb and be able to regularly travel back and forth between the United States and Japan. She consulted her husband first, who would have to manage without his wife half the time, and his reply was, "You should do as you wish, since this is your passion." He even helped her take out a substantial loan to start her own company to manage her performance schedule and to train others to do similar work, which Minemoto-san could not have done on her own, as she had no income.

"I never planned anything, one thing just led to another," Minemoto-san said cheerfully. But is that really how a person comes to own an international performance company?

"Apparently so," she laughed. "I never made any effort myself—I'm too lazy for that. Other people came to me and offered opportunities, so I consulted with my husband whether I should do it, and he said go for it. So I borrowed money to establish a company and let things happen."

Minemoto-san was, it turned out, another example of the transformative experience prompted by motherhood. She raised three children in the United States and struggled through her child-rearing years to give her children a sound educational foundation on which they could become well-rounded adults who are comfortable in their own country and also in an intercultural milieu. This goal turned out to be a major challenge. In the 1970s and early 1980s, when her children were still young, very few Japanese cultural resources were available to expatriate Japanese families in most U.S. cities. Minemoto-san realized that her children and their Japanese friends, who spent five days a week in the English-language environment of local schools, picked up colloquial English very quickly, but only at the expense of their Japanese-language development. She became concerned that these children had very little exposure to anything Japanese other than their interaction with their immediate family members. They were becoming, in Minemoto-san's mind, strange hybrid creatures who belonged neither in the United States nor in Japan, whose veneer of Americanness had no solid support of rich cultural heritage underneath on which to base their cultural and personal identities.

Minemoto-san's concern for cultural heritage may seem conservative at first, but her concerns are, in fact, realistic and practical. Expatriate Japanese children are, after all, raised by Japanese parents and most likely will have to return to Japan some day. They will "never be completely American," and if that is the case, they will suffer later in their lives without basic understandings of Japanese ways. Minemoto-san pointed out that my own situation was significantly different from those of her children, because I came to the United States as an adult, after I had established my identity as a Japanese: "Kurotani-san, you knew where you came from and where you belonged [when I came to the United States]. What you choose to do with it as an adult is your business. But you have to know first who you are, and it's my job [as a parent] to provide that to my children." In fact, she told me, her story-telling activities were *tsumihoroboshi*, an effort to compensate for past sin. She felt that she had failed in her duty as a parent to give that solid foundation to her children who grew up "in between" Japan and the United States. Telling Japanese stories would, she hoped, help Japanese children overseas in some small way to develop and maintain their Japanese cultural identity that she felt her children lacked. In other words, she acknowledged the imperfection of her motherhood, but also turned it into the drive for her volunteer work to effect some real changes in the world and to contribute to the lives of children other than her own.

Her transnational family continues to evolve and change, as Minemoto-san as a storyteller, her husband as a busy businessman, and her children as bicultural adults all live in perpetual motion. Over the years, Minemoto-san came to accept the in between nature of her children's identity, and while her regrets would never disappear, she seemed, at the time of our encounter, at peace with the unique ways in which her three children were exploring their biculturalism. The transnationality in Minemoto-san's life is defined not only by physical mobility between Japan and the United States, but by the fact that she and her family reworked implicit assumptions about their relationships and found meanings in their life in the two countries that they have all considered home for almost twenty years.

CONCLUSION: GLOBALIZING THE LOCAL

Understanding the motives of Japanese corporate wives at the end of their "vacation" takes careful consideration of agency as the complex interplay of personal desire and relational concerns. The notion of agency as the ability or will of the individual to act on his or her own interest is of very limited use here. Marilyn Strathern (1988) offers an alternative model of agency based on the notion of the "dividual," a person made up of multiple relationships that include simultaneously multiple vantage points other than his or her own.[5] In such a constitution of personhood, agency is not about acting for one's own cause; rather, a person's agency resides in acting with "another's vantage point in mind," or acting in a way that embodies one's relationship to the other; thus, the split between cause and action should not be considered "simply as the manifestation of a power that some have over others" (273). In any given social relationship, the accumulation of "earlier, specific differentiating acts" establishes a form of action to achieve this goal; therefore, to be a wife, for instance, is to choose to *act* as a wife in that recognized form (273–279). This notion of agency implicates the limitation of methodological individualism, as the cause that motivates a social actor may not reside in the self, but in one's relationships with others. Kawagoe-san and other Japanese wives' decision to do what is best for their family should not be interpreted simply as an indication of their subordination, but as the manifestation of their agency to activate their relationship with their husband and children. Reflecting the newly developed closeness with their husband and children, expatriate Japanese wives and mothers are compelled to exercise their relational agency and to make decisions of *their own* from their family's vantage point. The actual content of their decision is relationally determined: in some husband-wife relationships, it means immigration to America; in most others, prompt return to Japan.

However, relational agency leaves out important questions of power. Through what historical process are certain, and only certain, signs and actions made permissible for any given type of social interaction, and what do those signs and actions reveal about the possible inequity in the social relationship? Hegemonic power, as Gramsci theorizes, works quietly and thus insidiously so that subjects will internalize it and act upon it as though it is their own free choice, as though it is part of who they are. It appeared in many instances that the ideology of feminine domesticity permeates Japanese women's sense of self through and through, to the extent that they have incorporated that notion of self as their own. The particular form in which middle-class Japanese women activate their newly found sense of closeness with their family members, playing the part of a dedicated caretaker, is itself the product of Japan's modern history through which the essentialized notion of femaleness was naturalized. Their choice to privilege the wishes and well-being of their husband and children over their own fits comfortably with the ideal of middle-class femininity and helps further the agenda of Japanese transnational capitalism by doing precisely what they are expected to do as a wife and mother.

James Scott (1976, 232) proposes that such a disparity between behavior and consciousness is typical of the oppressed and that "[much] of what passes as deference" must be interpreted carefully in the context of sociocultural, economic, and political "constraints" at work. We can expand Scott's insight to explain the seemingly contradictory choices of middle-class Japanese women, whose social and economic constraints, albeit different from those of Scott's peasants, are nonetheless felt as quite limiting (also see Kondo 1990; Lock 1993). The most significant constraint at work is cultural as well as economic, whereby women are primarily defined in their roles as homemakers and caretakers whose labor, as virtuous as it may be, has no recognized value in the capitalist economy. For the majority of these full-time housewives, to ignore or to overtly transgress this dictate is to lose their subjecthood as well as their *livelihood* under the current social conditions in Japan, which leave very little room for divorced women to achieve economic independence (Brinton 1993; Lam 1992). Most Japanese corporate wives with whom I worked were keenly aware of their position as financially dependent on their husband, and some were also quite vocal about the clear and definite boundary within which they could exercise their own choices. Even if they did not buy into the "good wife and wise mother" ideology, they may have been compelled to perform that social identity, given these constraints.

The process through which the notion of uchi is challenged during kaigai chuuzai appears to contradict the naturalized notion of domesticity itself. In the foreign environment of the United States, the everydayness of middle-class domestic life loses its appearance of innocence and stability; as the routine homemaking practices become more intentional, the everyday becomes not so everyday, and the mundane takes on a new significance. While the corporate practice of kaigai chuuzai makes explicit the relationship between the global and the domestic, the shift of domestic responsibilities in expatriate Japanese households also blurs the naturalized division between male work and female work. As an expatriate Japanese husband and wife actively participate in each other's work, their conjugal relationship also begins to change into a more egalitarian partnership. At that moment, expatriate Japanese wives come to recognize, to varying degrees, the problematic of uchi as a closed space of cultural reproduction and begin to question the ideological underpinnings of their own femaleness based on domestic labor. Thus, this location of subjectivity making can—if fleetingly—also become a space for unexpected change and subversion. In some of the cases I have described, the experience of transnational migration opens up otherwise unavailable avenues of self-expression, the possibility of the transformation of family relations and cultural identities, and leads ultimately to a new life course in a place that women originally thought of as foreign. In other words, when the global comes into the home, the home can also become the space of reworking the global.

This turning of the tables against the global is predicted in Michael Hardt and Antonio Negri's (2000) grand scheme of resistance against the global power. Empire, as a deterritorialized form of biopower, reconfigures subjectivity, social organization, and space in its interest, producing increasingly mobile and hybrid subjects, weakening national boundaries, and developing communication networks that make possible instantaneous connections around the world. Against this seemingly all-encompassing power, the opportunity of resistance for its political subjects is in the workings of Empire itself. The hybrid subjectivity of the "multitude" allows them to transcend divisive national identities and be united in a common goal of "true democracy," taking advantage of the transnational communication networks built by Empire (Passavant 2004, 3–4).

Similarly, by delegating the identity-maintenance tasks to the domestic sphere and exposing uchi to a foreign soto, transnational corporations may, quite inadvertently, have initiated a transformation in their corporate subjects' sense of uchi, thus undermining its own structure of power from the inside out. At the same time, my ethnography takes Hardt and Negri (2000) to task for forgetting the domestic. While situating biopolitics at the center of their theoretical agenda, they include in their revolutionary agenda only "the right to the reappropriation of the means of production" (406–407) but not the right to the reappropriation of the means of *re*production. Given the intertwined nature of the domestic and the political, this omission can prove their liberation agenda fatally flawed. The domestic space, where the forces of globalization, identity production, and the daily work of reproduction converge, must be one of the most critical battlegrounds against Empire, whose strength comes, in their own words, from the global integration of the "political, the social, the economic, and the vital" (407). Quite aside from a large-scale process of change, the global, which increasingly affects life's most trivial details in all corners of the world, is also undermined precisely at the same location in which it intervenes with the minute, most mundane details of daily life.

If so, whether in Japan or the United States, Japanese wives and mothers have an opportunity to bring into the very location of identity making a sense of self and home that is more open to change, and to nurture a new Japanese identity that is truly global and not predicated on the rigid distinction between uchi and soto.

Notes

1 DOMESTICATING THE GLOBAL

1 Throughout this book, I use the term "expatriate" to refer to this group. This word is used in two different ways. Generally, it means those who reside outside of their native country. More specifically, it also means those who were forced to leave their country or to denounce their allegiance to their native country (Webster's Ninth New Collegiate Dictionary). My use of the term in this book follows the more general usage without the connotation of exile or the political positions.

2 By contrast, many women in industrialized societies have worked outside the home for wages, despite the hegemonic views of family and division of labor that were mainly applicable to women of the middle and upper classes. However, the naturalized conception of women's domestic tendencies often carries over into the domain of paid labor, too. Women are relegated to secondary roles at the workplace and limited to the duties of assisting, preparing for, and cleaning up after male workers. These tendencies are quite salient in male-dominant Japanese workplaces, where women often take the positions of unskilled support workers and part-timers (Brinton 1993; Kelsky 2001). Although directly contributing to the capitalist production of exchange value, these "feminine" kinds of labor are considered secondary to male labor and do not readily connect to social power (Thorne 1982, 4). With the recent advent of flexible capitalism, the hierarchy of industrial labor has become increasingly transnationalized and feminized. That is, the manufacturing process often takes place across national borders to utilize inexpensive and docile labor outside the core industrial nations, such as the United States. In these global assembly lines, local women are the favored choice

of transnational capital, as they are considered more docile, patient, dexterous, and cheaper than male workers. The newly created opportunities for wage labor may lead to increased autonomy and open up options to exercise an individual choice that was not available to young women in a traditional socioeconomic system, but paid work for transnational corporations may also have negative effects on these female workers' lives in the long run. The conflict between culturally defined femininity and the newly acquired freedom of young, unmarried women may lead to a tightened surveillance over female bodies, and the harsh working environment in unregulated transnational workplaces may have a debilitating effect, both physically and psychologically (Freeman 2000; Ong 1987).

3 In the past ten years or so, an increasing number of Japanese women have made headway into professional tracks. But many obstacles remain for women's professional aspirations, including informal yet persistent gender discrimination in the workplace. See Kelsky (2001) and White (2002) for further discussion.

4 Among over 120 expatriate Japanese families in my field research, I found only one case in which the husband and wife were sent to the United States on separate kaigai chuuzai assignments by the same Japanese corporate employer.

2 MANAGING TRANSNATIONAL WORK

1 I borrowed this expression from the description of the British colonial rule of India by Richard Fox (1985). There is something akin to the way British colonial administrators tried to manage the colony with the lowest cost with how Japanese corporations manage transnationality, in that they wish not only to appropriate the productivity of their workers, but to do so with minimum investment.

2 Corporate paternalism, although it is often naturalized as an innate characteristic of Japanese employers, has a relatively short history, and its benefit to employees varies greatly by the size of the corporation and the occupational category of the workers. For detailed historical analysis, see Beck and Beck (1994), Cole (1977), and Gordon (1991).

3 HOMEMAKING AWAY FROM HOME

1 Chuuzai returnee children often encounter long-term effects of their residence overseas in their educational and career endeavors. For further discussion, see, for example, Osawa (1986) and Taga (1995).

2 I do not describe the details of this case to avoid any possibility of inadvertently disclosing the second location of my fieldwork. For the current discussion, it is more important to note that the reasons that expatriate Japanese informants cited for the incident were all circumstantial and that the local police department was not convinced by their "cultural" explanation.

4 PLAYING HER PART

1   Japanese women usually referred to me by my first name, while they addressed one another by last name. This is one of the linguistic indications of my marginality.

2   This may seem to contradict the steadily declining birthrate in Japan. The analysis indicates, however, that the demographic change is caused more by delayed marriage and childbearing among a large number of Japanese women than a decrease in the number of women who have children.

3   I would like to thank Donald Nonini, whose comments on an earlier version of my writing helped me consider the disciplinary aspects of the women's community.

5 ON VACATION

1   I would like to thank one of the anonymous reviewers of this manuscript, who correctly identified Japanese corporate families abroad as sojourners and urged me to think more carefully about different types of mobility.

2   Japanese typically perceive their nation to be homogeneous and free of racial tension and violence, erasing the existence of cultural and ethnic minorities (Creighton 1997; Yoneyama 1995).

3   -*Kun* is a male suffix placed after a Japanese family name. Less formal than -*san*, it is used among peers, particularly at a younger age.

4   This, in turn, suggests that there is a certain limit to the surveillance mechanism in the expatriate community. Privacy of the domestic space remains a barrier that protects these women from watchful peers and neighbors; while family members may interfere with one another.

5   Postwar generations of Japanese eagerly acquired and surrounded themselves with consumer goods that embodied their economic and social progress toward middle-classness. The changing sets of novel commodities—from a TV set and washing machine in the 1950s, to an air conditioning unit and microwave oven in the 1980s—were the measure of progress and a step toward the glittering goal of the American-style consumer society. Increasing interest in leisure activities, including domestic and international travel, was another important component of this postwar consumer modernity (Havens 1994). Foreign travel became increasingly accessible and affordable to ordinary Japanese through the 1960s, and purchasing high-quality consumer goods as souvenirs became a standard practice. At least until the 1970s, a trip to the United States—Hawaii being the closest destination—constituted a dream vacation for the majority of Japanese. In this context, bags of commodities as souvenirs embodied the consumability and attainability of this particular brand of modernity that Japan pursued in earnest through the 1950s and 1960s.

1   I counted eleven out of more than 120 female informants in this category. I strongly suspect that this category of women is significantly underrepresented in my informant pool because those who had the most difficulty in the United States tended to decline my request to participate in my research.

2   For a thoughtful discussion of broader cultural and institutional ramifications of *Heisei Fukyo,* see Yoda (2001).

3   It had been a long-standing practice of the Japanese national government to protect first-tier companies in key industries, as it was perceived necessary to promote economic growth throughout the postwar era. This practice has been under attack since the collapse of the bubble economy as one of the factors that reduced the competitiveness of Japanese corporations in the global economy (e.g., Takeuchi 1998).

4   This is a symptom of guaranteed lifetime employment and other paternalistic practices that Japanese corporations have used to nurture employee loyalty. Although an economic sea change has reduced the certainty of employment, the general perception remains negative toward those who switch jobs.

5   As I discussed in chapter 4, the notion of the relational self has been a focal point in many anthropological studies of Japan. I have chosen to bring in Marilyn Strathern's (1988) conceptual framework, developed in the cultural context of Melanesia, because of its careful consideration of agency. Instead of merely observing "relationality" and assuming the significance of social relations in self-construct, Strathern grapples with the question of how to capture the social experience of a self that is inherently "dividual" without turning him or her into an automaton who simply follows the dictates of his or her social role and the needs of social others. To achieve this effect, Strathern develops a complicated understanding of "agency" that defies the expectation of individualism, a strong yet often unrecognized undercurrent in social thought.

References

Allison, Anne. 1994. *Nightwork: Sexuality, Pleasure and Corporate Masculinity in a To-kyo Hostess Club.* Chicago: University of Chicago Press.

——. 1995. "Producing Mothers." In Anne Imamura, ed. *Re-Imaging Japanese Women.* Berkeley: University of California Press.

——. 2000. *Permitted and Prohibited Desires: Mothers, Comics and Censorship in Japan.* Berkeley: University of California Press.

Althusser, Louis. 1971. *Lenin and Philosophy and Other Essays.* London: NLB.

Appadurai, Arjun. 1990. "Disjuncture and Difference in the Global Cultural Econ-omy." *Public Culture* 2, no. 2: 1–24.

——. 1991. "Global Ethnoscapes: Notes and Queries." In Richard Fox, ed. *Recaptur-ing Anthropology.* Santa Fe, N.M.: School of American Research Press.

Appadurai, Arjun, and Carol Breckenridge. 1988. "Why Public Culture?" *Public Culture* 1, no. 1: 5–10.

Bachnik, Jane, and Charles Quinn Jr., eds. 1994. *Situated Meanings: Inside and Outside in Japanese Self, Society, and Language.* Princeton, N.J.: Princeton University Press.

Bammer, Angelika, ed. 1994. *Displacements: Cultural Identities in Question.* Indi-anapolis: Indiana University Press.

Battaglia, Debbora, ed. 1995. *Rhetorics of Self-Making.* Berkeley: University of Cal-ifornia Press.

Beck, John, and Martha Beck. 1994. *The Change of a Lifetime: Employment Patterns among Japan's Managerial Elite.* Honolulu: University of Hawaii Press.

Benedict, Ruth. 1974. *The Chrysanthemum and the Sword.* New York: Meridian.

Bestor, Theodore. 1989. *Neighborhood Tokyo.* Stanford: Stanford University Press.

Bhabha, Homi. 1994. *The Location of Culture.* New York: Routledge.

Bourdieu, Pierre. 1977. *Outline of a Theory of Practice.* Cambridge, England: Cambridge University Press.

Bourdieu, Pierre, and Loïc Wacquant. 1992. *An Invitation to Reflexive Sociology.* Chicago: University of Chicago Press.

Bowman, Mary, and Osawa Machiko. 1986. *Developmental Perspectives on the Education and Economic Activities of Japanese Women.* Report prepared for the Office of Educational Research and Improvement, Washington, D.C.

Brinton, Mary. 1993. *Women and the Economic Miracle: Gender and Work in Postwar Japan.* Berkeley: University of California Press.

Brown, Judith. 1975. "Iroquois Women: An Ethnohistoric Note." In Rayna Reiter, ed. *Toward an Anthropology of Women.* New York: Monthly Review Press.

Butler, Judith. 1990. *Gender Trouble.* New York: Routledge.

Carrithers, Michael, Steven Collins, and Steven Lukes, eds. 1985. *The Category of the Person.* Cambridge, England: Cambridge University Press.

Chodorow, Nancy. 1989. *Feminism and Psychoanalytic Theory.* New Haven: Yale University Press.

Cieraad, Irene, ed. 1999. *At Home: An Anthropology of Domestic Space.* Syracuse, N.Y.: Syracuse University Press.

Clammer, John. 1997. *Contemporary Urban Japan: A Sociology of Consumption.* Oxford: Blackwell.

Clifford, James. 1997. *Routes: Travel and Translation in the Late Twentieth Century.* Cambridge, Mass.: Harvard University Press.

Cole, Robert. 1977. *Japanese Blue Collar: The Changing Tradition.* Berkeley: University of California Press.

Comaroff, Jean, and John Comaroff. 1991. *On Revelation and Revolution: Christianity, Colonialism and Consciousness in South Africa.* Chicago: University of Chicago Press.

Constable, Nicole. 1997. *Maid to Order in Hong Kong.* Ithaca, N.Y.: Cornell University Press.

Consulate General of Japan in New York. 1997. *Zairyuu Houjinsuu Chousa no Kekka* [The results of the survey on the number of expatriate Japanese]. New York: Consulate General of Japan.

Creighton, Millie. 1997. "*Soto* Others and *Uchi* Others: Imagining Racial Diversity, Imagining Homogeneous Japan." In Michael Weiner, ed. *Japan's Minorities: The Illusion of Homogeneity.* London: Routledge.

Crick, Malcolm. 1989. "Representations of International Tourism in the Social Sciences: Sun, Sex, Sights, Savings, and Servility." *Annual Review of Anthropology* 18: 307–344.

Davidoff, Leonore, and Catherine Hall. 1987. *Family Fortunes: Men and Women of the English Middle Class 1980–1850.* London: Huchinson.

Davis, Mike. 1990. *City of Quartz.* New York: Vintage.

de Certeau, Michel. 1984. *The Practice of Everyday Life.* Berkeley: University of California Press.

de Certeau, Michel, Luce Giard, and Pierre Mayol. 1998. *The Practice of Everyday Life, Volume 2: Living and Cooking.* Minneapolis: University of Minnesota Press.

De Vos, George. 1973. *Socialization for Achievement.* Berkeley: University of California Press.

Dirlik, Arif. 1999. "Globalism and the Politics of Place." In Kris Olds, Peter Dicken, Philip Kelly, Lily Kong, and Henry Wai-chung Yeung, eds. *Globalisation and the Asia-Pacific.* London: Routledge.

Doi, Takeo. 1973. *Anatomy of Dependence.* Tokyo: Kodansha International.

Dower, John. 1999. *Embracing Defeat: Japan in the Wake of World War II.* New York: Norton.

Draper, Patricia. 1975. "!Kung Women: Contrasts in Sexual Egalitarianism in Foraging and Sedentary Contexts." In Rayna Reiter, ed. *Toward an Anthropology of Women.* New York: Monthly Review Press.

Dumont, Louis. 1986. *Essays on Individualism: Modern Ideology in Anthropological Perspective.* Chicago: University of Chicago Press.

Dundes, Alan. 1980. *Interpreting Folklore.* Bloomington: Indiana University Press.

Eagleton, Terry. 1991. *Ideology.* London: Verso.

Esse. 1998. "Okane o Umidasu Waza 188" [188 tricks to create money]. June.

Farkas, Jennifer, and Morio Kohno. 1987. *Amerika no Nihonjin Seitotachi: Ibunkakan Kyouikuron* [Japanese students in the United States: Discussion on cross-cultural education]. Tokyo: Tokyo Shoseki.

Featherstone, Mike. 1996. "Localism, Globalism, and Cultural Identity." In Rob Wilson and Wimal Dissanayake, eds. *Global/Local: Cultural Production and the Transnational Imaginary.* Durham, N.C.: Duke University Press.

Flory, Michael. 1989. "More Japanese than Japan." Ph.D. diss., Columbia University.

Foucault, Michel. 1978. *The History of Sexuality: An Introduction.* New York: Random House.

Fox, Richard. 1985. *Lions of the Punjab: Culture in the Making.* Berkeley: University of California Press.

Freeman, Carla. 2000. *High Tech and High Heels in the Global Economy: Women, Work, and Pink-Collar Identities in the Caribbean.* Durham, N.C.: Duke University Press.

Friedl, Ernestine. 1967. "The Position of Women: Appearance and Reality." *Anthropological Quarterly* 40: 97–108.

Friedman, Jonathan. 1999. "Class Formation, Hybridity and Ethnification in Declining Global Hegemonies." In Kris Olds, Peter Dicken, Philip Kelly, Lily Kong, and Henry Wai-chung Yeung, eds. *Globalisation and the Asia-Pacific.* London: Routledge.

Fukunaga, Katsuko. 1990. *Aruhi Kaigai Funin* [One day, a foreign assignment]. Tokyo: Japan Times.

Goffman, Erving. 1959. *Presentation of Self in Everyday Life.* New York: Doubleday Anchor.

Goodman, Roger. 1990. *Japan's "International Youth": The Emergence of a New Class of Schoolchildren.* Oxford: Clarendon Press.

Gordon, Andrew. 1991. *Labor and Imperial Democracy in Prewar Japan.* Berkeley: University of California Press.

Gramsci, Antonio. 1971. *Selections from the Prison Notebooks.* New York: Lawrence and Wishart.

Gupta, Akhil, and James Ferguson. 1992. "Beyond 'Culture': Space, Identity, and the Politics of Difference." *Cultural Anthropology* 7, no. 1: 6–23.

———, eds. 1997. *Anthropological Locations: Boundaries and Grounds of a Field Science.* Berkeley: University of California Press.

Hall, John, ed. 1988. *The Cambridge History of Japan.* Vol. 4. *Early Modern Japan.* Cambridge, England: Cambridge University Press.

Hamada, Tomoko. 1992. "Under the Silk Banner: Japanese Company and Its Overseas Managers." In Takie Sugiyama Lebra, ed. *Japanese Social Organization.* Honolulu: University of Hawaii Press.

Hamaguchi, Eshun. 1982. *Kanjinshugi no Shakai Nihon* [Japan: A society of interpersonalism]. Tokyo: Tokyo Keizai Shimpo.

Hane, Mikiso. 1972. *Japan: A Historical Survey.* New York: Scribner.

Hannerz, Ulf. 1996. *Transnational Connections.* New York: Routledge.

———. 1998. "Reporting from Jerusalem." *Cultural Anthropology* 13, no. 4: 548–574.

Hara, Hiroko. 1989. *Katei no Keiei* [Home management]. Tokyo: Nihon Hoso Shuppan Kyokai.

Hardt, Michael, and Antonio Negri. 2000. *Empire.* Cambridge, Mass.: Harvard University Press.

Harkin, Michael. 1995. "Modernist Anthropology and Tourism of the Authentic." *Annals of Tourism Research* 22, no. 3: 650–670.

Harootunian, H. D. 1993. "America's Japan/Japan's Japan." In Masao Miyoshi and H. D. Harootunian, eds. *Japan in the World.* Durham, N.C.: Duke University Press.

———. 2001. "Japan's Long Postwar: The Trick of Memory and the Ruse of History." In Tomiko Yoda, ed. *Millennial Japan: Rethinking the Nation in the Age of Recession.* Durham, N.C.: Duke University Press.

Harvey, David. 1989. *The Condition of Postmodernity.* Cambridge, Mass.: Blackwell.

Havens, Thomas. 1994. *Architects of Affluence.* Cambridge, Mass.: Council on East Asian Studies, Harvard University.

Hettinger, James, and Stanley Tooley. 1994. *Small Town, Giant Corporation: Japanese Manufacturing Investment and Community Development in the United States.* Lanham, Md.: University Press of America.

Hosoya, Chihiro, and Nagayo Homma, eds. 1991. *Nichibei Kankeishi, Shinban* [History of Japan-U.S. relations, new edition]. Tokyo: Yuikaku Shobo.

Ikeda, Yoshiko. 1984. *Tsuma ga Abunai: Shufu no Seishin Eisei Soudan* [Wives in danger: Mental health consulting of housewives]. Tokyo: Koubundou.

Imamura, Anne. 1987. *Urban Japanese Housewives.* Honolulu: University of Hawaii Press.

Inoue, Teruko, and Yumiko Ebara, eds. 1995. *Josei no Deeta Bukku, Dai Niban* [Women's data book, second edition]. Tokyo: Yuikaku.

Itami, Juzo, director. 1988. *Tampopo* [Dandelion]. Tokyo: Itami Production. Original motion picture.

Jameson, Fredric. 1984. "Postmodernism, or The Cultural Logic of Late Capitalism." *New Left Review* 146: 53–92.

Jameson, Fredric, and Masao Miyoshi, eds. 1998. *The Cultures of Globalization*. Durham, N.C.: Duke University Press.

Johnson, Sheila. 1988. *The Japanese through American Eyes*. Stanford: Stanford University Press.

Kanter, Rosabeth Moss. 1977. *Work and Family in the United States: A Critical Review and Agenda for Research and Policy*. New York: Russell Sage Foundation.

Kawai, Takeo. 1992. *Ginkouin Nyu Yoku Monogatari* [A banker's New York story]. Tokyo: Gakuseisha.

Kearney, Michael. 1995. "The Local and the Global: The Anthropology of Globalization and Transnationalism." *Annual Reviews of Anthropology* 24: 547–565.

Kelsky, Karen. 1996. "Flirting with the Foreign: Interracial Sex in Japan's 'International' Age." In Rob Wilson and Wimal Dissanayake, eds. *Global/Local: Cultural Production and the Transnational Imaginary*. Durham, N.C.: Duke University Press.

———. 2001. *Women on the Verge*. Durham, N.C.: Duke University Press.

Kim, Choong Soon. 1995. *Japanese Industry in the American South*. New York: Routledge.

Kinoshita, Ritsuko. 1983. *Oukoku no Tsumatachi: Kigyou Joukamachi Nite* [The wives of the kingdom: At corporate castle towns]. Tokyo: Komichi Shobou.

Kondo, Dorinne. 1990. *Crafting Selves*. Chicago: University of Chicago Press.

Koyama, Shizuko. 1994. "The 'Good Wife and Wise Mother' Ideology in Post–World War I Japan." *U.S.-Japan Women's Journal, English Supplement* 7: 31–52.

Kristeva, Julia. 1991. *Strangers to Ourselves*. New York: Columbia University Press.

Kumon, Shumpei, and Henry Rosovsky, eds. 1992. *Political Economy of Japan*. Vol. 3. *Cultural and Social Dynamics*. Stanford: Stanford University Press.

Kuroda, Junichiro. n.d. "North Carolina's Recruitment Policy of Japanese Companies: A Report to Steve Brantley, International Development Representative." North Carolina Department of Commerce, Business and Industry Development Division.

Lam, Alice. 1992. *Women and Japanese Management: Discrimination and Reform*. London: Routledge.

Lebra, Takie Sugiyama. 1976. *Patterns of Japanese Behavior*. Honolulu: University of Hawaii Press.

———. 1984. *Japanese Women*. Honolulu: University of Hawaii Press.

Levitt, Peggy. 2001. *Transnational Villagers*. Berkeley: University of California Press.

Lifson, Thomas. 1992. "The Managerial Integration of Japanese Business in America." In Shumpei Kumon and Henry Rosovsky, eds. *The Political Economy of Japan*. Vol. 3. *Cultural and Social Dynamics*. Stanford: Stanford University Press.

Lock, Margaret. 1993. *Encounters with Aging: Mythologies of Menopause in Japan and North America*. Berkeley: University of California Press.

MacCannell, Dean. 1976. *The Tourist: A New Theory of the Leisure Class.* New York: Schocken.

——. 1992. *Empty Meeting Grounds.* New York: Routledge.

Mannari, Hiroshi, and Harumi Befu, eds. 1983. *Challenge of Japan's Internationalization: Organization and Culture.* Tokyo: Kodansha International.

Marcus, George. 1995. "Ethnography in/of the World System: The Emergence of Multi-Sited Ethnography." *Annual Review of Anthropology* 24: 95–117.

——. 1998. *Ethnography through Thick and Thin.* Princeton, N.J.: Princeton University Press.

Markusen, Ann, Yong-Sook Lee, and Sean DiGiovanna, eds. 1999. *Second-Tier Cities: Rapid Growth beyond the Metropolis.* Minneapolis: University of Minnesota Press.

Martin, Emily. 1997. "The End of the Body?" In Roger N. Lancaster and Micaela di Leonardo, eds. *The Gender/Sexuality Reader: Culture, History, Political Economy.* New York: Routledge.

Mead, George H. 1934. *Mind, Self, and Society.* Chicago: University of Chicago Press.

Milkman, Ruth. 1991. *Japan's California Factories: Labor Relations and Economic Globalization.* Monograph and Research Series 55. Los Angeles: Institute of Industrial Relations Publication Center, University of California, Los Angeles.

Miller, Daniel, ed. 1995. *Acknowledging Consumption: A Review of New Studies.* New York: Routledge.

——. 1998. *A Theory of Shopping.* Ithaca, N.Y.: Cornell University Press.

Minami, Hiroshi. 1994. *Nihonjinron: Meiji Kara Konnichi Made* [Theory of Japaneseness: From Meiji to today]. Tokyo: Iwanami Shoten.

Ministry of Foreign Affairs of Japan. 1997. *Kaigai Zairyuu Houjinsuu Chousa Toukei* [Statistical survey of the number of expatriate Japanese]: *1980–1996.* Tokyo: Ministry of Foreign Affairs.

Ministry of International Trade and Industry of Japan (MITI). 1996. "Summary of 'The Survey of Trends in Overseas Business Activities of Japanese Companies.'" International Business Affairs Division, MITI.

Mintz, Sidney. 1985. *Sweetness and Power: The Place of Sugar in Modern History.* New York: Viking.

——. 1996. *Tasting Food, Tasting Freedom: Excursions into Eating, Culture, and the Past.* Boston: Beacon Press.

Miyoshi, Masao, and H. D. Harootunian, eds. 1990. *Japan in the World.* Durham, N.C.: Duke University Press.

Mori, Rie, and Hibari Saike. 1997. *Chuuzaiin Fujin no Deepu na Sekai* [The deep world of expatriate wives]. Tokyo: Media Factory.

Morita, Akio, and Shintaro Ishihara. 1989. *"No" to Ieru Nihon* [Japan that can say "no"]. Tokyo: Koubunsha.

Motoyama, Chisato. 1995. *Kouen Debyuu: Hahatachi no Okite* [Play park debut: The unspoken rules among the mothers]. Tokyo: DHC.

Muta, Kazue. 1994. "Images of the Family in Meiji Periodicals: The Paradox Underlying the Emergence of the 'Home.'" *U.S.-Japan Women's Journal* 7: 53–71.

Nakane, Chie. 1967. *Tate Shakai no Ningen Kankei* [Human relations in vertical society]. Tokyo: Kodansha.

Nakasone, Yasuyuki, and Shintaro Ishihara. 2001. *Eiennare, Nippon* [Forever Japan]. Kyoto: PHP Kenkyujo.

Newman, Katherine. 1993. *Declining Fortunes: The Withering of the American Dream.* New York: Basic Books.

Nippert-Eng, Christena. 1996. *Home and Work.* Chicago: University of Chicago Press.

Ogura, Chikako. 1998. "Hanayome Sugata ha 'Iiko' no Akashi: Joshidaisei no Shin-Sengyo Shufu Shikou" [The bridal costume is the symbol of a "good girl": The neo-housewife orientation among female college students]. *Yomiuri Shimbun, Satellite Edition* April 9: 10.

Ohayou Okusan. 1998. "Ie ni Inagara Moukaru Hon" [Book of how to make money while at home]. June.

Ohinata, Masami. 1992. *Bosei ha Onna no Kunshou Desuka* [Is motherhood women's badge of honor]? Tokyo: Sankei Shinbun Seikatsu Jouhou Sentaa.

Ohnuki-Tierney, Emiko. 1997. "McDonald's in Japan: Changing Manners and Etiquette." In James Watson, ed. *Golden Arches East.* Palo Alto, Calif.: Stanford University Press.

Okada, Mitsuyo. 1993. *Nyuu Yoku Nihonjin Kyoiku Jijo* [Circumstances of the education of Japanese in New York]. Tokyo: Iwanami.

Okada, Mitsuyo, and Makiko Shimamoto. 1993. *Amerika Chuuzai Monogatari* [American job assignment story]. Tokyo: Kenkyusha.

Okifuji, Noriko. 1986. *Tenkinzoku no Tsumatachi* [Wives of the corporate transfer tribe]. Osaka: Sougensha.

Ong, Aihwa. 1987. *Spirit of Resistance and Capitalist Discipline.* New York: State University of New York Press.

——. 1998. *Flexible Citizenship: The Cultural Logics of Transnationality.* Durham, N.C.: Duke University Press.

Ong, Aihwa, and Donald Nonini, eds. 1997. *Ungrounded Empires: The Cultural Politics of Modern Chinese Transnationalism.* New York: Routledge.

Ortner, Sherry. 1974. "Is Woman to Man as Nature Is to Culture?" In Michelle Rosaldo and Louise Lamphere, eds. *Woman, Culture and Society.* Stanford: Stanford University Press.

Osawa, Chikako. 1986. *Tatta Hitotsu no Aoi Sora: Kaigai Kikoku Shijo ha Gendai no Sutego ka* [The one and only blue sky: Are overseas returnee children the orphans of the contemporary era]? Tokyo: Bungei Shunjuu.

Passavant, Paul. 2004. "Introduction: Postmodern Republicanism." In Paul Passavant and Jodi Dean, eds. *Empire's New Clothes: Reading Hardt and Negri.* New York: Routledge.

Pinches, Michael, ed. 1999. *Culture and Privilege in Capitalist Asia.* London: Routledge.

Piot, Charles. 1999. *Remotely Global: Village Modernity in West Africa.* Chicago: University of Chicago Press.

Pratt, Mary Louise. 1986. "Fieldwork in Common Places." In James Clifford and George Marcus, eds. *Writing Culture.* Berkeley: University of California Press.

Rapp, Rayna. 1978. "Family and Class in Contemporary America: Notes Toward an Understanding of Ideology." *Science and Society* 42, no. 3: 278–300.

Rapport, Nigel, and Andrew Dawson, eds. 1998. *Migrants of Identity: Perceptions of Home in a World of Movement.* Syracuse, N.Y.: Syracuse University Press.

Ribeiro, Gustavo. 1994. *Transnational Capitalism and Hydropolitics in Argentina.* Gainesville: University Press of Florida.

Robertson, Jennifer. 1991. *Native and Newcomer: Making and Remaking a Japanese City.* Berkeley: University of California Press.

Rohlen, Thomas. 1974. *For Harmony and Strength: Japanese White-Collar Organization in Anthropological Perspective.* Berkeley: University of California Press.

———. 1989. "Order in Japanese Society: Attachment, Authority, and Routine." *Journal of Japanese Studies* 15, no. 1: 5–40.

Rosaldo, Renato. 1989. *Culture and Truth.* Boston: Beacon Press.

Rosenberger, Nancy. 1995. "Antiphonal Performances? Japanese Women's Magazines and Women's Voices." In Lise Skov and Brian Moeran, eds. *Women, Media and Consumption in Japan.* Honolulu: University of Hawaii Press.

———. 2000. *Gambling with Virtue: Japanese Women and the Search for Self in a Changing Nation.* Honolulu: University of Hawaii Press.

Russell, John. 1996. "Race and Reflexivity: The Black Other in Contemporary Japanese Mass Culture." In John W. Treat, ed. *Contemporary Japan and Popular Culture.* Surrey, England: Curzon Press.

Sacks, Karen. 1975. "Engels Revisited: Women, the Organization of Production, and Private Property." In Rayna Reiter, ed. *Toward an Anthropology of Women.* New York: Monthly Review Press.

Sanday, Peggy. 1981. *Female Power and Male Dominance.* Cambridge, England: Cambridge University Press.

———. 1990. *Fraternity Gang Rape: Sex, Brotherhood, and Privilege on Campus.* New York: New York University Press.

Schneider, David. 1968. *American Kinship: A Cultural Account.* Englewood Cliffs, N.J.: Prentice-Hall.

Scott, James. 1976. *The Moral Economy of the Peasant.* New Haven: Yale University Press.

Sen, Krishna, and Maila Stivens, eds. 1998. *Gender and Power in Affluent Asia.* London: Routledge.

Shimizu, Hiroko. 1996. *Otto ha Teinen Tsuma ha Sutoresu* [The husband's retirement, the wife's stress]. Tokyo: Aoki Shoten.

Shweder, Richard, and Robert LeVine, eds. 1984. *Culture Theory.* Cambridge, England: Cambridge University Press.

Smith, Robert. 1983. *Japanese Society.* Cambridge, England: Cambridge University Press.

Stoler, Ann Laura. 1997. "Carnal Knowledge and Imperial Power: Gender, Race, and Morality in Colonial Asia." In Roger Lancaster and Micaela di Leonardo, eds. *The Gender/Sexuality Reader.* New York: Routledge.

Strathern, Marilyn. 1981. "Self-interest and the Social Good: Some Implications of Hagen Gender Imagery." In Sherry Ortner and Harriet Whitehead, eds. *Sexual Meanings*. Cambridge, England: Cambridge University Press.

——. 1988. *Gender of the Gift*. Berkeley: University of California Press.

Taga, Mikiko. 1995. *Kikokushijo no Shuushoku Hakusho* [White paper on the employment of returnee children]. Tokyo: Kenkyusha.

Takeuchi, Yasuo. 1998. *"Nippon" no Owari* [The end of "Japan"]. Tokyo: Nihon Keizai Shimbunsha.

Taniguchi, Etsuko. 1985. *Madame Shosha: Kaigai no Chuuzaiin Fujin tachi* [Madame Shosha: Wives of corporate employees stationed abroad]. Tokyo: Gakuseisha.

Thorne, Barrie. 1982. "Feminist Rethinking of the Family: An Overview." In Barrie Thorne and Marilyn Yalom, eds., *Rethinking the Family*. New York: Longman.

Tobin, Joseph. 1992a. "Introduction: Domesticating the West." In Joseph Tobin, ed. *Re-made in Japan: Everyday Life and Consumer Taste in a Changing Society*. New Haven: Yale University Press.

——. 1992b. "Japanese Preschools and the Pedagogy of Selfhood." In Nancy Rosenberger, ed. *Japanese Sense of Self*. Cambridge, England: Cambridge University Press.

Tsing, Anna. 1993. *In the Realm of the Diamond Queen*. Princeton, N.J.: Princeton University Press.

Tsurumi, Yoshihiro. 1994. *Datsu Daifukyo* [Getting out of the major recession]. Tokyo: Kodansha.

Ueda, Miho. 1992. *Tokyo Shufu Monogatari* [Tokyo housewife story]. Tokyo: Geibunsha.

Ueno, Chizuko. 1987. "Genesis of the Urban Housewife." *Japan Quarterly* April–June: 130–142.

——. 1996. "The Collapse of 'Japanese Mothers.'" *U.S.-Japan Women's Journal English Supplement* 10: 3–19.

Uno, Kathleen. 1999. *Passage to Modernity: Motherhood, Childhood, and Social Reform in Early Twentieth-Century Japan*. Honolulu: University of Hawaii Press.

Vogel, Ezra. 1979. *Japan as Number One*. New York: Harper.

Watson, James, ed. 1997. *Golden Arches East*. Stanford: Stanford University Press.

White, Merry. 1992. *The Japanese Overseas: Can They Go Home Again?* Princeton, N.J.: Princeton University Press.

——. 2002. *Perfectly Japanese*. Berkeley: University of California Press.

Wilson, Rob, and Wimal Dissanayake, eds. 1996. *Global/Local: Cultural Production and the Transnational Imaginary*. Durham, N.C.: Duke University Press.

Wolf, Eric. 1982. *Europe and People without History*. Berkeley: University of California Press.

Wulff, Helena. 1998. *Ballet across Borders*. Oxford: Berg.

Yamazaki, Tetsuo. 1984. *Nyuuyooku Nihonjinmura Soncho Funsensu* [The head of New York Japanese village fights well]. Tokyo: Shinchousha.

Yoda, Tomiko, ed. 2001. *Millennial Japan: Rethinking the Nation in the Age of Recession*. Durham, N.C.: Duke University Press.

Yomiuri Shimbun, New York local edition. 1998a. "Kyuyo yori Jiyu wo Sentaku: Chuuzaiin no Tenshoku Aitsugu" [Choosing freedom over wage: Increasing job change among expatriate workers]. March 28.

———. 1998b. "Bei-Chuuzaichuu ni Okiru Youyou na Mondai" [Various issues that arise during job assignments in the United States]. April 18.

Yoneyama, Lisa. 1995. "Memory Matters: Hiroshima's Korean Atom Bomb Memorial and the Politics of Ethnicity." *Public Culture* 7, no. 3: 499–528.

Yoshimoto, Mitsuhiro. 1989. "The Postmodern and Mass Images in Japan." *Public Culture* 1, no. 1: 22.

Yoshino, Kosaku. 1992. *Cultural Nationalism in Contemporary Japan.* London: Routledge.

Yoshitake, Teruko, ed. 1994. *Nohon no Kazoku wo Kangaeru: Onna, Otoko, Kazoku no Yukue* [Thinking about Japanese family: The direction for women, men and family]. Kyoto: Minerva Shobou.

Index

middle-class families: husband-wife relationships in; Expatriate Japanese middle-class wives, and returning to Japan; Food preparation; Homemaking; *Kaji*; Kidnapped Japanese wife story; Motherhood; Obligation, and love; Travel/traveling; Vacation(s)

Expatriate Japanese middle-class wives, and returning to Japan, 193–94; problems during, 199–200; unmaking a home and, 198–201

Expatriate Japanese workers. See *Kaigai chuuzai*

Femaleness, 136, 148, 219

Female subjectivity, 113–15, 146; dualistic, 129

Femininity, 14, 189, 221–22 n.2; domesticity and, 16–17; Japanese, 218–19; motherliness and, 134

Flexible labor: ambiguity of, 54–59; Japanese corporate workers and, 55–56

Food preparation, 90–96; availability of Japanese food, 91; dislike of American food, 92–93, 95; labor intensity of, 91–92; as requirement of Japanese motherhood, 94; "scientific" explanation of, 95; *uchi/soto* dichotomy in, 93–94, 95

"Fordism," 17

Fox, Richard, 222 n.1 (ch. 2)

Friedman, Jonathan, 55

Fuji Photofilm, 30

Fukoku kyohei, 127

Fukunaga Katsuko, 81

Fundamentalism, 8

Furusato, 21

Futsuu no koto, 108

Global, the, local construction of, 7

Globalization, 3, 187, 220; class and, 4; culture and, 6–10; domestic space and, 4–5; of Japanese capitalism, 22, 51–52, 56–58

Global-local articulation, 7–8

Goffman, Erving, 114

Goto Machiko (Goto-san), 131, 161–62, 199; home work schedule of, 83, 84–85

Gramsci, Antonio, 192, 218

Greater New York area, 24, 28–33, 106, 107, 117–18, 120, 165, 204, 212, 213; educational resources, 32–33, 210; preferred residential areas for Japanese families, 30–31; services provided for expatriate Japanese families in, 31–32; traffic conditions in, 101

Green Mountain Photographics (GMP), 53, 69

Gurobaruka. See Globalization

Hardt, Michael, 187, 219–20

Heisei Fukyo, 205–7

Henna nihonjin, 203

Himajin, 151

Home, concepts of, 21

Homemaking, 4, 13, 20, 73–74, 85–86, 154; corporate interests and, 68–70, 190–91; function in physical and psychological health, 96–97; as *shigoto*, 79–81; transnational, 184; traveling and, 158–60; work-home connection and, 190–92, 193

Hoshuukou, 27

Ichigaya-san, 92, 98, 99–100, 156, 166–67, 183

Ichiji kikoku, 165–68

Ichiji taizai, 23

Ichiji taizaisha, 23

Identity: performative construction of, 115, 220; place-based, 8. *See also* Mobility: national collective identity and

Ikuji noiroze, 141

and, 99; Japanese manufacturing in, 42–45; as a *kowai tokoro*, 168, 170–71; "mixedness" of, 175; racial hierarchy in, 172–73

Urashima Taro, 22, 204

Vacation(s), 23–24, 38–39, 152–55, 223 n.5; "long" vacations, 178–82. See also *Ichiji kikoku*; *Rongu Bakeeshon*

Wabishisa, 139

Westchester County, New York, 109

Women: avoidance of marriage among Japanese, 16–17; defined roles of, 218–19; as mediators between nature and culture, 134; professional, 222 n.3; reproductive roles and, 16–17, 38, 68–70, 220

Women's community, 116–23, 144, 223 n.3 (ch. 4); company-sponsored women's groups, 118–19; corporate-

based hierarchy of, 119–20; economic and educational factors of, 117–18; gender roles and, 124; group activities with children, 120–22; homosocial, 38, 147; importance of reliable friendships, 117; nature of *kaigai chuuzai* influence on, 123

Yakume, 79–80, 182, 183

Yamagata-san, 186

Yamaichi Securities, 206–7, 208, 224 n.3

Yamazaki, Tetsuo, 171

Yaohan Plaza, 32

Yokota-san, 209

Yokoyama Kazue, 131; home work schedule of, 82, 84–85

Yomiuri Culture Club, 121

Yomiuri Shimbun, 212

Yoshimoto Mitsuhiro, 176

Yutori, 210, 211

Sawa Kurotani is Assistant Professor of
Anthropology at the University of Redlands
in Redlands, California.

Library of Congress Cataloging-in-Publication Data

Kurotani, Sawa.

Home away from home : Japanese corporate wives
in the United States / Sawa Kurotani.

p. cm.   Includes bibliographical references and index.

ISBN 0-8223-3630-8 (cloth : alk. paper)

ISBN 0-8223-3622-7 (pbk. : alk. paper)

1. Executives' spouses—Japan. 2. Executives' spouses—United States.

3. Homemakers—Japan. 4. Japanese—United States.

5. Japanese—Employment—United States. 6. Employment in
foreign countries—Social aspects. 7. Transnationalism.

8. National characteristics, Japanese.

I. Title.

HQ759.6.K87 2005   305.48'9622'0973—dc22

2005013584